Subregional Economic Cooperation in Central and Eastern Europe

For Liz, Sophie and Kate

Subregional Economic Cooperation in Central and Eastern Europe

The Political Economy of CEFTA

Martin Dangerfield

University of Wolverhampton, United Kingdom

Edward Elgar

Cheltenham, UK • Northampton, MA, USA

Published by
Edward Elgar Publishing Limited
Glensanda House
Montpellier Parade
Cheltenham
Glos GL50 1UA
UK

Edward Elgar Publishing, Inc.
136 West Street
Suite 202
Northampton
Massachusetts 01060
USA

A catalogue record for this book
is available from the British Library

Library of Congress Cataloguing in Publication Data

Dangerfield, Martin.
    Subregional economic cooperation in central and Eastern Europe : the political economy of CEFTA / Martin Dangerfield.

    Includes bibliographical references and index.
    1. Central European Free Trade Agreement (Organization)
    2. Europe, Eastern–Economic integration.
    3. Europe, Central–Economic integration. I. Title

    HC244.D336 2001
    337.1'4–dc21

                                                                                          00–061738

ISBN 1 85898 900 0

Printed and bound in Great Britain by MPG Books Ltd, Bodmin, Cornwall

Contents

Tables

Abbreviations

BEAC	Barents Euro–Arctic Council
BFTA	Baltic Free Trade Area
BSEC	Black Sea Economic Cooperation
CACM	Central American Common Market
CARICOM	Caribbean Community of West Indian States
CBSS	Council of Baltic Sea States
CEE	Central and Eastern Europe
CEE5	Bulgaria, Czechoslovakia, Hungary, Poland, Romania
CEE10	The 'Europe Agreement' countries: Bulgaria, Czech Republic, Estonia, Hungary, Latvia, Lithuania, Poland, Romania, Slovakia, Slovenia
CEFTA	Central European Free Trade Agreement
CEI	Central European Initiative
CMEA	Council for Mutual Economic Assistance
CPE	Centrally Planned Economy
CSCE	Conference for Security and Cooperation in Europe
DDR	German Democratic Republic
EBRD	European Bank for Reconstruction and Development
EC	European Community
EEC	European Economic Community
EFTA	European Free Trade Association
EU	European Union
FDI	Foreign Direct Investment
IBEC	International Bank for Economic Cooperation
ISDL	International Socialist Division of Labour
MNC	Multinational Corporation
NAFTA	North American Free Trade
OECD	Organisation for Economic Cooperation and Development
OSCE	Organisation for Security and Cooperation in Europe
RIF	Regional Integration Framework
SEI	Socialist Economic Integration
SRG	Subregional Groupings
TR	Transferable Rouble
UN	United Nations
UNECE	United Nations Economic Commission for Europe
V4	The Visegrad Four (Czech Republic, Hungary, Poland, Slovakia)
WTO	World Trade Organisation

Preface and Acknowledgements

My interest in subregional economic cooperation in Central and Eastern Europe (CEE) was rekindled following a conference on CEFTA held in Warsaw during November 1996, sponsored by the Friedrich Ehbert Foundation. During the subsequent attempt to carry out further research into CEFTA it soon became clear that apart from the interest in subregional initiatives involving CEE being shown by certain scholars working on the emerging security structures for the 'new Europe', CEFTA was clearly keeping a very low profile. Yet there were many reasons why the CEFTA topic should have been getting far greater coverage. From the point of view of studies of transition, for example, subregional trade and economic cooperation was a dimension of the broader transformation process which in general was attracting the attention of large numbers of researchers. Also, the fact that CEFTA was a new addition to the family of subregional economic associations in Europe and was created to support its member states' approaches to the EU meant that the topic was highly relevant for scholars interested in the European integration process too, especially in the context of a mushrooming literature on the EU's eastward enlargement. Fortunately, the team at Edward Elgar and their expert reviewers agreed with these arguments, liked my proposal for a book to help bridge this gap in the literature and in late 1997 gave me the go ahead to begin the work. Three years on, the timeliness and topicality of this study have been further enhanced by developments connected to the EU enlargement which are creating new agendas and problems for subregional cooperation.

CEFTA is not an easy topic to research. There is no headquarters, no web-site, no secretariat and therefore no place where the requisite supply of information and official materials can be easily accessed. It has been necessary to spend a lot of time tracking down and talking to those people in the CEFTA countries who are actually engaged in the implementation of CEFTA and/or are involved in policy on multilateral economic relations. I am most grateful to all the people who have been open to my requests to visit their offices to discuss aspects of CEFTA or have responded to my written requests for relevant materials. In particular I would like to mention the following individuals: Mr Peter Hodul of the Slovak Ministry of Economy (to whom I am most indebted in this respect), Ms Erica Piller of the Hungarian Ministry of Economic Affairs, Dr Ishtvan Balogh of the Hungarian Ministry of Foreign Affairs, Dr Atanas Batakliev of the Ministry of Trade and Tourism of Bulgaria, Ms Carmen Turturea of the UK Embassy of Romania, staff at the Ministry of Industry and Trade of Romania and HE Justas Paleckis, Lithuanian Ambassador to the UK. Thanks also to the Central Statistical Offices of Poland, Slovakia and Slovenia for providing crucial data on their countries' trade within CEFTA. I have also been able to benefit from extremely helpful discussions with scholars based in CEFTA countries who I would like to mention. They include Dr Miroslav Had and Dr Vladimir Handl, both from the Institute for International Relations, Prague; Dr Judit Kiss, Institute for World Economy, Budapest, Dr Tamas Reti, Kopint Datorg, Budapest; and Dr Richard Outrata, Institute of Slovak and World Economy, Bratislava to name a few. Thanks also to the Public Relations and Media Office of the Slovenian government and Media & Karlson for giving permission to reproduce the logo developed for the 1997 Slovenian CEFTA presidency which I have used for the cover of this book.

I would also like to record my gratitude to the various bodies and organisations which have provided financial and other forms of assistance. They include: the University of Wolverhampton which has provided crucial practical support, mainly in the form of funds to buy some time, including a one-semester period of sabbatical leave in the academic year 1998/99, to work on the project and to pay for the vital field visits to the CEFTA countries. Particular thanks to the Research Committee for European Studies of the School of Humanities, Languages and Social Sciences, which was the main channel for the institutional support I received, for having enough faith in me and for general encouragement; the British Academy and the Hungarian Academy of Sciences for funding and arranging a two-week research visit to Budapest in June 1999 and to the Institute for World Economy for hosting me; the Freidrich Ehbert Foundation who kindly supported my attendance at the 1996 Warsaw conference; the Institute of International Relations, Prague and the Association for the Study of International Relations, Prague for organising the May 1999 conference 'The Role of CEFTA in the Process of EU Enlargement' and to the various sponsors who funded the participants' attendance.

Sincere thanks also to Professor Neil Malcolm, formerly head of the Russian and East European Research Centre (REERC) and these days Director of International Education at the University of Wolverhampton. The guidance and inspiration of Professor Malcolm, and also Professor Philip Hanson of the Centre for Russian and East European Studies, University of Birmingham, as my PhD research (on the then CMEA countries' foreign economic strategies) was steered to a successful conclusion were simply invaluable. The subsequent support and encouragement I have received from Professor Malcolm go far beyond the duties of a supervisor. Finally, many thanks to Luc Bonenfant of the University of Wolverhampton for help with the proofreading and also to Mr

Tony Clemson at the Print Services Unit of the University of Wolverhampton for producing the camera-ready version of the text.

Any errors and misconstructions contained in the following pages are, of course, purely my responsibility and nothing to do with the people mentioned above.

Chronology

1/1/91	Intra-CMEA trade 'switches over' to world market prices and settlement in convertible currencies.
28/6/91	Forty-sixth, and final, CMEA session in Budapest. Members decide to disband CMEA within 90 days.
6/10/91	'Declaration of Cracow'. Visegrad leaders announce their intention to form a free trade area.
30/11/91	Visegrad countries' ministers for foreign economic relations agree to commence trade liberalisation negotiations.
21/12/92	CEFTA treaty signed in Cracow. Target is free trade in industrial products by 2001.
1/3/93	Implementation of CEFTA commences.
1/7/94	CEFTA enters into force.
9/4/94	Additional Protocol No. 1 signed in Budapest. Transition period to free trade in industrial products cut from eight to five years.
25/11/94	First CEFTA summit (Poznan, Poland).
18/8/95	Additional Protocol No. 2 signed in Warsaw. Transition period to free trade in industrial products cut by a further year.
11/9/95	Second CEFTA summit (Brno, Czech Republic).
11/9/95	CEFTA treaty is amended. CEFTA becomes an open organisation.
25/11/95	Treaty for accession of Slovenia signed in Ljubljana.
21/12/95	Additional Protocol No. 3 signed in Warsaw. Principle of free trade in agricultural products adopted with target date of 1/1/2000.
1/1/96	Slovenia becomes fifth member of CEFTA.
13–14/9/96	Third CEFTA summit (Jasna, Slovakia).
12/4/97	Treaty for accession of Romania signed in Bucharest.
1/7/97	Romania becomes sixth member of CEFTA.
12–13/9/97	Fourth CEFTA summit (Portoroz, Slovenia).
18/7/98	Treaty for accession of Bulgaria signed in Sofia.
24/8/98	CEFTA countries' agricultural ministers meet in Prague. The movement to free trade in agricultural products is suspended.
11–12/9/98	Fifth CEFTA summit (Prague, Czech Republic).
1.1.99	Bulgaria becomes seventh member of CEFTA.
18–19.10.99	Sixth CEFTA summit (Budapest, Hungary).

Introduction

Together with the introduction of the euro, eastward enlargement of the European Union (EU) stands out these days as the foremost issue on the European integration agenda for the new millennium. Despite the many obstacles still in the way of a smooth incorporation of the Central and East European (CEE) candidates into the EU, it is nevertheless true that the repositioning of these countries in the European integration process has progressed remarkably over a relatively short period of time. After all it was just nine years ago that EU membership for countries emerging from the CMEA and Warsaw Pact seemed like a pipe dream rather than the tangible event it is today, and the drama was how to manage the economic disintegration of the former Soviet bloc. Following the *de facto* dismantling of socialist economic integration triggered by the pricing and payment system 'switchover' of 1 January 1991, the pre-eminent Western analysts of socialist and post-socialist international economic relations lacked confidence in the CEE countries' ability to rapidly reorient trade to the OECD area and were therefore far more concerned with measures to quickly restore rather than reorient the economic ties of the post-socialist area.

Against the background of the 'pull' of the EU and 'push' of political considerations (usually encapsulated by the idea of the so-called 'Yalta/CMEA syndrome') policy-makers within CEE quickly became firmly committed to a reorientation strategy. The rejection of proposals for multilateral schemes to recover the considerable loss of mutual trade which marked the early years was also founded on some powerful intellectual arguments. The widely accepted view of the pre-existing exchanges as a 'mutual exchange of inefficiency' served to legitimise their demise, and economists within the region, in Hungary in particular, had long stressed that the economic opening strategy had to focus on the OECD countries since they alone could supply the imports, investment and competitive impulses so crucial for the transformation. Not only that, but it was beyond question that the core market of the past – the ex-USSR – would not be able to transform itself into the core market of the future in any reasonable time scale, if at all. Furthermore, newly independent enterprises in the environment of the decentralised trading environment had to learn how to do business for themselves and many practical obstacles to a renewal of trade within the post-communist area, connected to payment for example, were manifest.

The process of rebuilding multilateral economic ties within CEE officially began in February 1991 when the 'Visegrad' countries (Czechoslovakia, Hungary, Poland) placed economic affairs on their agenda for cooperation. A breakthrough came in October 1991 with the affirmation that it was their intention to liberalise their mutual trade, though the actual agreement to do so was not signed until more than a year later. The Cracow treaty of 21 December 1992 created the Central European Free Trade Agreement (CEFTA) which came into force on 1 March 1993. It was clearly the case, however, that the formation of CEFTA was based less on a conviction that it remained a vital measure to support economic recovery and restructuring, and more on the desire to send the correct signals to the main Western organisations coveted by the post-communist leaders. Having rapidly adopted the neo-liberal orthodoxy in their economic relations with the OECD countries, it would have seemed absurd to further delay applying the same principles to their mutual trade.

The activation of post-CMEA regional economic cooperation in CEE therefore had its roots in the 'Visegrad' cooperation and the EU's preference for aspirant members to engage in subregional cooperation as a forerunner. Not surprisingly, CEFTA (like other subregional cooperation initiatives involving CEE) has tended to maintain a low profile. It is in the shadow of, and indisputably circumscribed by, the main integration task of furthering relations with the EU; it accounts for only a small proportion of its member states' total trade (except for the special case of the Czech and Slovak Republics whose mutual economic relations are anyway not governed by CEFTA but by their own customs union); it is a low-level form of integration and appears to have a transient existence due to the fact that when its members join the EU they will be obliged to withdraw from CEFTA. At the same time, certain factors suggest that the nature and role of subregional initiatives such as CEFTA, which is after all a part of the European integration process, have been over-neglected and merit some investigation.

For one thing, CEFTA has been in existence for over six years and, according to official statements from within CEE at least, despite its inauspicious beginnings has emerged as an important framework for the reconstruction and development of intra-regional economic ties. Indeed, during their (September) 1998 CEFTA summit meeting, the Prime Ministers of the CEFTA countries declared that they 'appreciated the significant contribution of the Central European Free Trade Agreement to the development of mutual trade and to the increase of the level of mutual economic co-operation among the signatory countries. They underlined that CEFTA contributes to the integration process in Europe and to the strengthening of market economies in their countries.' Therefore it seems reasonable to ask some questions about the impact of CEFTA so far and the ways, if any, in which it has developed. What have been the effects on intra-CEFTA trade? Has CEFTA in any way managed to compensate for the sidelined Visegrad cooperation by generating any non-economic by-products? Have there been pressures to 'deepen' the integration? What factors have been at work as far as the enlargement of CEFTA has been concerned? How has CEFTA cooperation interacted with the main task of furthering integration with the EU?

In addition, the CEFTA experience has helped break down some of the early barriers to multilateral economic cooperation in CEE. One of the early hindrances to reactivation of subregional economic cooperation, even among the Visegrad countries, was an idea that it would compromise ambitions to accede to the EU in double-quick time, a fear which contributed to the original treaty's lack of provision for CEFTA to expand. The fact that these fears have proved to be unfounded contributed to the Visegrad countries' conclusion that CEFTA cooperation could not only intensify but also take in other CEE cooperation. Accordingly, CEFTA has enlarged, expanding its membership to include Slovenia (1 January 1996), Romania (1 July 1997) and Bulgaria (1 January 1999), and some of the other countries in the CEE area who have sought to become part of CEFTA (Croatia, FYR Macedonia, Moldova) have managed to get 'one foot in the camp' through bilateral free trade agreements with certain CEFTA states. CEFTA is also linked to the Baltic Free Trade Area (BFTA) through a network of bilateral free trade agreements.

Next, and somewhat paradoxically, rather than signal the demise of and further diminish attention to issues of subregional cooperation the green light for EU eastward expansion seems to have had the opposite effect. The revitalisation (since late 1998) of the 'Visegrad group' and the increasingly regular meetings of the senior members of negotiating teams of the CEE candidates who began EU accession negotiations in 1998 are both indicative of the new subregional cooperation agenda being generated. At the same time, this new agenda also involves potential disruptions to subregional relations due to the requirements of EU membership. For example, CEFTA countries' visa-free border regimes with eastern neighbours are under threat as are current or proposed trade agreements with non-CEE countries that do not conform with the CEFTA countries' EU arrangements. The new divisions threatened by the EU enlargement programme can potentially be offset by subregional initiatives which can include the more peripheral CEE states in the broader European integration process. The war in Kosovo and ensuing (and at the time of writing still vaguely defined) 'Balkan Stability Pact' project have further undermined the validity of a global EU approach to CEE and it seems that subregional cooperation will have a useful role to play in that context too. CEFTA has been one of the more significant and successful subregional organisations which have emerged in post-cold war Europe but how will it fit in this new climate for subregional cooperation – as an active player or as a model for other groups of post-communist countries?

Finally, subregional economic cooperation in CEE provides an interesting and, again virtually ignored, case study of the 'new regionalism' for which international relations theorists are currently having to develop new explanatory frameworks due to changing motivations for development of new inter-state cooperation arrangements in the post-cold war era, and the apparent contradiction between simultaneous trends growth of both regionalisation *and* globalisation over the last decade. In what ways, if any, does the CEFTA experience conform with or dissent from current views on the nature and dynamics of contemporary regionalism? Are subregional actions in post-communist Europe the unique products of the extraordinary circumstances of transformation or are there reference points in other parts of the globe? Though it is beyond the scope of this study to more than touch on these issues I would hope that a fuller understanding of the CEFTA experience can inform these broader academic research agendas or at least encourage greater coverage of CEFTA in future studies of comparative regionalism.

The structure of the book is as follows. Chapter 1 surveys the integration experiences of central and eastern Europe in the era of the now-defunct Council for Mutual Economic Assistance (CMEA). Chapter 2 discusses integration strategies in the post-communist period, from the collapse of the CMEA to the formation of CEFTA, highlighting the main reasons why a transformation of the CMEA was not possible and restoration of regional economic links inevitably commenced on the basis of a subregional, low-ambition form of cooperation. Chapter 3 covers the CEFTA in detail. It outlines the aims and objectives of CEFTA, the main features of the CEFTA agreement and the various modifications which have been introduced, and how CEFTA is implemented and monitored. Chapter 4 provides an assessment of the effects of CEFTA during its first six years of operation under the broad theme of the reintegration effects of CEFTA, which include both the direct contributions at the subregional level and the indirect contributions to the broader reintegration strategy (that is, the 'return to Europe' otherwise known as integration with the EU). From the economics perspective, Chapter 4 includes a review of the main developments in intra-CEFTA trade, including the commodity structure aspects, since 1993 and some observations on the relationship between CEFTA and FDI inflows. The discussion of the political dimension of CEFTA, which draws on and develops the recent work on the functions of subregional cooperation in the new Europe, will operate at two levels: the role of CEFTA in the EU pre-accession strategy and the subconscious contributions to 'soft security' and better political understanding within the CEFTA and wider CEE region.

Chapter 5 attempts to throw more light on the nature of CEFTA cooperation and the forces shaping its agenda and development by considering some of the main issues and controversies which have arisen during CEFTA's relatively short existence. The three specific themes of this chapter are the debate over institutionalisation, integration 'deepening' in the CEFTA context and the CEFTA enlargement process. Chapter 6 speculates about the future development of CEFTA in the context of the current stage of the EU eastward enlargement process, focusing on the questions of not only whether there is scope for the existing members to further enhance their integration in the CEFTA arena but also whether there are any real prospects for CEFTA to develop a more pan-European and even independent role in the evolving European integration process. On the first of these questions, there is enough unfinished business in implementing CEFTA as it stands to keep the internal CEFTA agenda alive for a while yet, at least until the end of 2001 which is the target date for completing the implementation of the remaining Articles. It is clear that qualitative leaps forward in mutual integration will be incorporated into the process of attaining EU membership and it may well be the case that the attempts to fully liberalise agricultural trade between the CEFTA countries will be finalised in that context too. As for the role of CEFTA cooperation beyond the first phase of EU enlargement, the main findings appear pessimistic. While CEFTA has been an extremely useful vehicle for assisting the transition from integration in the CMEA to eventual integration into the EU (at least for those CEFTA countries which make it), the idea that CEFTA may evolve in such a way that it can help compensate for the new divide in Europe runs up against a number of problems which are mainly to do with the lack of prospects for taking in new countries. The strong interplay between CEFTA development and the EU enlargement process have ring-fenced CEFTA's enlargement to the CEE10 and have more or less turned it into another expression of the EU's current projected boundaries. However, though the success of CEFTA has been such that it has now become rather exclusive, the CEFTA experience is a positive message for subregions cognate enough to emulate the CEFTA model. The best policy is to find ways to encourage relevant countries to develop subregional economic associations along the lines of CEFTA now rather than wait for a time when what will in any case be a much diminished CEFTA might be able to extend southwards and eastwards. In the meantime, the EU side must set an example by being creative and generous enough in its own relations with the non-associated CEE and/or flexible enough in its negotiations with relevant CEE10 so as to allow the existing networks of economically and politically useful bilateral free trade agreements in the CEE region to continue and even further develop. The concluding remarks contained in Chapter 7 complete the agenda of this study.

The appendices found at the end of the book include some extracts from various official CEFTA documents (including some pages of the basic CEFTA text and records of the agendas and resolutions of both the CEFTA Joint Committee and summit meetings of 1997 along with an extract from the CEFTA countries' own survey of the first five years of CEFTA) and further details of the Czech–Slovak customs union which operates inside CEFTA. There is also a collection of statistical tables which offer a comprehensive picture of each of the member countries' trade within CEFTA.

Finally, a point of clarification. As is well known, the term 'region' is notoriously difficult to pin down, sometimes used to refer to very large geographic areas comprising a number of states and at the same time denoting sub-units of states. There is a tendency in the literature for CEFTA, together with the Visegrad group, CEI and other initiatives, to be referred to as both 'subregional cooperation' and 'regional cooperation' and clearly there is a need to be flexible and view them as legitimately interchangeable terms. In opting for the use of subregional I am simply deferring to the terms of reference used by Cottey (1999) who adopts UN/OSCE configurations according to which (Cottey, 1999, 5–6) 'Europe is a "region" of the world ... (and) "subregional" refers to a geographically and/or historically reasonably coherent area within the OSCE space as a whole. The term is not exact, since it is clear that the definition of any subregion (like that of a region) reflects not only geography, but also history and politics – often making the issue contentious. Nevertheless in this sense the BEAC, the CBSS, the Visegrad group, CEFTA, the CEI and the BSEC may reasonably be defined as subregional groups.' Where there is reference to 'regional' or the 'region' in this book I am usually following the OSCE convention though in some places, especially Chapters 1 and 2, the terminology reflects cold-war era divisions in Europe and identifies the CMEA/Warsaw Pact zone as a former region of Europe at least.

1. Socialist Economic Integration

INTRODUCTION

By 1960 three separate economic areas had been established in Europe. Within the capitalist part, the European Economic Community (EEC) included those countries whose initial integration ambitions were most far reaching, while the European Free Trade Area (EFTA) was occupied by countries which favoured a rather more minimalist approach and at that time did not support the long-term goal of political unity implicit in the Treaty of Rome. The years since these economic spaces were convened have witnessed the ongoing erosion of this divide as one by one EFTA countries have become part of the EEC, which had become known as the European Union (EU) by the time the last major enlargement to EFTA countries took place in 1995. A different sort of fault line separated Western from Eastern Europe, where an altogether more fundamentally different process of integration was on the agenda, based on the alternative economic order practised by the member states of the Soviet-dominated Council for Mutual Economic Assistance (CMEA). Though trade patterns show that certain of the more outward-looking members of the CMEA (principally Hungary, Poland and Romania) clearly intensified their economic links with EC countries during the second half of the communist period, the countries of Central and Eastern Europe did not make any significant moves towards becoming an integral part of the dominant European economic integration project until after the political revolutions of 1989. This chapter provides an overview of socialist economic integration (SEI), as it developed in the framework of the CMEA which existed between January 1949 and June 1991. It covers the following topics: the genesis of the CMEA; the main phases of its evolutionary path; the salient characteristics of the economic integration process and the impediments to successful development of trade and cooperation; and, finally, the relevant aspects of the breakdown of the CMEA.

1.1 GENESIS OF THE CMEA

The CMEA was formally convened in Moscow in January 1949. Its original members were Bulgaria, Czechoslovakia, Hungary, Poland, Romania and the USSR. The organisation was subsequently extended to Albania (1949 but becoming 'inactive' in 1961), the German Democratic Republic (1949), Mongolia (1962), Cuba (1972) and Vietnam (1978). Of course the international socialist economic community defined by the CMEA was a restricted concept of the socialist world, incorporating as it did only those socialist countries under the direct or indirect tutelage of the USSR. China, Yugoslavia and later Albania remained outside socialist economic integration thus defined. In fact the desire to ostracise Yugoslavia from the mainstream socialist commonwealth has been put forward as one of several reasons to explain the particular timing of the CMEA's formation.

The existence of the CMEA was a logical consequence of the political and ideological divide of Europe which emerged after the 1939–45 war. The political obstacles in the way of any of the 'People's Democracies' joining the US-backed programmes to support post-war economic recovery programmes in Europe took, of course, the form of the Soviet veto. At the same time, to present the formation of the CMEA purely as a product of Soviet power politics would only cover part of the story. Once Soviet-style socialist regimes had become established across Central and Eastern Europe, the establishment of an alternative international economic complex was not only necessitated by political and ideological factors but also because an alternative economic system to the market economy, based on state ownership and centralised planning, was under construction in the east. The idea of an international socialist economic community had always been an explicit part of socialist thinking, as Kornai (1992, 355) explained:

> (t)he classics of socialist thinking proclaim the idea of internationalism. Ever since the *Communist Manifesto* of Marx and Engels, 'Workers of the world, unite!' has been one of the main slogans of the socialist movement. Before history produced a situation in which several socialist countries, segregated in national states, try to build economic relations with each other, many people hoped that the significance of national frontiers would decline and a supranational socialist economic community would emerge.

As it happened, a mixture of pragmatic economic and political considerations were the real imperatives behind the early formal launch of socialist integration in 1949. Since the creation of the CMEA was a very limited affair in that no coherent concept of integration or concrete measures for economic cooperation were elaborated, this fitted well with the idea that the creation of the CMEA was best explained as a product of international political considerations, principally those of the USSR. Not only was there no blueprint for integration, there was not even a treaty. Instead, a communiqué issued by the Soviet news agency, TASS, was the main evidence that the CMEA had been formed. It included a brief statement about the main tasks, which were to be (Kaser, 1965, 12): 'exchanging economic experience, extending technical aid to one another and rendering mutual assistance with respect to raw materials, foodstuffs, machines, equipment etc.'

In line with the lack of substance about how the CMEA would actually function, what its institutions would be and so on, the first phase of the CMEA's existence was characterised by its inactivity and little evidence that it was leading any kind of meaningful existence. Trade rose considerably within the CMEA region during the early 1950s but this was the result of bilateral agreements and was principally bilateral trade between the USSR and its new satellites. The CMEA 'itself served no real function in relation to trade' (Robson, 1980, 132). This period of dormancy also linked in well with the general view that a desire for active regional economic cooperation was not the prime factor behind the formation of the CMEA. Apart from the Yugoslavia factor, one of the most commonly cited imperatives for the timing of the creation of the CMEA was the European Recovery Programme/Marshall Plan together with the Western economic boycott of Eastern Europe following the Berlin Blockade. Yet, as the studies of Brabant (1980, 1989) showed, strong internal impulses for regional economic solutions were evident even before the main external factors came into play. War devastation and the necessary scale of reconstruction gave rise to a search for regional solutions and in the years immediately preceding the formation of the CMEA, several concrete cooperation projects were conceived, of which (Brabant, 1989, 12)

> the best-known examples are the Czechoslovak–Polish confederal or federal plans and the Balkan Federation schemes, which consisted of various combinations among Albania, Bulgaria, Greece, Romania, Turkey and Yugoslavia ... (b)ut, as with the desire to join the Marshall Plan or Western integration schemes, efforts designed to promote integration and regionalism without the USSR were prematurely scrapped, apparently on Stalin's personal orders.

As well as aborted precursors of regional economic cooperation, during the first year or so of the CMEA's existence there were debates about many practical aspects of implementing regional economic cooperation in the CMEA with the assumption that specialisation and trade would play an important role. With Stalin unwilling to entertain multilateral relations within the socialist camp, the outbreak of the Korean war provided the perfect excuse to put the idea of a regional division of labour into cold storage, and also set the stage for the emergence of the 'radial' pattern of trade as the USSR took firm control over the economic development strategies of the other CMEA members. Even when, under Khrushchev, Soviet attitudes changed in favour of activating the CMEA as a vehicle for regional integration, it was already the case that the legacy of the very early years would never really be overcome.

1.2 CONCEPTS OF SOCIALIST ECONOMIC INTEGRATION

Despite their differences, the economic integration projects in Western Europe (EFTA and EC) could both lay claim to clear theoretical underpinnings in the form of classical trade theory and later customs union theory. This meant that the process of integration had a logical starting point and there were relatively clear policy guidelines for governments which prescribed the removal of impediments to free international trade. In contrast, the intellectual foundations for socialist economic integration were normative and the CMEA project could not draw on any blueprint for action. As is well known neither Marx nor Lenin provided the detailed guidelines of how socialist planning would work at the level of domestic economy let alone for the conduct of international economic relations between socialist states.

In theory, three broad approaches to socialist integration are identifiable. First, supranational planning, which entails a regional planning commission taking responsibility for resource allocation. Under this model, participating states transfer considerable sovereignty to the supranational institutions and national interests give way to the regional rationale. Second, plan coordination, in which economic planning remains primarily a national competence. In this model, the national plans incorporate provisions for exchanges of current production according to state trading contracts negotiated prior to the commencement of each five-year planning cycle. In principle, exchanges of current production are the product of longer-term coordination of investment strategies. The third model, involving decentralisation of decisions to the level of the firm and relying primarily on market levers rather than state directives was relevant for reformist socialist economies retaining social ownership but utilising market forces rather than plans as the prime resource allocation mechanism. All three models figured in the CMEA integration debate at various times and it is correct to say that even though all the CMEA countries officially accepted the plan coordination approach, at no time was there a genuine consensus on the most appropriate model.

Following the initial period of dormancy, in the mid 1950s the Soviet leadership began the process of developing an active role in regional trade and cooperation for the CMEA. The array of economic difficulties in the socialist region and popular uprisings in Poland, Hungary and the DDR all contributed to a change from the Stalinist course, including a reappraisal of the basis of Soviet economic relations with the rest of the CMEA countries. The principle of autarky gave way to that of regional autarky meaning self-sufficiency for the CMEA as a whole but division of labour within it. Breathing new life into the CMEA also had a political purpose. Soviet supervision through the 'embassy system' could be replaced by a more indirect control to be exercised via Soviet dominance of multilateral organisations. The newly created Warsaw Pact could serve this purpose in the military sphere and the CMEA could be utilised for the economic dimension. Finally, action was needed to counteract any unhealthy interest the Soviet satellite countries may have had in economic integration developments in Western Europe, which were progressing with the formation of the EEC and EFTA.

The pre-eminence of regional autarky was confirmed with the approval of the 'Basic Principles of the International Socialist Division of Labour (ISDL)' in June 1962 at a Moscow CMEA summit meeting. The ISDL set out five objectives as follows: to determine the correct proportions in each national economy; to ensure rational location of the factors of production available in the CMEA; the effective utilisation of labour and strengthening of defensive power; to guarantee each country a dependable market for its specialised output; to guarantee each country dependable supplies of necessary inputs. Brabant (1989, 66) wrote that '(f)or the first time in their post-war cooperation, in basic principles the CPEs codified basic rules and regulations of intragroup cooperation as well as the purposes to be promoted in this way'. Nevertheless, the implementation of the ISDL fell foul of disagreements about the process of integration which became a matter of serious dispute throughout the 1960s. Three issues in particular more or less created an impasse that endured for the whole of that decade. First, the issue of supranational planning as formally proposed by Khrushchev in late 1962. In November of that year he proposed 'the establishment of a common single planning organ ... fully empowered to put together common plans' (Smith, 1979, 7). Second, the contradictory interests of, on the one hand, the most industrialised countries and, on the other, the less developed economies. Czechoslovakia and the DDR favoured a division of labour which would concentrate production of industrial goods in their economies and avoid oversupply of industrial goods in the CMEA, while Bulgaria and Romania had industrialisation ambitions which were at odds with their potential roles as primarily suppliers of agricultural and food products. The third dimension of conflict ranged the more reformist regimes (Hungary and, until 1968, Czechoslovakia, who by the mid 1960s were developing a preference for an integration process which would rely on market levers rather than joint planning), against the more conservative CMEA members who were not following any radical domestic economic reform programmes.

The debate about the integration process seemed to be finally settled when the CMEA members signed the 'Comprehensive Programme for Socialist Economic Integration' at the 25th CMEA Council Session in Bucharest during

July 1971. The 'Comprehensive Programme' confirmed that the principles of sovereignty and voluntarism would prevail, and that integration was to be based on plan coordination to be achieved via government negotiations. A central role would be played by the new 'CMEA Committee for Cooperation in Planning Activity' in which the heads of the national central planning commissions would resolve coordination of their five-year plans. As Smith (1979, 9) wrote, the 'basis of plan coordination was therefore to be the voluntary cooperation of national planning bodies in formulating long term forecasts which would form the basis for coordinating five year plans and would only receive a directive character when introduced into members annual plans by the planning bodies of the member countries themselves'.

The signing of the Comprehensive Programme did not, however, really signal an end of the debate over the process of SEI which in fact was going to be on the CMEA agenda (though not always officially acknowledged) for the whole of its existence. Underlying differences of national interest remained, in terms of both incompatible developmental objectives and the agenda for change created by the Hungarian market socialist experiment (not to mention the generally more independent/nationalist inclinations of the Romanian leadership). In addition, by the time the Comprehensive Programme appeared, a further major centrifugal force had also emerged by the late 1960s/early 1970s. The CMEA countries' common interest in developing trade with the OECD countries (itself in part a consequence of the inadequacies of regional integration in the CMEA) created problems of how to reconcile the two competing trends in foreign economic relations, an issue which became increasingly relevant in the 1980s when the Hungarian 'turning outwards' preference came into conflict with the Soviet push for a more inward-looking CMEA-oriented strategy following the ill-fated 'import-led growth' experiment of the 1970s. Thanks to over a decade of fast growth in East–West trade while intra-CMEA trade stagnated, by the 1980s Hungary and Poland were already conducting around half of their total foreign trade with the developed market economies. It is true to say that the intellectual roots of the external dimension of the post-communist economic transformation were firmly established as a result of the 'turning inwards' versus 'turning outwards' debate of the early 1980s.

The next phase of serious debate took place between 1985 and 1989. 'Perestroika' of the CMEA came onto the agenda in the context of the advent of Gorbachev and the convergence of the official Soviet and Hungarian approaches to economic reform. Even though the dominant CMEA partner now endorsed and intended to engage in rather than tolerate radical economic reform, any meaningful and effective change to CMEA trade and payment mechanisms was still blocked by a number of factors. First, the more conservative regimes either failed to emulate perestroika or did so in disingenuous fashion. Thus the long-standing problem of lack of consensus on CMEA reform was perpetuated.

Second, the introduction of currency and commodity convertibility, the necessity of which was inescapable, was simply not possible while communist regimes remained in power, irrespective of whether they were reformist. Perestroika opened the door to real change, but real change could only come after communism. This was largely true for the CMEA too, though there was a breakthrough of sorts as far as external relations were concerned. The political barriers to formal relations with the EC were removed with the signing of the CMEA–EC Accord in June 1988. The Accord provided the political framework for a series of bilateral trade and cooperation agreements which were signed between the EC and certain CMEA countries (Hungary, Poland, Czechoslovakia and the USSR) in 1988 and 1989. Ironically Romania, the one CMEA country which had defied the norm by having signed a bilateral agreement concerning trade in industrial products in 1980, was frozen out of these negotiations because of the excesses of the Ceaucescu regime.

1.3 SOCIALIST ECONOMIC INTEGRATION IN PRACTICE

During the communist era there were, of course, official views of the CMEA which naturally painted a somewhat rosy picture. A Czech analyst (Henys, 1974) wrote the following on the 25th birthday of the CMEA: '(t)he twenty five year record of the Council for Mutual Economic Assistance has demonstrated without a doubt that it has become an indispensable organisational factor in speeding the development, perfecting the structure, and increasing the effectiveness of its members' economies, while simultaneously closing, by degrees, the gaps in economic level'. No serious analyses of the time or since have accepted this as an accurate representation of the reality of the CMEA, though the views of the CMEA from the outside contained some serious misconceptions too. It was not uncommon for the CMEA to be referred to as Eastern Europe's equivalent of the EC, for example. In fact the discrepancies were substantial including the fact that the CMEA was in fact a global rather than a purely European organisation, and had no formal supranational authority although, again unlike the EC, it did contain one exceptionally dominant member which dwarfed the other countries in every sense. Furthermore both the results and the methods of integration were fundamentally different, reflecting the alternative economic systems upon which they were constructed. Since the literature on the CMEA is substantial, including many detailed analyses of the process and problems of trade and integration, a brief summary of the key features of SEI in practice will suffice here.[1]

The fact that SEI was attempted in the context of an economic system which was fundamentally not conducive to international trade generated additional complications for trade between the planned economies themselves. The main rules, which were seen as 'absurd but necessary' (Lavigne, 1995, 75), for trade and payments were as follows. First, intra-CMEA trade was the result of intergovernmental bargaining and was based on governmental protocols rather than contracts between enterprises. Trade flows reflected five-year agreements covering volumes and values of exchanges, broken down into annual components for operational purposes. Second, transactions were priced in transferable roubles (TRs) but the TR did not have the essential attributes of money. TRs were not freely convertible for currencies or commodities either inside or outside the CMEA. Third, official intra-CMEA foreign trade prices were derived from prevailing world market prices for the goods being traded. Between 1965 and 1975 prices were fixed every five years and thereafter every year, though to reflect average world market prices over the previous five years. To the extent that this system was practicable at all, it applied mainly to primary goods. Intra-CMEA trade, predominantly bilateral, was effectively a system of barter with prices and monetary values of exchanges determined ex post.

The rules of the game for the players in the intergovernmental negotiations were to aim for bilateral balance, that is avoid any trade surpluses or deficits. The fact that this system actively discouraged maximum exploitation of export opportunities was one of the most damning distortions of SEI and one which played a major role in holding back the development of intra-CMEA trade.[2] It was also necessary to play the game of structural bilateralism, reflecting the two categories of goods which circulated in the CMEA. There was a tendency to match imports and exports of 'hard' goods (goods which could be sold on the world market without subsidies and for which there was strong demand and limited supply within the CMEA) and to do the same for 'soft' goods (usually low quality manufacturers which were difficult to sell on competitive markets). The golden rule was to avoid receiving soft goods in return for hard goods. Similarly, transactions settled in convertible currencies (generally estimated to account for around 5 per cent of intra-CMEA trade) related to hard goods purchases. Any deviance from these rules of the game could only be explained by reference to non-economic motivations.[3]

Though the range of critical literature contains different interpretations of the nature of the CMEA, there is a complete consensus that as an exercise in economic integration the CMEA was an unequivocal failure, whatever terms of reference are used. The main influences on the modus operandi of SEI in the CMEA – central planning and the political economy that it generated, the dominant position of the USSR in intra-CMEA activity and divergent national interests – were at the same time the roots of its failure. The absence of reliable price signals to guide the division of labour was a central problem. Without prices reflecting supply and demand (or even a common methodology for price calculation) or accurate exchange rates there was no accurate information about the true value of goods being exchanged. Central planning and currency and commodity convertibility are incompatible, thus preventing multilateral trade and payments and causing import requirement to prevail over export potential in bilateral trade relations. The CMEA was essentially an administrative solution to SEI unable to rely on the information required to make it work effectively. Furthermore, national interests worked against resource allocation patterns which would have made sense at the bloc level, and both a general fear of total loss of sovereignty and specific fears of developmental solutions which would have prevailed under supranational planning prevented national development patterns from following a regional rationale. Trade and specialisation were further hindered by powerful sectoral lobbies which were not only able to resist any scaling back of their sectors which would have been justified by the ISDL, but were even able to achieve new investments regardless of the capacity elsewhere in the CMEA.[4] These sectoral lobbies were part of the broader set of vested interests which made up the opposition to radical reform of the economic system and also prevented any serious economic opening even under reform socialism (Hungary) thus demonstrating how far marketisation still had to go there. Smith (1992, 110) wrote that the impracticability of the solutions at hand indicated why 'it proved so difficult to raise the level of integration in the CMEA – the full market solution would have greatly weakened the role and authority of central planning bodies, while the full planning solution would effectively have involved the incorporation of Eastern Europe into the USSR'.

Lavigne (1995, 76) asks: 'we have seen that Comecon was just non-existent as an economic body: it was neither a market, nor a supranational instrument of planning. Had it any reality whatsoever?' Viewing the CMEA as a catch-all for international economic relations between its member states rather than in specific organisational terms, there have been various interpretations of the CMEA experience. Attempts to analyse SEI on the basis of mainstream integration theory was problematic because the latter assumed integration between capitalist economies. Nevertheless some interesting interpretations were put forward. Using the standard Viner approach, Holzman labelled the CMEA as a 'trade-destroying customs union' in which major losses from trade diversion were experienced by the East European countries during the early period of the CMEA and since the late 1950s by the USSR. Holzman also argued that 'the system leads to absolute "trade destruction" instead of trade creation, with all the countries suffering from the resultant losses' (Lavigne, 1991, 62). This approach also utilised the ideas of 'development creation' and 'development diversion' to illustrate the consequences of combining the inward-looking nature of the CMEA and the Soviet-type economic system, with argument going as follows. The less economically advanced CMEA (in particular Bulgaria and Romania) were able, at least in the 1950s and 1960s, to undertake an accelerated programme of industrialisation – development creation – as a result of intensive trade relations with more developed countries in the CMEA. On the other hand, right from the start the economic development prospects of the more advanced states (especially the DDR and Czechoslovakia) were held back – development diversion – because their foreign economic relations were oriented towards industrially and technologically retarded states.

The issue of which countries gained and which lost as a result of CMEA exchanges was hotly debated. In one of the most controversial studies of the CMEA, Marrese and Vanous (1983) argued that by the 1960s the CMEA had evolved into an international regime, the basis of which was Soviet economic subsidisation of the other European CMEA in order to secure their loyalty to Moscow. Accordingly the value of the subsidy (which was reflected in the real cost of Soviet energy – mainly oil – and raw material supplies) varied across the CMEA, with the least loyal members (for example, Romania) losing out and the most loyal and strategically important members (Czechoslovakia and DDR) gaining most. While analysts of the CMEA were in overall agreement that the USSR was incurring losses, and that these losses were at their greatest during the 1970s (the era of high oil prices) there were debates over the magnitude of the loss and whether it was a deliberate Soviet strategy.[5] Economists within the region, most notably the Hungarian expert Köves, rejected the notion of East European gains from CMEA dealings, pointing out that the subsidies analysis only approached the issue of winners and losers from a static perspective. Much more important were the consequences of the smaller CMEA members having been forced to adopt a perverse long-term development strategy which locked a significant proportion of their economic activity into producing goods for the Soviet market, much of which could not be sold on any other markets. CMEA exchanges were more a cause of long-term poverty and instability rather than the other way round. These views, in conjunction with the idea that the CMEA also served as an instrument for protectionism, that is to crowd out the impact of the global economy on the CMEA, were to prove most influential when the reintegration versus reorientation debate came onto the agenda in the early 1990s.

1.4 TRANSFORMATION AND DISINTEGRATION

The main act of the 46th session of the CMEA, held in Budapest on 28 June 1991, was to set a date for the winding-up of the organisation, though the effective termination of the CMEA as a framework for trade and payments had in fact already happened. In the summer of 1990 the Soviet leadership announced that it had decided to impose payment in convertible currencies and world market prices in its transactions with the rest of the CMEA.[6] The activation of these new conditions as of 1 January 1991 (the so-called 'switchover') is often cited as the real point at which the CMEA as a system failed to exist. It must also be stressed that, regardless of the Soviet policy, the reform and transformation environment across the former socialist bloc was already eroding the central pillars of the CMEA system. In place or forthcoming were the abandonment of state direction of enterprises and control over distribution of output, abolition of the state monopoly of foreign trade, price liberalisation and currency convertibility for current account purposes.

The end of the trading regime was, of course, only part of the explanation behind the collapse of East European economic integration. The political priority previously given to intra-regional trade no longer applied, and CEE countries were free to intensify trade and integration to the developed West. The Soviets too were interested in developing their own relations with the global economy and a 30 per cent cut in oil deliveries to CEE in 1990 demonstrated that as well as subsidised prices, guaranteed supplies to CEE were also now a thing of the past. The CEE responded by restricting their own exports to the USSR ranging from a cut of around 42 per cent in the case of Romania to 11 per cent in the case of Poland (Richter, 1992). Thus mutual trade was in serious decline even before the new arrangements were introduced. Equally important, the USSR also amassed a sizeable deficit in its CMEA trade in 1990 indicating that intensifying problems of the Soviet economy were already undermining its ability to cover its pre-existing levels of imports from the CMEA.

According to some estimates Soviet imports from the CEE declined as much as 60 per cent and exports by 50 per cent during the first quarter of 1991 compared with the same period in 1990 (Dabrowski, 1991a, 31). The USSR was generally unable to substitute imports from elsewhere and shortages of vital inputs soon began to compound the general paralysis gripping output. Thus the new system of trade and payments antagonised the economic chaos already beginning to engulf the Soviet Union but it was not in itself the fundamental cause of the collapse of the CMEA market. It was more a question of timing. As Toth (1994, 16) observed, the 'phenomenon called the collapse of the CMEA must, therefore, be carefully used as a general explanation to the developments in the dynamics of intra-regional trade within the CMEA. The economic disruptions in Soviet and post-Soviet markets must be separated from problems related to the complete overhaul of the trading regime, and subsequent dissolution of the CMEA'.

Concerning the reactions and responses of the CEE countries to the events within the CMEA during 1990 and 1991, it is clear from the literature that to drastically sever trade relations with the USSR was not premeditated.[7] It might be fair to say that for CEE during the very early phase of post-communism, development of relations with the OECD area seemed to have the greatest political significance and long-term strategic economic importance, while for trade and economic relations with the east (meaning the USSR) though the ideological significance had disappeared, considerable short-term economic imperatives were perceived. At the domestic level, there were strong social and political incentives to manage the impending transition of regional economic arrangements in the least painful way.

As soon as it was clear that attempts by those countries more exposed to the Soviet market to postpone the switchover or introduce it more gradually were clearly futile, the ambitions of the Central and East European five (CEE5) – bearing in mind that the expected outcome at the time was not a trade collapse of the magnitude which actually occurred but a huge terms of trade deterioration for the CEE5 and a hard currency windfall for the USSR – , were as follows. First, to fashion 'some kind of safety net to help finance the costs of the transition in its first and most difficult phase,' (Köves, 1992, 65) and, second, to 'minimise or at least monitor the trade-reducing effects of the transition to dollar-accounted trade' (ibid). Following the meltdown of intra-CMEA trade which occurred in the aftermath of the switchover, the debate shifted to whether it was possible to achieve a significant recovery of these exchanges and whether it was appropriate to try to do so. Even though policy at the tactical level was inevitably shifting towards a retreat from the Soviet market in favour of the full-bloodied strategy of trade reorientation, throughout 1991 the governments of the CEE5, their firms and other official organisations nevertheless worked hard to find ways to 'cut through or circumvent the economic chaos that reigns in the USSR and renegotiate trading links' (Dabrowski, 1991b, 29). It is a crucial point that the various strategies employed by CEE actors were a continuation of the traditional bilateral approach which had characterised CMEA cooperation. While CEE governments clearly wanted those companies that could continue to operate in the Soviet and post-Soviet markets to do so, a multilateral institutionalised approach to regional economic cooperation was not forthcoming. Indeed, the CMEA broke up when the debate about the need for an alternative body was still live, a development which, as Richter (1992, 264) observed, 'clearly indicated the lack of consensus in the countries concerned about future economic cooperation in the region'.

NOTES

1. There will be no detailed description of the CMEA's institutions both for the reasons just stated and because of the prevailing consensus that very few of them had any meaningful role. Interested readers should consult Brabant chapters 7 and 8, (1989).
2. The value of trade within the CMEA was relatively small vis-à-vis the achievements of other regional economic associations. This reflected the general low level of economic openness characteristic of the CMEA countries where exports per capita and exports as a proportion of GDP were much lower than in the case of the developed capitalist countries. Moreover, the share of mutual trade in total began diminishing at an early stage. Following the high point of the early 1950s where the share of intra-CMEA trade was as high as 80 per cent of the total, regional trade became increasingly less dynamic and in 1980 had actually fallen to less than 50 per cent recovering to nearer 60 per cent in 1987 mainly because of an enforced fall in trade with the OECD area (data from Robson, 1980 and Lavigne, 1991). As far as other areas of cooperation were concerned Marrese (1986) notes that in particular scientific and

technical cooperation remained way below potential due to the lack of enterprise to enterprise contacts and absence of proper incentives. Joint investment programmes had yielded some limited success but only for primary products and energy in particular, citing the examples of the oil, gas and electricity infrastructure.

3. The strategy of avoiding trade surpluses and hard good for soft good exchanges was not rigorously applied by the USSR, which led some analysts to infer a Soviet strategy of deliberately subsidising its oil supplies to the other CMEA members in return for certain political benefits. See discussion of the Marrese/Vanous approach below.

4. In this respect Kornai (1992, 358) wrote that '(I)n a good many fields, different member countries set up parallel facilities with the same function, despite all the CMEA's declarations of principle prescribing a division of labour. Discounting a few joint projects, there was hardly any joint investment and no appreciable flow of capital between member countries'.

5. The Soviet subsidy worked mainly through the price of oil in intra-CMEA trade. It could also be mentioned that the subsidisation argument was seemingly compromised by the mid to late 1980s when the price of Soviet oil to the other CMEA countries moved above world levels.

6. The relevant decree was issued by Gorbachev on 24 July 1990 (Rosati, 1992, 59).

7. Dependence on Soviet supplies of oil and gas could not be reversed in the short term.

2. Integration Strategies in Post-communist Europe

There is no way to restore former trade links without returning to central planning. The flow of trade in CMEA was not based on comparative advantages and cannot be renewed without direct coercion (former Czech premier Vaclav Klaus, May 1993, quoted in Metcalf, 1997, 168).

INTRODUCTION

The declaration of the October 1991 Cracow summit meeting of the leaders of Czechoslovakia, Hungary and Poland seemed to close a debate on the future integration strategies of countries that had belonged to the former CMEA. Two main issues were settled, at least as far as the central European 'three' were concerned. First, there would be no reintegration of the former CMEA countries based on institutionalised multilateral cooperation or even preferential treatment of their mutual trade; the strategic priority was the development of economic integration with the EC, already proceeding apace in the real economic sense. Second, there *would* be an active resumption of economic cooperation but only in the form of a free trade area to 'level the playing field' for their mutual trade and trade with the EC and EFTA. The eventual outcome was the Central European Free Trade Agreement (CEFTA), signed by the Prime Ministers of the Czech Republic, Hungary, Poland and Slovakia in Cracow on 21 December 1992.

When CEFTA came into force in March 1993, post-communist economic cooperation of former CMEA countries therefore amounted to a subregional and, from the point of view of types of economic integration possible, a seemingly minimalist project. Moreover, the markets of the CEFTA four remained firmly biased against the rest of the ex-CMEA. Thus several CMEA countries had essentially been successful in their resistance of the many pressures to transform rather than abandon their (CMEA-wide) multilateral cooperation as a means to reverse the devastation of their mutual trade that had accompanied the collapse of communism. Even CEFTA was entered into somewhat reluctantly. Yet the incentives to restore trading links seemed rather compelling, including the extent to which the decline of CMEA trade severely aggravated – some would argue caused – the transformational recession together with pressures coming from Western organisations with which closer links were desired, not to mention policy advice in that direction from eminent Western experts. This chapter discusses a range of issues pertinent to the lack of prospects for intra-regional economic cooperation following the demise and abolition of the CMEA. It includes an account of the debate over alternative models of post-CMEA economic cooperation and identifies the main factors which inevitably prevented CMEA-wide solutions and determined the nature and scope of the more limited economic cooperation embarked upon by the Visegrad countries in 1993. The final section of the chapter includes a discussion of the differences between the CEFTA countries in terms of how their national approaches to regional cooperation were perceived when CEFTA began its implementation, a matter of importance not only because of the influence on early perspectives on CEFTA cooperation but also on subsequent debates about its further development.

2.1 ALTERNATIVE MODELS OF POST-CMEA ECONOMIC COOPERATION

2.1.1 The Organisation for International Economic Cooperation

Various multilateral initiatives were discussed during the different stages of the breakdown of regional integration. The first was connected to the early attempts to re-fashion the CMEA. Although, as Brabant (1991) pointed out, the exploration of 'CMEA reforms had been on the debating table since the early 1980s' the old constraints to meaningful reform had now vanished. The 45th Council Session of the CMEA, held in Sofia in early January 1990, rejected the Soviet proposal for the 'switchover' as not radical enough (sic) and convened a commission to prepare reform proposals consistent with the overall economic transformation agenda. A year later, statutes for an organisation to replace the CMEA were signed by the CMEA Executive Committee. As formulated, the so-called Organisation for International Economic Cooperation (OIEC) would have been little more than a data gathering and disseminating centre. In the end the OIEC did not materialise, a casualty of its own irrelevance and the changing agenda for the CMEA which had progressed from reform/replacement to abolition.

2.1.2 The Central European Economic Union

The second multilateral solution, which originated from outside the CMEA circle and which was associated most strongly with analysts working at the United Nations Economic Commission for Europe (see Brabant, 1991), argued for the creation of a Central European Economic Union (CEEU). This proposal envisaged a continuation of preferential intra-regional trade, to be supported by a multilateral clearing system which provisionally became known as the Central European Payments Union (CEPU).[1] Assuming hard currency shortages on the part of CEE were the main hindrance to sustaining intra-regional trade and that a successful rapid, liberal opening to the developed capitalist economies was unrealistic, the CEEU would tackle the trade-reducing impact of the switchover and facilitate a more gradual adjustment to global economic conditions. The CEEU and CEPU ideas were discussed intensively in academic circles for a period and the balance of opinion seemed to cast doubt on whether it would ever have been really practical even if the Soviet economic situation had not developed the way it did in 1991. In any case, the CEEU was inevitably a non-starter because, as Richter (1992, 267) informs us, the proposal simply had no political support among CEE officials.

2.1.3   A 'Small' Integration

The third proposal (see Köves, 1992, also Drabek, 1992, Rosati, 1992, Csaba, 1992) was for a free trade area, to be established when conditions permitted, to foster the development of regional trade in a non-discriminatory, rational (that is, according to competitiveness) way. The main concern was to take action to ensure that the portion of trade which was viable was not lost forever and 'in view of this situation we are suggesting some version of free trade within central and eastern Europe' (Köves, 1992, 85–6). This more modest (compared to CEEU) concept was, however, eventually translated into action, but only three of the former CMEA countries – Czechoslovakia, Hungary and Poland – were involved at the outset and the initial basis was not preferential trade but to remove the discrimination they faced on each other's market vis-à-vis imports from EC and EFTA countries. The Visegrad free trade initiative was a product of the complex mixture of centrifugal and centripetal forces at work in the initial phases of the post-communist transformation. Why was it that this model of cooperation was able to emerge and why was it, at least initially, restricted to a small subset of ex-CMEA countries? The account of the origins of CEFTA must begin with a discussion of the general set of obstacles to a resurrection of regional economic cooperation which were a key aspect of the communist aftermath.

2.2 OBSTACLES TO POST-CMEA ECONOMIC COOPERATION

2.2.1 The 'CMEA Syndrome'

Machowski (1997, 9) has written that the 'economic and political joining of the Central and East European countries continues to be heavily burdened by post-war history'. The post-communist elites in CEE have regarded the post-war integration experiences as intrinsically negative, having played a significant role in retarding economic growth and development. The general aversion to and mistrust of regional (particularly institutionalised) cooperation characteristic of CEE in the post-communist era have been cited in some circles as symptoms of a condition known as the 'CMEA syndrome'. This term is often used in conjunction with the 'Yalta syndrome' which traces the corruption of the CEE countries' social, economic and political development back to the post-war partition of Europe which placed them under the Soviet sphere of influence. The greatest fear, at least in the early post-communist phase, was that regional cooperation would perpetuate the idea and practice of an Eastern bloc, and compromise integration into mainstream European structures. Since some countries of the region in any case regarded themselves as historically and culturally part of Western rather than Slavic Europe, the negative attitudes have affected not only attitudes towards ties to the former Soviet Union but also to the other former CMEA partners.

Factors such as the CMEA–Yalta syndromes are intangibles and as such hard if not impossible to gauge yet there seems to be no doubt that they represented a powerful psychological impediment to regional cooperation between the CEE countries. It is perhaps worth making a couple of observations at this point. First, the passage of time and positive experience of regional cooperation has seemed to counter the CMEA–Yalta syndromes, especially as nowadays it is absolutely clear that regional cooperation exerts no negative influence on progress towards membership of the EU. Second, to what extent was the latent aversion to regional cooperation universal across and within CEE political elites? When ex-communists returned to office in certain CEE countries in the mid-1990s (Poland 1993, Hungary 1994) it was noticeable that their policy statements included references to the importance of rediscovering markets of the former CMEA, including the CIS. In this connection, Kolankiewicz (1994, 491) wrote that: '(f)or many, it is no accident that the emergence of an ex-communist government in Poland in 1993 and in Hungary in 1994 should lead to a re-examination of eastern policy in the Visegrad countries'. It is unlikely that the 'CMEA syndrome' was so relevant for politicians who were comfortable in the capitals of the former CMEA countries and who could still look to networks in the region, albeit to a lesser degree than in communist times. In both respects, the softening of the CMEA syndrome would have gone hand in hand with some of the setbacks being experienced in relations with the EU (growing deficits with the EU, use of various anti-trade weapons against CEE, and perceived foot-dragging on the question of EU membership).

2.2.2   Developments in Relations with the European Community

As Inotai (1997a, 129) and others have often stressed, CEE has always relied on an external anchor for both security and economic modernisation. For the new elites, disengagement from their post-war anchoring arrangements was indivisible from the departure from communism and a replacement anchor was needed. The new anchor had not only to carry out traditional functions but also play an important role in guiding and ensuring the irreversibility of the crucial process of political and economic transformation. Clearly, there was only one choice, the European Community (EC) which, even as the political revolutions swept across CEE in late 1989, had almost unwittingly taken on leadership of the West's contribution to supporting the economic and political rehabilitation of CEE. The mere existence of the EC made it a magnet for those CEE countries whose new elites aspired to the EC states' economic prosperity and democratic credentials.[2] There was practical support to the region available immediately too, in the form of the PHARE technical assistance programme, and the EC provided additional encouragement by moving quickly to extend the Generalised System of Preferences (GSP) to improve CEE producers' access to EC markets.[3] Yet though the CEE countries were (Avery and Cameron, 1998, 15) 'grateful for this assistance, the new reform leaderships in the CEECs were determined to push for full membership as swiftly as possible'.

The drive to further integration with the EC was the other side of the coin to the CMEA syndrome, pull–push factors respectively. As Linden (1992, 7) put it:,

> [the]movement against the system was in most cases complemented by a movement *for* something: the European model. The most powerful force exerted both on the political systems and the peoples of East Europe was the pull of the idea of Europe itself. As the revolutions of 1989 spread, the sentiment was increasingly voiced by those making the changes that they wanted their country to be 'European', to join or rejoin a political continent from which they had been forcibly cut off.

To the extent that any regional economic cooperation was possible, it would inevitably be the secondary trend and subservient to the main priority. Through 1990 and 1991 the debate over regional cooperation was progressively circumscribed by the rapid development of CEE relations with the EC. Thus by the time the statutes for the IOEC, itself already a much-watered down regional economic body, were ready, the situation had moved on considerably from the time the CMEA reform commission was entrusted with its task. Most significant in this respect was that by this stage the EC had already offered to discuss associate membership, with free trade as its centrepiece, with those CEE countries where economic and political reform was most advanced. In February 1991 discussions were opened with Czechoslovakia, Hungary and Poland, seriously weakening the immediate relevance of regional economic cooperation for the Visegrad three states in particular. On the 'push' side, there were also some disturbing developments in the Soviet Union around this time, including the clearly weakening internal position of Gorbachev during late 1990 and violent action against secessionist movements in Latvia and Lithuania in January 1991.

Some concrete economic developments were also strengthening the case for reorientation rather than reintegration. First and somewhat unexpectedly, trade between the EC and certain CEE countries had grown very rapidly since the transformation began. The CEE5 exports to the EC grew by 29.8 per cent in 1990 and imports by 47.5 per cent in the same year (Grabbe and Hughes, 1997, 27). Second, in June 1990 Czechoslovakia, Hungary and Poland put their relationships with the European Free Trade Association (EFTA) on a new footing by signing cooperation agreements containing provisions to develop free trade agreements. Third, the European Bank for Reconstruction and Development (EBRD) was founded in May 1990 and commenced operations in May 1991. The creation of this institution suggested at least that external sources of capital to underwrite the restructuring tasks would be forthcoming. Fourth, while foreign direct investment was largely static in 1990, there was a notable increase in this activity in 1991 as far as the Visegrad three were concerned, though there were considerable differences even within that group. The pre-eminence of reorientation over reintegration was formally confirmed in October 1991 when the Czechoslovak, Hungarian and Polish political leaders governments (*Declaration of Cracow*, October 1991, II) stated that they considered

> an all-round development of relations with the European Community the primary objective of their foreign policies. The countries of the Central European Three express the hope for a speedy conclusion on talks on association with the European Community. They also express the conviction that the association agreement should result in the integration of the Czech and Slovak Federal Republic, the Republic of Hungary and the Republic of Poland into the system of European political cooperation and in future full-fledged membership in the Community.

In reality, once the Europe Agreements were signed, the future agenda of the Visegrad three was irreversible from their viewpoint at least. By the time Romania and Bulgaria had shown themselves to be on the same course with the signing of their Europe Agreements in February and March 1993, respectively, the agenda had already moved on to the question of when full membership of the EC could be offered to CEE candidates.

2.2.3 The Problem of the Central and East European 'Region'

As is well known, the argument that regional economic integration should be maintained was prominent in many Western circles. Some commentators even went so far as to suggest that external financial assistance and the prospect of closer relations with mainstream European integration structures should only be forthcoming in the event of successful intra-regional cooperation (see Köves, 1992). Apart from all the other factors hindering an early resumption of regional collaboration, there was the very important complication of how the 'region' should be defined in the sense of the countries it encompassed. Indeed, now the artificially unifying communist edifice was gone, was it even strictly correct to speak of a region? As Maresceau (1997, 4) wrote: 'the expression "Central and Eastern Europe" is not well defined and it certainly has a geographical and perhaps above all a geopolitical connotation. One of the most fundamental questions in this respect concerns the precise place of the former USSR within the notion "Central and Eastern Europe"'.

While it was certainly the case that any schemes that equated the CMEA with a region were non-starters because of the political sensitivity of any idea that the CEE were still part of an 'Eastern bloc', this did not point to the automatic formation of a 'small' integration of the CMEA minus the USSR. Notwithstanding the feeling that any initiatives confined to a breakaway group of CMEA countries were not really politically feasible while the CMEA itself still existed, it was also the case that the CEE5 were differentiated into two groups. This differentiation had both an economic dimension, according to the speed of reform and level of development, and a political one according to whether the new governments represented a genuine break from communist regimes, as was the case for the Visegrad three, on the one hand, or continuity with the former regimes, as was the case with Bulgaria and Romania, on the other. Some contested whether even the Visegrad three lacked a really solid foundation for cooperation, both in terms of post-war and longer-term historical experiences and traditions.[4]

Furthermore, it should not be forgotten that many new states were emerging out of former federal structures. Where did the Baltic states fit in, or for that matter the newly independent components of the former Yugoslavia? Finally, the picture was blurred further by the emergence of some apparently regionally defined initiatives with cross-cutting (both the east–west and intra-east divides) configurations. For example the Alps–Adria group (later to evolve into the Central European Initiative) formed in November 1989 in Budapest by Italy, Hungary, Austria and Yugoslavia was suggestive of a new concept of Central Europe by the time it had evolved into the 'hexagonale' with the membership of Czechoslovakia and Poland and also for a while 'seemed a likely candidate for the role of establishing some kind of regional cooperation at state level ... Thus the idea of Central Europe penetrated the realm of institutional politics on the state-to-state level as well' (Dunay, 1998, 5). All in all, any possible regional economic cooperation in Central and Eastern Europe was inevitably bound to be fragmented and the main question was what kind of region/subregion-building if any was on the agenda.

2.2.4 How Strong was the Economic Case for Reintegration?

Many analysts argued, some at the time and some later when reflecting on the end of the CMEA, that from the economic point of view both the USSR and CEE had sufficient interests to justify finding ways to continue regional economic cooperation. For some, this even extended to security interests since it soon materialised that there would neither be early CEE admission to NATO nor creation of pan-European security arrangements based on the CSCE. Metcalf (1997, 144) concluded that 'their [Soviet and CEE] economic and security interests did provide support for the continuation of some form of economic cooperation'.

Whatever the assessments of the real interests at stake at the time, the establishment of voluntary multilateral frameworks for regional economic integration presupposes that there are strong political and/or historical foundations underpinning the cooperation as well as sound economic arguments for it. In the post-CMEA environment, centrifugal forces prevailed to such an extent that the considerable short-term economic costs were outweighed. Moreover, there was serious opposition to the assumption that the economic case for efforts to maintain the level of regional trade was so clear-cut. This included a rejection of the idea that there was a technically feasible multilateral solution to the problems afflicting mutual trade in the transformation environment and elaboration of the inverse argument that it was actually necessary to accept that the collapse of intra-CMEA trade, with all the implications for output, employment and recession, was unavoidable if the central mission of economic and political transformation and integration into the EC and broader global economy was to be achieved.

On the first of the objections to the economic case for rescuing regional economic ties, since the shock attributed to the breakdown of intra-CMEA trade was mainly due to the collapse of the individual trade of each of the CEE5 with the former USSR, only multilateral schemes covering the whole of the CMEA (or at least the European part of it) were relevant. Since the free trade model (at least CMEA-wide) was obviously not practicable in the early transformation phase the debate came back to the only serious multilateral model which came forward, the CEEU. This scheme's lack of political feasibility was decisive, but it was also contested on economic grounds, even assuming the Soviet economy could have carried on functioning normally in 1991 and after. The justification for the CEPU component was presented in two ways. First, that it could actually mediate against trade collapse through its clearing function and thus target the central impediment to maintaining a good level of intra-regional trade. Second, the historical precedent of the European Payments Union which greatly assisted the post-war recovery of trade and economic reconstruction in Western Europe. Without elaborating the arguments, which were set out at length by various economists at the time, it was argued that the CEPU could never have worked because, inter alia, the structural large-scale surpluses in favour of the USSR would have undermined the clearing function.[5] The historical justification was mainly rejected on the basis of the very different conditions in Eastern Europe compared with post-war Western Europe.

The proposal for preferential treatment of trade between the post-CMEA members garnered little open support from within CEE. Though the broader debate over foreign economic strategy included different opinions concerning, say, the speed with which overall external liberalisation should be implemented, there was a common conviction that the long-term economic health of the former CMEA countries necessitated an extrication from artificially guaranteed markets since the inward-looking CMEA- oriented development strategy was a key cause of the distorted and retarded character of their economies.[6] Officials and members of the Hungarian and Czechoslovak academic communities were particularly vocal in the opposition to the CEEU concept. A Czech contribution (Drabek, 1992, 71) put it as follows:

> (t)he solution cannot lie in an arrangement which ensures a market for these countries; rather, it must lie in one which simultaneously leads to a reallocation of resources, reduction of costs through elimination of waste, an increase in productivity and improvements in quality. This cannot be achieved by preferential treatment of the former CMEA area, which would merely encourage existing inefficient production and provide incentives for maintaining the existing inefficient production structures.

Hungarian contributors included Köves (1992) who argued that even

> under more normal (post-) Soviet conditions they (schemes for [CEEU and CEPU] might have had a negative impact on systemic transformation and economic policy. They would have raised hopes in central and eastern Europe that the pains of reorientation and restructuring could be avoided and the traditional pattern of exports maintained. As the lessons of 1991 suggest, this was an illusion. The attempt would have resulted not in easing the adjustment process but in postponing the important decisions. In this sense, the idea of new integration would have hindered the emerging reorientation and restructuring; it would have been inconsistent with the five's basic aim of becoming integrated into a different community, the EC.

Clearly, then, many eminent economists in the Central European countries rejected the basic premise behind the proposals for a CEEU. For many of them, particularly in Hungary, this was nothing particularly new as they had in any case been calling for a reversal of the CMEA countries' inward-looking strategy ever since the early 1980s. It is important to note that this was not a case of rejecting the markets of the former Soviet Union purely because of political risks since 'a Russian come-back in Eastern Europe ... would certainly not result from an increase in trade relations' (Köves and Oblath, 1994, 18), rather it was a rejection of preferential trade with ex-CMEA partners in order to rectify what had been politically motivated over-trading together with a realistic assessment of how accessible the former Soviet markets were going to be in the foreseeable future.[7] As Csaba (1992, 46) saw it, 'if one accepts the established theory that the purpose of international trade is improved welfare, importing more advanced technological solutions and opening new opportunities for profitable business, there is nothing to be restored'.

Though with the benefit of hindsight the reorientation strategy has turned out to be justified, not least because the CEE are no longer so vulnerable to the kind of direct shock the Russian economic crisis of 1998 would have delivered, the purpose of this section has not been not so much to pass judgement on one strategy or another but to stress the existence of powerful intellectual arguments against post-CMEA reintegration. We should also bear in mind that even in Central Europe there were considerable vested interests in the form of large companies whose prospects for survival were connected to the former Soviet market and who posed a real threat to the political sustainability of the reorientation strategy. The intellectual arguments for reorientation and against reintegration were therefore an important factor in sustaining the reformist course.

2.3 TOWARDS A 'SMALL' INTEGRATION

2.3.1 What Kind of Integration?

Though the policy-making communities in CEE were not able to accept the rationale for a restoration of integration that was based on CMEA-type configurations, the debate tended to be somewhat less proscriptive as far as cooperation between countries at a similar stage of reform progress was concerned. The issue of a payments union for the CEE5 was raised but such a project was regarded as largely unnecessary because their mutual trade was generally balanced and also made up only a small component of overall CMEA trade, making the case for convertibility rather than multilateral clearing even stronger in the case of a smaller-scale post-CMEA integration. From the point of CEE at least, the only realistic measure on the agenda was 'a free trade area covering selected CMEA countries with the most compatible market economic systems and relatively balanced economies' (Rosati, 1992, 80).

Given the nature of the economic transformation, which targeted the creation of economies based on freedom of enterprise and driven by national and global market forces, and bearing in mind the basis of trade relations with the EC and

EFTA, the free trade area seemed the natural avenue for regional economic cooperation to follow. Indeed no other model of capitalist economic integration would have really been feasible at that stage of the reform process irrespective of whether or not the countries' integration ambitions were targeted outside the region. As far as reform harmonisation was concerned, the very experimental nature of economic transformation and intensive debate in and outside the region over a number of fundamental aspects of the process (for example, methods and speed of privatisation), together with the national specifics of transformatory endeavours, made the idea of coordinated fine detail of economic transformations fanciful. In addition, anything beyond a free trade area would have entailed institutions and a measure of transfer of sovereignty both of which were not realistic for countries which had had no meaningful sovereignty during the post-war period. Furthermore, bearing in mind that the model of subregional economic cooperation was to be determined according to which formula had most efficacy as a way to collectively approach the European Union, it should also be mentioned that the formation of a free trade area was supported by the experience of the Benelux countries. As Dunay (1998, 14) explained, interaction with the Benelux countries through joint projects in 1992 'served the socialisation of the Visegrad countries by learning from the experience of the Benelux concerning several issues, both as far as their cooperation and their integration in the Union are concerned, among others in establishing a free trade area'. The main questions then seemed to be whether and when this proposal could be translated into action, which CEE countries could join it and whether the free trade area would be a platform for further types of cooperation (for example to coordinate applications for EC membership).

2.3.2 Five or Three?

Three factors determined the concept of Central Europe as far as which countries would join the first reintegration initiative. First, as we noted above, the free trade area would be restricted to the states which had made most progress in their departure from communism. Bulgaria and Romania were still more or less at the starting line of economic and political reform and were not even at the stage of formulating their policies towards regional cooperation. Second, the EC's policy towards CEE singled out the Visegrad three, at least for a while. Maresceau (1997, 4) informs us that the 'launching of the Europe Agreements policy as something special for a number of Central and Eastern Europe countries constitutes at least implicitly a clear separation of the USSR from these countries'. The fact that Europe Agreements were concluded first with the Visegrad three reinforced those countries own ideas that they were the avant garde in every sense. Third, leaders from Czechoslovakia, Hungary and Poland were meeting regularly in the framework of the 'Visegrad Troika' which had convened because the central European three recognised the clear advantages of close cooperation as far as security matters were concerned.[8] Though the Visegrad cooperation was in the form of (Vachudova, 1993, 38) 'intergovernmental negotiations and rapprochement to western institutions' and was 'thus confined to what could be called the external sphere', the process nevertheless provided an important platform for the development of economic cooperation, not least by providing a forum where it could be discussed at the highest level and giving the EC a target for its pressure to do so. Economic cooperation came into the frame as soon as the agenda progressed from purely security issues and questions connected to NATO, the Warsaw Pact and the CSCE and took in relations with the EC as part of the broader process of strategic reorientation.

2.3.3   The Road to CEFTA

Though discussions about a free trade area between the Visegrad three were carried out at governmental as well as academic levels from early 1991 onwards, there was no real urgency as far as putting the idea into practice was concerned. In fact, there were still many obstacles to overcome, not least the fact that the CMEA syndrome meant that even (Köves, 1992, 91) 'the idea of any Central European integration faces quiet opposition on the part of the governments of the respective countries'. The recommendations for a free trade area as made by leading economists/policy advisers were of course put forward in the context of discussions of the general issue of post-CMEA arrangements and rejection of the CEEU. In other words it was a form of cooperation to which there was no logical objection rather than something which merited a high priority on economic grounds. In fact, it was more common to find the argument that the benefits from a 'small integration' would be marginal anyway because trade dependence among the CEE5 had never been very significant. The declines in the mutual trade of the CEE5 and their trade with the USSR were problems of completely different magnitudes. In 1989, exports to the European CMEA excluding the USSR and the DDR ranged from 9.9 per cent of total exports in the case of Romania to 16.7 per cent in the case of Czechoslovakia (see Table 2.1). Besides the much smaller significance of the mutual trade of the CEE5 compared with their trade with the USSR and OECD area, there were additional reasons to claim that the implications of reducing the levels of this trade were less serious. In 1990 this mutual trade fell, 'mysteriously', more dramatically than trade between the CEE5 and the USSR. Richter (1992, 260) observed that

> a quarter, one third (in extreme cases even one half) of this turnover simply vanished. While it is not easy to explain this phenomenon, it might be mentioned that in Poland and Hungary, and to some extent in Czechoslovakia, an export boom to the West took place which diverted part of the former intra-COMECON trade. The economies

of Bulgaria and Romania were nearly crippled by the uncertainties of the political transition. Finally, perhaps there was no room left for the traditional exchange of 'soft' goods; the mere fact that in mutual trade of 'soft' goods the disadvantages deriving from poor quality are balanced out did not provide a motivation strong enough to maintain the traditional level of trade.

Table 2.1   Territorial structure of CMEA countries' exports, 1989 (% of total exports)

	CEE5	USSR	DME	DEVC
Bulgaria	11.8	65.2	8.0	8.0
Czechoslovakia	16.7	30.5	31.2	13.9
Hungary	10.5	25.1	43.1	15.1
Poland	9.9	20.8	49.1	15.8
Romania	10.8	22.6	36.8	23.0
USSR	36.4	–	23.8	21.0

Notes:
DME = Developed market economies.
DEVC = All other countries.

Source: Rosati (1992).

Certain political economy factors were also relevant. Vested interests in CEE were mostly concerned with the Soviet and post-Soviet markets and the long-term priority for trade with the USSR had created a 'large and influential group of economic agents with a vital interest in this trade' (Köves and Oblath, 1994, 16). While CEE governments therefore would face pressure to make attempts to restore those export outlets, the lobbies concerned with the rest of the ex-CMEA market were smaller and therefore less influential.[9] Also the firms involved had had most success in diverting their output to Western markets. In fact, due to the emergence of neoprotectionism in 1991, the greatest pressures were against reopening markets to producers from the region. Okolicsanyi (1993, 21) wrote that '(d)omestic producers had already been complaining about the liberalisation of regulations on imports coming from the EC countries, which had resulted in a number of factory closures ... state-owned firms, citing high unemployment figures, were by no means eager to confront still more competition as a result of the new free-trade zone'.

It was also the case that in 1991 the Visegrad three were preoccupied with the negotiations for their free trade agreements with the EC. The chances of an early conclusion of a mutual free trade agreement were not only limited because it was a much lower priority but for practical reasons also. The latter was not only a question of administrative capacity. Whatever the strategic priority, it was the case that CEE needed to bridge their knowledge gaps concerning the business of negotiating international free trade agreements by engaging first with experienced partners in the global economic community. This was more or less proved by the extent to which the mutual free trade agreements relied, both for content and form, on the trade chapters of the Europe Agreements and also aimed to (World Economy Research Institute, 1996, 187) 'synchronise liberalisation of trade between the Central European countries with the elimination of tariff and non-tariff barriers under these countries' association agreements with the (European) Community'.

At the same time, the Europe Agreement negotiations and the run-in to their activation helps explain why the array of excuses available and competitive rather than cooperative tendencies did not result in a longer delay. A crucial external pressure on the Visegrad three to act on the issue of their mutual economic cooperation was brought into play. It was made clear at an early stage that their future ambitions vis-à-vis Western organisations would in part depend on their willingness and ability to cooperate with each other. In the economic sphere, this did not mean preferential trade with each other, but it did demand serious attention to the discriminatory bias their more open policies to OECD countries had created and which would be intensified with the implementation of free trade with the EC and EFTA countries. This pressure did not necessarily convince those inside CEE that their mutual economic cooperation was really vital, and it even gave rise to the objection that this pressure was part of a plot to forestall their accession to the EC. Nevertheless, pressure from Brussels was far more potent than the advice of Western academics and other policy advisers, and this was the main source of the political impetus, thus leading to the expectation that the leaders of the Visegrad three would enhance their case for a rapid move to EC Associate membership by announcing their intention to form a free trade area at their summit meeting of February 1991. The actual outcome was a general reference to the need to engage in economic cooperation rather than a concrete proposal or dates for implementation. Richter (1992) stated that this may have been down to a mixture of 'intra-triangle politics' (differences over the nature and extent of this cooperation for example) and the wish to avoid provoking the USSR, particularly at that time.[10] Dunay (1998, 3), pointing out that the Visegrad summit was convened mainly to discuss the urgent problem of how to secure the dissolution of the Warsaw Pact, reached a similar conclusion: '(m)ultilateral interstate cooperation in Central Europe, among members of the Warsaw Treaty and the COMECON, could not be instituted as long as the two integrative elements of the socialist world functioned. It was not only the revolutions of 1989 that made regional cooperation possible but the virtual collapse of the two organisations integrating the so-called socialist countries as well'.

In sum, economists and policy-makers in the Visegrad three recognised that measures to put their mutual trade on an equal footing with trade relations with the OECD area were logical. But the assessments of the economic effects were clearly not persuasive, especially at a time when the transformatory measures, agenda was also extremely crowded, and were being countered by anti-cooperative tendencies at governmental level, emerging political economy factors and the fact that each of the Visegrad three had reason to believe that they would enter the EC first.[11] Nevertheless, since the Visegrad three could not ignore the connection between mutual economic cooperation and their efforts to move closer to the EU and other Western organisations, the Visegrad free trade area stayed firmly on the agenda. The dissolution of both the CMEA and Warsaw Pact in June and July 1991 respectively, together with the end of the Soviet Union itself during the events following the abortive August 'putsch', helped to move events on.[12] As well as confirming that the debate over reorientation versus reintegration was formally over by stating that relations with the EU were the strategic priority for all three countries, the Cracow Declaration also included the following passage (*Declaration of Cracow*, October 1991, II):

> the nearing conclusions of talks on a free trade zone held with the European Community and the European Free Trade Association necessitates a speedy removal of barriers hindering mutual trade. All three states declare their will to conclude agreements on mutual liberalisation of trade as quickly as possible. The aim of these agreements will be the achievement of liberalisation of trade similar to that included in agreements with the European Community and the European Free Trade Association.

The Visegrad countries' ministers for foreign economic relations met in Warsaw one month later to discuss the concrete aspects of the free trade project. This meeting achieved a genuine breakthrough by establishing four main principles which would be the basis for the forthcoming negotiations. These were as follows (Rudka and Mizsei, 1995, 13):

1. A trilateral agreement to create a free trade area to cover all industrial and agricultural products;
2. Gradual elimination of barriers to trade to cover both tariffs and non-tariff restrictions;
3. The trilateral agreement was to be modelled on the Central European countries' agreements with EC and EFTA, but – unlike in those agreements – the principles of symmetry and equivalence of mutual benefits were to be followed;
4. The transition period to full liberalisation of trade was initially set for five to ten years.

It was, however, impossible for the Visegrad three to meet the original target date (July 1992) for the activation of their free trade agreement. Although there were difficult issues to confront,[13] this was not really due to specific problems in the negotiations, especially since the content of the trade chapters of the Europe Agreements were the basis for the detail. Against the background of the transformational recession and general worries about further import penetration, the overall pace of liberalisation was more of an issue, remembering that unlike the Europe Agreements duty reductions would have to be symmetrical. The regional political climate of 1992 was not especially conducive to an early conclusion of the agreement, either. There were difficulties in Poland in the form of frequent changes of government and in Czechoslovakia where the June 1992 elections brought to power a Czech team less supportive of regional cooperation, and placed the division of the country at the top of the political agenda. Long-standing disputes between Hungary and Czechoslovakia (principally the Slovak half) were also causing problems in bilateral relations. This background left (Rudka and Mizsei, 1995, 14)

> the actual signing of the agreement by all countries in doubt almost until the last moment ... When the signing finally happened, it was a truly symbolic act. This was the first economic agreement concluded by a group of former CMEA countries. It was also the first international accord signed separately by the two not yet fully independent political entities, the Czech Republic and Slovak Republic.

The CEFTA Treaty was eventually signed on 21 December 1992, in Cracow, and the process of dismantling trade barriers began on 1 March 1993. The original target of CEFTA was to eliminate tariffs and quotas on industrial products by 1 January 2001, and to partially liberalise trade in agricultural products. Notable features of the CEFTA agreement were firstly that the details of the removal of customs duties were set out bilaterally in annexes to the document and, secondly, the general framework part of the agreement contained no articles dealing with enlargement, meaning that in its original formulation CEFTA was a closed organisation. Though the CEFTA text referred to the initiative having a role in the European integration process and included provision for the parties to explore ways to further develop their economic cooperation (the 'Evolutionary Clause' – see Chapter 5) at that point there was no explicit commitment to a progressive integration project.[14] This seemed to confirm that the joint route to the EC was through their mutual market integration rather than any policy integration, be that concerning economic transformation measures or further development of relations with the EC.

2.4 CEFTA AND ALTERNATIVE PERSPECTIVES ON SUBREGIONAL COOPERATION

Some analysts have remarked that rather than being an *outcome* of the Visegrad cooperation, CEFTA represented an 'important shift in the concept of regional cooperation' (Richter, 1997, 2) and one which represented a victory for the Czechoslovak approach, synthesising a commitment to laissez-faire economics and antipathy to close political cooperation with other CEE countries while satisfying external (EU) demands for subregional initiatives. Insofar as there was a serious debate among the Visegrad three over the nature of their mutual economic cooperation it essentially concerned the most efficacious formula for supporting the primary goal of integration with the EU. This boiled down to whether cooperation in CEFTA should be restricted to a neo-liberal concept – free trade – or whether it would be a foundation upon which other layers of cooperation would be built; would CEFTA *replace* or be part of a broader economic agenda for Visegrad cooperation? The latter position was associated mainly with the Polish side and according to certain Polish analysts (World Economy Research Institute, 1996) would have included Visegrad acting as a vehicle for both coordinated negotiations for association, pre-accession and accession to the EU and harmonised economic transformation strategies. Certain members of the Polish political establishment of the time even suggested that Visegrad could evolve into a 'new Comecon' or 'EEC2'.[15]

Whatever the practicalities of augmenting the free trade area with other layers of cooperation, the crucial fact was that the CEFTA countries did not share a common approach to, nor possess similar levels of interest in, subregional affairs. This fact as much as any other prevented the further development of Visegrad political cooperation, whether the topic of discussion is coordination of economic, trade and integration policy or security matters, once its original role in securing the end of socialist international organisations and coordinating the early overtures to Western organisations was over. In this climate, theories of international cooperation tell us that cooperation of any sort is unlikely unless it is promoted by an outside influence, and in such circumstances the lowest common denominator usually prevails. Thus Inotai (1997a, 130) wrote that subregional cooperation in CEE is 'in most cases a reaction to impacts coming from the more developed and more powerful external factors ... (and) ... this reaction does not manifest itself as a group answer; it comes as a national answer, and only indirectly there is an impact on the group behaviour, or on the group level'. While the Visegrad countries clearly shared the baseline conviction that subregional economic cooperation should not and could not substitute for EU membership, there was nevertheless room for important differences in the national approaches to subregional cooperation. In the post-Visegrad period, the individual CEFTA states' overall approaches to subregional cooperation developed according to two factors. First, their perceptions of how subregional cooperation could further their approach to the EU and how far its role could be developed and, second, the extent to which their geopolitical location and other considerations involved them in potential or existing subregional problems.

The newly independent Czech Republic's Eastern agenda was now quite light. It no longer had a border with the former Soviet Union and most of its territory was next to EU and EFTA states, Germany and Austria, and acrimonious disputes with Hungary were now the concerns of Slovakia alone. This environment reinforced the Klaus government's self-confidence over the success of economic and political transformation in the Czech Republic which placed the country, in Prague's view, a clear front-runner in the EC accession competition. Poland, Hungary and Slovakia, however, had no such exit route from subregional affairs. All had substantial borders with Balkan and/or Eastern countries. Also, unlike during the Kadar regime, the Hungarian government was carefully monitoring the situation of Hungarian minorities in neighbouring post-communist states which was a source of tension in bilateral relations with certain of them (Slovakia, Romania). Poland's Eastern (Russia) and Western (Germany) questions clearly set it apart from the other Visegrad countries. The suspension of Visegrad cooperation in 1993 can be taken as proof that it was not seen as the most effective tool to deal with their intra-regional problems and underscores how its role was restricted to external relations. According to Kolankiewicz (1994), by the end of 1992, four different approaches to subregional cooperation were identifiable.

The Czech Republic's approach was classed as 'minimalist'. Relations between the Central European states should be managed primarily on the basis of bilateral relations which could be 'complemented by multilateral ties such as those of the Central European Free Trade Area (CEFTA)' (Kolankiewicz, 1994, 485). There was uncompromising opposition to any institutionalisation of subregional cooperation and to the deepening of integration in CEFTA. According to this perspective, the Czech Republic's positive attitude towards Slovenia's initial expression of interest in CEFTA was a tactic to keep subregional cooperation diluted.

Hungary's approach was seen as 'pragmatic/instrumental'. Like the Czech Republic, Hungary has remained firmly against creating any formal institutions for subregional cooperation and has consistently stressed that the CEE states cannot be judged for suitability to enter the EU or NATO en masse and so individual countries from the region must be judged according to their individual efforts and progress. Thus Visegrad cooperation should go along with 'noble competition' (that is, no actions to further one's own cause which disadvantage others) *vis-à-vis* external organisations and such subregional cooperation which exists is open to new members but only when they attain the economic and political reform standards of the existing members. Hungary's approach was to utilise subregional cooperation when and where it is a useful means to specified ends according to its own priorities. Thus its interest in Visegrad cooperation was ignited in March 1990 when the Hungarian government of Josef Antall was mandated to withdraw from the Warsaw Pact; its proactive (with Poland) role in getting the Visegrad free trade talks organised in 1992 during a phase when the Czechoslovak leaders were stalling the tendency to use Visegrad summit meetings to discuss bilateral relations with Czechoslovakia in the period before the Hungary–Slovakia bilateral treaty was signed.[16]

Poland was taking more of a 'maximalist' approach, based on the notion that subregional cooperation should be promoted because it is intrinsically productive. This has included not only the preference to maximise the use of the Visegrad framework but also the whole range of emerging subregional initiatives (CEI, Baltic Council) and bilateral treaties which can support Poland's acceptance in to the mainstream European structures. The Poles 'saw themselves as the moving spirit behind the Visegrad Four, taking a lead which is understandable in that they have to go to greater lengths in defining themselves out of the sphere of Russian interest'(Kolankiewicz, 1994, 484). This maximalist approach has also been linked to Poland's potential as a leading subregional power (see below).

Finally, Slovakia, for which the links to subregional cooperation represented a 'lifeline'. The velvet divorce left the country faced with the challenge of state-building at a time when it was in danger of falling behind in its relations with the West since it was assessed as the economically disadvantaged and less politically stable half of the former Czechoslovakia. The Slovaks saw Visegrad as their main chance for staying in the leading group of post-communist states. During the Meciar regime, the Slovaks' tendency to push for an upgrading of CEFTA's substance and profile was often interpreted as an attempt to fashion a counterweight to its diminishing prospects *vis-à-vis* the EU and NATO.

Of course these different approaches interacted with each other. The idea that some kind of Central European security framework might be possible, popular for a while with certain members of the Polish political elite, gave rise to the idea that Poland was harbouring ambitions to be a major subregional power. This naturally only served to reinforce negative attitudes to subregional cooperation elsewhere in the Visegrad group. According to Vukadinovic (1996, 14)

> [the Polish]maximalist approach to co-operation within central Europe has not been accepted well by other partners, and some arguments have emerged in Poland regarding the creation of a greater Polish interest, stretching from the Baltic to the Black Sea. If only for this, Polish advocation for Romania and Ukraine joining the Visegrad group has been instantly judged as an attempt to draw closer countries that would support this Polish attitude and its maximalist concept of relations.

Despite differences in the focus and levels of concern with subregional affairs which made certain states at least more disposed to the idea that the Visegrad group could stay active and that its role might include adding extra layers of cooperation to the CEFTA framework, the Czechs' refusal to continue with political cooperation at the Visegrad level and insistence on restricting economic cooperation to the neo-liberal concept prevented these ideas being taken further. However, with or without the veto of individual countries the main factor, as noted earlier, was the sheer impracticality of any attempts to coordinate the course of reform. In many respects it was already too late anyway. CEFTA was clearly the only feasible course of action as far as the first moves to activate the revival of CEE states' mutual economic relations was concerned, and the main questions therefore were whether CEFTA could be made to work, what results it might generate and whether the different national approaches to subregional cooperation might exert an influence on CEFTA development at a later stage.

NOTES

1. There was a strong feeling in certain Western circles that a lasting breakdown of intra-CMEA trade could derail the transformation process by prolonging and adding to the scale of the recessionary phase. From the point of view of those who argued for a large-scale exit from the Soviet market would amount to throwing away decades of investment (Brabant, 1991) and, irrespective of the willingness of OECD countries to offer CEE genuine market access, supply inelasticities within CEE would prevent compensatory trade growth occurring for some years to come. Even those who were less convinced by the logic for protecting regional trade recognised that it was not only genuinely non-viable trade which would disappear.
2. As was noted in Chapter two, in real economic terms the reorientation in the direction of the EC on the part of certain CEE states (Hungary and Poland) was already a fact in the 1980s and therefore preceded the political revolutions. In the case of Hungary, in 1985 22.6 per cent of exports and 29.9 per cent of imports were with the EC/EFTA area and by 1989 this applied to 33.6 per cent of exports and 39.7 per cent of imports. For Poland the respective figures were 29.0 per cent and 39.6 per cent for exports and 25.3 per cent and 42.2 per cent for imports (data from Richter, 1997).
3. Some analysts argued that the granting of GSP had a more significant impact on CEE exports to the EC than the free trade provisions included in the Europe Agreements. See Faini and Portes (1995).
4. For example, contrast the (Polish) perspective of Perczynski who wrote that (1993, 1) 'subregional cooperation of the Visegrad group nations is not an unexpected historical incident. It grew out of meaningful experiences and traditions, and represents an endeavour to devise solutions to new problems of regional development. It is more than a mere symbol that the meeting of Poland's, Hungary's and Czechoslovakia's leaders took place in Visegrad. For it was at the same place where their ancestors convened in 1335: these were the kings – Poland's, Casmir The Great, Czechia's, Jan Luxembourg, and Hungary's, Charles Robert, who assembled there to face together the threats of their time' with the remarks of (Czech) commentator Stepanovsky (1995, 93) that the 'historical experience and memory of the Czech people – and, with some differences, also of the Slovaks – differed from that of the Poles. While throughout the centuries the latter's traditional enemy was Tsarist and then Soviet Russia (and, at times, German militarism), the Bohemian kingdom or the Czechoslovak Republic had never shared a common border with the Russian or Soviet Empire and, therefore, had not suffered from invasions, acts of aggression, or territorial or minority rights, disputes. Until the communist takeover and, in particular, the Russian invasion, occupation and humiliation of the Czechs and Slovaks in 1968, a broad stratum of people were inclined to see the giant Russian power as a friendly Slavic state ready to offer its helping hand to aid the Czechs who were being oppressed by German imperialism of either Prussian or Austrian origin'. Bakos, representing a Hungarian view, wrote (1993, 1025) that '(b)efore and after World War II the small countries in Central Europe were always tied to some greater power outside the region and could not have developed significant mutual cooperation even if they had wished to'.
5. Readers interested in looking at the arguments for and against the CEEU/CEPU in more detail should consult the contributions to Flemming and Rollo (1992).
6. These analyses, using gravity models or inter-war trade patterns as support, stressed that the level of trade among the CMEA countries had been way in excess of 'normal' levels.

7. Referring to the Europe Agreements, critics of the CEEU also pointed out that preferential trade for the ex-CMEA region was inconsistent with trade policies being pursued towards other sets of countries and could contravene international agreements.

8. For detailed discussion of the Visegrad cooperation see Dunay (1998), Vachudova (1993), Weydenthal (1992) and Cottey (1996, 1999).

9. Foreign direct investment brought in new actors in these policy processes. On the one hand, pressures to liberalise trade with the regional market came from inward investors following the 'headquarters' strategy, and on the other there were inward investors following the 'landlocked' approach who looked to reduce competition on domestic markets.

10. This suggests that the Visegrad three's determination to stress that they were not or would not become a new 'bloc' was serving not only policy to the West but to the East as well.

11. Hungary had over 20 years of experimentation with market forces; Czechoslovakia looked like it had the best post-communist economic legacy in terms of internal balance and foreign debt; Poland's case was more to do with strategic position and history.

12. It should be acknowledged that the preparation of the Europe Agreements provided a lesson on the benefits of cooperation rather than competition. Joint Visegrad negotiating positions reduced the negotiation period by one year and therefore facilitated early signature and implementation. See Handl (1999, 3).

13. These included problems such as different degrees of price liberalisation. Domestic energy, for example, was still receiving considerable state subsidies in Czechoslovakia whereas in Hungary this was no longer the case. See Okolicsanyi (1993).

14. Integration within the CEFTA area has always been differentiated because of the Czech–Slovak customs union formed on 1 January 1993. This rather than the CEFTA agreement governs their mutual trade and, moreover, the two countries have continued to operate free movement of labour. The Czech–Slovak situation has, however, really been a case of disintegration rather than progressive integration within CEFTA, as the countries had, by virtue of the division of the federal state, put their integration into reverse. Independent economic policies and reform strategies and a very short-lived common currency were obvious aspects of this. Their mutual trade has been in general decline, in terms of a proportion of their total trade, since 1993, despite the existence of a customs union which usually leads to an intensification of mutual trade.

15. Former Polish President Lech Walesa (though not the Polish Foreign Ministry) favoured institutionalised cooperation and during the Prague (6 May 1992) summit made a suggestion that the Visegrad could develop into an 'EC mirror-like organisation for economic and political integration' (Dunay, 1998, 16).

16. According to Okolicsanyi (1993, 22) Hungary and Poland warned that the two of them would go ahead and form their own free trade area if they (the Czechs and Slovaks) remained too preoccupied with the impending division of Czechoslovakia.

3. CEFTA: Aims and Objectives, Structure, Content and Implementation

INTRODUCTION

This chapter offers a detailed description of CEFTA cooperation, covering its aims and objectives, the form and content of the CEFTA treaty itself, and the operational aspects. It begins with an overview of the structure and provisions of the Cracow treaty, including details of the specific provisions for liberalisation of industrial goods and the concessions for agricultural goods together with an outline of the general provisions contained in the agreement. The second part covers the various amendments which have been introduced since CEFTA entered into force, most of which have been concerned with decisions to accelerate and enhance the trade liberalisation programme. The next stage is to explain how CEFTA functions in terms of arrangements for the supervision and monitoring the implementation of its provisions. This entails discussion of the roles of the three main layers of the CEFTA executive and administrative machinery which consists of the CEFTA summit, the CEFTA Joint Committee and the units responsible for CEFTA which are located in the individual countries' ministries with responsibility for external trade relations. The final section examines progress in realising the liberalisation targets which have been set, mainly using data on changes in the customs rates applying to industrial and agricultural products between 1993 and 1997. Before moving on to all these detailed aspects, it is useful to briefly outline the broad aims and objectives of CEFTA.

The aims of CEFTA, as set out in the preamble of the Cracow treaty, state that it was brought into existence to serve the signatories' 'intention to participate actively in the process of economic integration in Europe and ... their preparedness to co-operate in seeking ways and means to strengthen this process' (CEFTA, 1). To this end, the original objectives of CEFTA were described in Article 1 of the Cracow treaty as follows (CEFTA, 2): to gradually establish, by 1 January 2001 at the latest, a free area which conforms to GATT Article XXIV and, through the agreement to do so: (a) to promote trade expansion in order to develop the parties' economic relations, advance economic activity, improve living and employment conditions, increase productivity and financial stability; (b) to eliminate non-tariff obstacles to trade and ensure markets are genuinely competitive; (c) to contribute to the broader process of world-wide trade liberalisation.

The trade liberalisation timetable in CEFTA was originally linked to that of the Visegrad countries and the EU which is scheduled to be finally completed by 2001. Also in common with the EU arrangements, the principle of complete removal of protection was to be applied to industrial products only.[1] With one or two exceptions which allow an extra year for a small number of products the original deadline for the end of the transition period still stands. The liberalisation process has, however, been considerably accelerated and some pairs of countries already have achieved total duty removal or will do so earlier than 2001. Since the countries which have acceded to CEFTA have been also bound to the broad timetable agreed by the original members, trade liberalisation involving non-founder CEFTA countries has therefore been subject to a compressed transition period, particularly in those cases where there were no prior (to CEFTA accession) bilateral free trade agreements in force. While the extent of liberalisation of industrial goods trade achieved so far is such that the implementation of CEFTA is generally on course, there have been setbacks where liberalisation of agricultural trade has been concerned. Full liberalisation of agricultural products was brought onto the CEFTA agenda in December 1995 but subsequently suspended, in August 1998, due to the sheer sensitivity of certain agricultural items and influence of the broader context of intra-CEFTA trade in agricultural products.

3.1　THE CRACOW TREATY

The main influences on the design of the CEFTA treaty were the trade chapters of the Visegrad countries' Europe Agreements, the EFTA text, WTO rules for regional trade arrangements (Article XXIV of the GATT), and the CEFTA states' preference for bilateral timetables for liberalisation of trade in specific products.[2] The basic text of CEFTA is made up of the following three components: (a) the multilateral parts of the agreement, Chapters I, II and III, which set out the generic rules and regulations for the trade liberalisation process; (b) the protocols, which deal with specific trade liberalisation schedules between pairs of countries and certain technical and definitional issues; and (c) the annexes, which include elaboration of some of the articles in the general agreement and the fine detail of the protocols (for example, lists of products covered by certain categories identified in the bilateral trade protocols). The constituent parts of the original CEFTA text and their organisation are as follows:

Joint Declaration

Preamble which includes Article 1 (the objectives)

Chapter I – 'Industrial Products', which covers (in Articles 2 to 10) the specific provisions regarding liberalisation of industrial products.

Chapter II 'Agricultural Products', which covers, (in Articles 11 to 15) the specific provisions regarding concessions for agricultural products.

Chapter III – 'General Provisions', which includes the standard set of clauses about the terms and conditions of the trade liberalisation process. Articles 16 to 32 cover the following: 'rules of origin', 'internal taxation', 'general exceptions', 'security exceptions', 'state monopolies', 'payment rules', 'rules of competition concerning undertakings', 'state aid', 'government procurement', 'protection of intellectual property', 'dumping', 'general safeguards', 'structural adjustment', 're-export and serious shortage', 'fulfilment of obligations', 'procedure for the application of safeguard measures', and 'balance of payments difficulties'. Chapter III also includes the 'evolutionary clause' (Article 33) which clarifies the procedures concerning proposals to extend/enhance cooperation; the details of the role and procedures of the Joint Committee (Articles 34 and 35); 'trade relations covered by this and other Agreements' (Article 36) which includes confirmation that the Czech and Slovak Republics are one entity from the point of view of CEFTA; confirmation of the integral status of the annexes and protocols (Article 37); 'territorial application' (Article 38); the procedure for introducing amendments to the CEFTA (Article 39); and articles 40, 41 and 42 which specify the date of entry into force, the procedure for withdrawal and the Depositary (Government of Poland).[3]

Protocols 1, 2 and 3, which set out the timetables for abolition of customs duties on industrial goods between the Czech/Slovak Republics and Hungary, the Czech/Slovak Republics and Poland, and Hungary and Poland respectively.

Protocols 4, 5 and 6, which detail the bilateral agricultural concessions granted by the Czech/Slovak Republics and Hungary, the Czech/Slovak Republics and Poland, and Hungary and Poland respectively.[4]

Protocol 7, which covers, in 93 pages of (27) articles and (8) annexes, procedures and definitions connected to rules of origin, including the definition of products which qualify for duty and quota free treatment, necessary documents (e.g. EUR.1 Movement Certificate), the arrangements for cooperation of the parties' customs administrations so as to ensure documentary authenticity etc., and details of the degree and type of working and processing necessary for qualification of non-originating materials.

The details of the actual trade liberalisation programme are set out in the relevant bilateral components of CEFTA. Looking first at the timetables for eliminating duties on industrial products as set out in Protocols 1 to 3, these differed slightly in each case. In the bilateral agreement between the Czech/Slovak Republics and Hungary there were six headings. Headings 1 and 4 referred to goods (List

A – low sensitivity to competition) for which imports of goods to the Czech and Slovak Republics[5] and Hungary respectively would become duty-free on the day the CEFTA agreement entered into force. Headings 2 and 5 referred to goods (List C – high sensitivity to competition) for which the progressive elimination of duties would commence on 1 January 1995 and be completed by 1 January 2001. Headings 3 and 6 referred to goods (List B – medium sensitivity to competition) for which the progressive elimination of duties would commence on 1 January 1995 and be completed by 1 January 1997. The agreement between the Czech and Slovak Republics and Poland included an extra heading for the Polish side, covering imports of passenger cars, which extended the transition period to 1 January 2002. The Hungary–Poland agreement added two further headings, one for each side, which included products to be subject to duty-free tariff quotas until the end of the transition period.

As far as food and agricultural products were concerned, the concessions set out in the Czech and Slovak–Hungarian agreement specified two lists, one covering those goods which would qualify for two successive 10 per cent duty reductions and the other covering those goods which would get five successive 10 per cent reductions. Both sets of goods were, however, to remain subject to quotas. The agricultural concessions between the Czech and Slovak Republics and Poland set out in Protocol 5 again included two lists following the same principles as the Czech and Slovak Republics–Hungary arrangements plus a further list of Polish exports which became free of duty and quotas upon the entry into force of CEFTA. Finally, the Hungary–Poland agreement had the same two main lists plus provision to harmonise the treatment of Poland's exports of 'seafish and marine products' with the provisions of Hungary's free trade agreement with EFTA. At this stage of CEFTA, though the tariff reduction schedules for each of the lists were symmetrical between each country, the product compositions varied both within and between each of the protocols.

Certain other general principles might also be mentioned. Bearing in mind that the broader framework for regional trade arrangements was the GATT, the reductions applied to the basic duty which was the Most Favoured Nation rate applying in February 1992. Also, in the case of industrial products the parties agreed to a standstill rule which stipulated that no new charges equivalent to customs duties should be applied in mutual trade relations. Finally, in order to at least start off with broadly symmetrical benefits, in the negotiations which established the details of the bilateral protocols the '(p)arties to the agreement aimed at reaching a balance in concessions reciprocally including the respective lists of goods, groups of products having similar turnover volumes in the previous years' (CEFTA Joint Committee, 1998, 2).

3.2   REVISIONS TO CEFTA

This section deals with the evolution of CEFTA in respect of the formal changes the agreement has undergone since its entry into force, most of which have been concerned with the scope and speed of trade liberalisation. Table 3.1, which chronicles all agreements signed in connection with CEFTA, shows that the first major alterations were introduced during April 1994. These particular changes were in fact put on the agenda before CEFTA had even entered into force. The Joint Declaration inserted into the Cracow treaty at the last minute on the insistence of the Czech side (Rudka and Mizsei, 1995, 14) stated that the parties would 'immediately start to discuss the reduction of the transitional period to five years' (CEFTA, 2). Consequently, Additional Protocol 1 (the 'Budapest Accord' of April 1994) established 1 January 1998 as the new target date for the end of the transitional period for industrial goods trade and enhanced food and agricultural goods concessions.

Further significant steps forward in the trade liberalisation schedule were embodied in Additional Protocols 2 and 3, which brought liberalisation of industrial goods a further year forward and considerably remodelled the agricultural goods component of CEFTA. These represented the last major advances in the trade liberalisation programme, though some relatively minor revisions agreed in Jasna were elaborated in Additional Protocol 5. Subsequent Additional Protocols were necessitated by the need to amend CEFTA regulations in line with external commitments (the pan-European cumulation zone) and to resolve some anomalies connected to Slovenia's position in CEFTA.[6]

The provisions of Additional Protocols 3 and 5, together with the Protocols setting out the liberalisation timetables for the subsequent CEFTA newcomers, Bulgaria and Romania, mean that the current state of play is as follows. For trade in industrial goods, since 1 January 1997 only a small percentage of goods – the 'lists of exceptions' – (around 5 per cent of total tariff items) have remained subject to duties. The timetables for reducing the duties on the lists of exceptions vary between the CEFTA countries (Table 3.2). The agricultural concessions are more complicated, but the products to which the concessions apply are now divided into those to which common duties are now applied across CEFTA (so-called Lists A and B) and those which are still set out bilaterally (so-called Lists C and D).[7] List A goods (including breeding animals, horses, rabbits, durum wheat and oilseeds) became duty-free as of 1 January 1996, while List B goods (poultry meat, wheat, barley, flour, pastry, some fruit and vegetables) qualify for tariff levels which are below MFN rates.[8] According to Additional Protocol 3 no quotas are applied to imports of Lists A and B goods.[9] Lists C and D refer to the bilateral concessions applying between pairs of countries.[10] Some of the goods covered by the bilateral concessions are duty-free, while those duties and/or quantitative restrictions which are applied tend to be more favourable than those applied generally.

Table 3.1   List of agreements signed in the CEFTA framework

Title of Document	Date of signing	Date of application	Outcome
Central European Free Trade Agreement concluded by the Czech Republic, the Republic of Hungary, the Republic of Poland and the Slovak Republic.	21/12/92 (Cracow)	1./3/93	Original CEFTA text.
Additional Protocol to the CEFTA concerning the amendment to Protocols 1 to 6.	9/4/94 (Budapest)	1/7/94	Replaced Protocols 1 to 6. The liberalisation timetable for most sensitive industrial products shortened from 8 to 5 years. Enhanced concessions for agricultural products.
Additional Protocol No. 2 to the CEFTA.	18/8/95 (Warsaw)	1/1/96	Replaced Protocols 1 to 3. The liberalisation timetable for most sensitive industrial products shortened from 5 to 4 years.
Agreement Amending the CEFTA.	11/9/95 (Brno)	11/9/95	Introduced provision for CEFTA to enlarge and established the CEFTA membership criteria.
Agreement on Accession of Slovenia to CEFTA.	25/11/95 (Ljubljana)	1/1/96	Admission of Slovenia to CEFTA. Added Protocols 8–10.
Additional Protocol No. 3 to the CEFTA.	21/12/95 (Warsaw)	1/1/96	Replaced Protocols 4 to 6. Targeted 1/1/2000 for full liberalisation of agricultural trade.
Additional Protocol No. 4 to the CEFTA.	13/9/96 (Jasna)	1/1/97	Replaced Protocol 7, abolished annex to Article 8 of Accession Agreement for Slovenia. Introduced new rules of origin in line with 'pan-European cumulation zone'.
Additional Protocol No. 5 to the CEFTA.	13/9/96 (Jasna)	1/1/97	Replaced Protocols 1 to 3 and 8 to 10. Abolished duties on trade in goods of medium sensitivity between Poland and Slovenia. Minor corrections to other trade liberalisation schedules.
Agreement on Accession of Romania to CEFTA.	12/4/97 (Bucharest)	1/7/97	Admission of Romania to CEFTA. Added Protocols 18 to 21.
Additional Protocol No. 6 to the CEFTA.	19/12/97 (Warsaw)	1/4/98	Replaced Protocols 11 to 13 and 21. Liberalisation of Slovenia's agricultural trade harmonised with the provisions of Additional Protocol No. 3.
Agreement on Accession of Bulgaria to CEFTA.	18/7/98 (Sofia)	1/1/99	Admission of Bulgaria to CEFTA. Added Protocols 22 to 26.

Table 3.2 **Dates for complete elimination of duties on industrial goods trade**

	Bulgaria	Czech/ Slovak R.	Hungary	Poland	Romania	Slovenia
Bulgaria		1/1/1999	1/1/2001	1/1/2002	1/1/2002	1/1/2000
Czech/ Slovak R.	1/1/1999		1/1/2000	1/1/2001	1/1/2001	1/1/1997
Hungary	1/1/2001	1/1/2000		1/1/2001	1/1/2002	1/1/2001
Poland	1/1/2002	1/1/2002	1/1/2002		1/1/2002	1/1/2002
Romania	1/1/2002	1/1/2001	1/1/2002	1/1/2002		1/1/2002
Slovenia	1/1/2000	1/1/1999	1/1/2001	1/1/2001	1/1/2001	

Note: Exporting countries are in the vertical (far left) column; importing countries are in the horizontal (top) row.

Sources: Additional Protocol to CEFTA No. 5; Agreement on Accession of the Republic of Bulgaria to the Central European Free Trade Agreement; Agreement on Accession of Romania to the Central European Free Trade Agreement

The fact that trade liberalisation has generally developed in a progressive way can be seen as one indicator of the success of subregional integration in CEFTA. The first acceleration of the CEFTA trade liberalisation timetable is often portrayed as a response to the advances in the Europe Agreement schedules agreed at the EU Copenhagen summit. Yet, as noted earlier, the first proposal to accelerate CEFTA trade liberalisation was in fact already on the table at the time of the signing of the Cracow treaty (therefore well before any alterations to EU–CEE schedules) and subsequent CEFTA liberalisation advances were not accompanied/preceded by corresponding EU–CEE developments. The moves to enhance the speed and coverage of the trade liberalisation were connected to pragmatic reasons to make mutual market access more preferential.[11] The CEFTA countries, first Poland and Hungary and later the Czech and Slovak Republics, began to post growing trade deficits after 1993 which renewed the imperatives for export growth. At the same time, the tendency, almost universal in CEE, for imports from the EU to continue growing faster than exports to it was compounded by the tendency of the EU to punish CEE for 'unfair' trading practices by reversing access to the EU market for certain important products. In addition, recessionary conditions in the main EU markets were slowing the momentum of CEE export growth there. In this context, all parties to CEFTA became increasingly well disposed to liberalising the CEFTA market at a faster pace. Moreover, as well as the general idea that a more accessible CEFTA market would increase export opportunities, from the collective point of view if the liberalisation process could not only prevent further trade diversion from regional to EU producers but also reverse some of the trade diversion which had already occurred, then the result should be net gains for all the CEFTA parties.

As far as the specific interests of individual countries were concerned, it can be noted that the Czechs and Slovaks were particularly voracious in the push for faster liberalisation due to their surplus trade positions in CEFTA (see Chapter 4) together with the need to compensate for declining mutual trade, and the Czech neo-liberal/open-door approach to foreign economic relations. At the same time, the Hungarian and Polish sides, though tending to be in less of a rush than the Czech/Slovak sides, anticipated that the decline in the mutual trade of the Czech and Slovak Republics could create additional export opportunities for their producers. At the political level, elections in Poland (1993) and Hungary (1994) brought about a term of office for governments of former communists who were not only comfortable with policies to resuscitate trade with former CMEA partners but positively encouraged it.[12] Since its entry into CEFTA, Slovenia has also demonstrated similar attitudes to the Czechs and Slovaks as far as industrial trade has been concerned, but along with Poland, has been far more cautious over the pace and extent of removing barriers for agricultural goods: 'liberalisation of agricultural trade has been much slower. Poland and Slovenia in particular have resisted changes which they fear would damage their inefficient farming sectors'(*Financial Times*, 14/9/98). On the other hand for Hungary, also with a significant but in its case relatively efficient agricultural sector which was being boosted by growing involvement of foreign direct investment and the country's export-oriented agricultural development strategy, CEFTA provided the perfect context to target former CMEA markets. As Kiss (1999, 88) wrote:

> (s)ince as a consequence of the demise of the CMEA and the economic and financial crisis in the former Soviet Union, a part of her traditional Eastern European markets was lost and as the EU – in spite of signing the Association Agreement – failed to provide an expanding market, Hungary's main endeavour became to regain the lost Eastern European markets, including the markets of the neighbouring countries. In order to achieve this goal Hungary revitalised her traditional relations.

3.3   SUPERVISION AND ADMINISTRATION OF CEFTA

There are three main levels of the CEFTA administration, which operates strictly according to intergovernmentalist principles. The supreme authority is the Summit meeting of Prime Ministers of the CEFTA countries, which takes place annually in the chair country. The main function of the CEFTA summit is to 'review and evaluate co-operation hitherto, the activities and results within CEFTA, and to outline the forms of co-operation and activities to be carried out before the next Summit' (Ministry of Economic Relations and Development of Republic of Slovenia, 1997). The agenda usually includes matters connected with the implementation of the CEFTA treaty and any major disputes, applications from interested countries and proposals to extend the extent of cooperation. The chair country may also view the summit as a chance to forward its own agenda for CEFTA.

From the point of view of the practical operation and implementation of CEFTA, the summit is really just a rubber-stamping occasion. The prime responsibility for overseeing the process of putting the free trade agreement into practice and dealing with disputes therefore essentially rests with the CEFTA Joint Committee. The Joint Committee, which is composed of the member states' ministers with responsibility for foreign economic relations, prepares most of the work for the summit and reaches decisions and resolutions which the latter approves. The Joint Committee operates a rotating presidency, following the alphabetical order of the CEFTA states, with a one-year term of office.[13] Article 34 of CEFTA sets out the terms of reference for the Joint Committee and says that as well as supervising and administering the CEFTA, the parties may exchange information and hold consultations through the Joint Committee which can also 'take decisions in the cases provided for in this Agreement. On other matters the Committee may make recommendations' (CEFTA, 17). The procedures of the Joint Committee (Article 35) state that meetings can take place whenever necessary but require them to happen at least once a year (the regular plenary sessions of the CEFTA Joint Committee usually take place a couple of months before the CEFTA summit – see Table 3.3) and that decisions must be unanimous. A long-standing problem has been that the modus operandi for the Joint Committee as set out in Article 35 is rather basic and there has been no clear guidance concerning, for example, aspects of agenda-setting, procedures for requesting an extraordinary session of the Joint Committee and responsibility for hosting extraordinary sessions once convened, use of written procedures for reaching certain decisions or recommendations, and so on. This was finally settled in Budapest in October 1999 when the CEFTA Prime Ministers formerly approved the comprehensive Rules of Procedure agreed by the Joint Committee during their meeting on 18 June 1999. The officials of the country holding the CEFTA presidency are also required to prepare a report on the 'Functioning and Implementation of CEFTA' covering their year of office and on the basis of this report, together with the decisions and recommendations of the CEFTA Joint Committee and summit meetings of the same year, the incoming CEFTA chair country prepares a 'Plan of Activities of the CEFTA countries' to serve as a framework for CEFTA work in the year ahead.

Table 3.3   **CEFTA summit and Joint Committee meetings**

	Meeting	Place and date(s)	Guest countries
1994	Joint Committee	Prague, 2 February Budapest, 29 April	
1994	Summit	Poznan, 25 November	Slovenia
1995	Joint Committee	Warsaw, 17–18 September Ljubljana, 25 November* Warsaw, 21 December	
1995	Summit	Brno, 11 September	Bulgaria, Lithuania, Romania, Slovenia
1996	Joint Committee	Bratislava, 5–6 June	
1996	Summit	Jasna, 13–14 September	Bulgaria, Latvia, Lithuania, Romania, Ukraine
1997	Joint Committee	Bucharest, 12 April* Bled, 3–4 July Warsaw, 21 December	
1997	Summit	Portoroz, 12–13 September	Bulgaria, Croatia, Latvia, Lithuania, FYR Macedonia, Ukraine
1998	Joint Committee	Prague, 3 July Sofia, 18 July*	
1998	Summit	Prague, 11–12 September	None
1999	Joint Committee	Budapest, 17–18 June	
1999	Summit	Budapest, 20 October	None

Notes:
Only CEFTA summits have been open to guest countries.

* Extraordinary meetings convened for signing of accession treaties.

Since the beginning of 1995, the second tier group of the CEFTA administrative machinery has expanded as different minister-level teams (including ministers for agriculture, finance and public procurement) have convened in connection with the expanding agenda of CEFTA. The Joint Committee is also able to call on the services of working parties, composed of relevant experts from the CEFTA countries, which it can convene for technical tasks or specialist investigations connected to the implementation and potential further development of CEFTA. There is a division of labour for the leadership of working parties and coordination of their tasks. Previous working parties have looked at proposals for CEFTA institutions (led by Slovakia), liberalisation of trade in services (led by the Czech

Republic), liberalisation of capital movements (led by Poland), preparation of the Joint Committee Rules of Procedure (led by Slovakia), implementation of CEFTA Article 23, which covers state aids (led by Slovenia). As well as working parties, the CEFTA Joint Committee can also convene sub-committees to deal with matters of outstanding importance. For example in June 1999, in the context of the need to further examine ways to improve the application of CEFTA provisions and coordinate the liberalisation of intra-CEFTA agricultural trade with the impending incorporation into the EU Common Agricultural Policy, the Budapest Joint Committee confirmed the formation of a subcommittee on agricultural trade.

Finally, as a consequence of the absence of any institutional framework for CEFTA (see Chapter 5) all of the appropriate work connected to CEFTA is carried out by government officials of the member states, including the functions that would normally be carried out by a permanent secretariat. This is the third tier of the CEFTA administrative machinery. Each member country has its own groups of experts, usually part of a department for multilateral trade or department for European integration, who are responsible for the detailed and technical aspects of CEFTA cooperation and, during their country's presidency, organising the main CEFTA annual meetings. The official working language for CEFTA is English. With regard to the informational aspect of CEFTA, which is generally scant, the main sphere of cooperation involves the national statistical offices of the CEFTA countries who cooperate to produce the quarterly *CESTAT* which covers a range of economic and social indicators for each of the CEFTA countries.[14]

3.4 IMPLEMENTATION OF THE CEFTA PROVISIONS

As far as realisation of the enhanced trade liberalisation programme is concerned, the CEFTA countries themselves have concluded that (CEFTA Joint Committee, 10)

> [the] functioning of CEFTA demonstrates that the Agreement has met the expectations and has been a decisive element in the increase of the volume of mutual trade among the CEFTA markets. The CEFTA provisions have been implemented thus the gradual abolition of trade barriers and the establishment of fair conditions of competition are proceeding in accordance with the objectives defined by the Parties.

Though the developments in intra-CEFTA trade since 1993 (covered in Chapter 4) have been sufficiently positive to suggest that CEFTA cooperation has produced the desired results, it must also be shown that liberalisation targets have been met in order to credit CEFTA as a key factor in generating this trade growth. According to the data available, the overall conclusion should be that the implementation of CEFTA has been a general success, though it is the case that while the liberalisation of industrial products has progressed relatively smoothly, the same cannot be said for agricultural products which has been a far more complicated affair.[15]

Looking at industrial products first, Table 3.4 compares the levels of protectionism applied to imports from CEFTA in 1993 and 1997. The data shows that the original CEFTA plus Slovenia were all close to complying with the objective of eliminating the majority of duties by 1997, and the most diligent duty removers had been Slovakia and Slovenia (98.5 per cent of overall CEFTA imports were duty-free) followed by the Czech Republic (98.3 per cent), Hungary (87.8 per cent) and Poland (72.5 per cent). Whereas the Czech Republic, Slovakia and Slovenia had already begun implementing bilateral free trade agreements with Romania, the Hungarian and Polish averages were held down by their arrangements with Romania, which only came into effect when Romania joined CEFTA in the second half of 1997 (interestingly, Romania recorded a higher average duty-free content of CEFTA imports (76.5 per cent) than Poland). Also noticeable is the high proportion of Slovak exports to Hungary and Poland included in the latters' lists of exceptions and not qualifying for duty-free treatment by the 1997 target. Since the excepted items tended to be in declining sensitive sectors (textiles, steel products and certain chemical products) this may have been indicative of some problems of lack of dynamism in the Slovak export structure.

The absence of quotas and the successful application of the standstill rule to the effect 'at present charges having equivalent effect to import customs duties are eliminated in mutual trade between the CEFTA parties' (CEFTA Joint Committee, 1998, 2) mean that the use of customs duty rates to indicate the extent of liberalisation gives a reliable picture of the state of play for industrial products trade in CEFTA. While this trade has been affected by sporadic protectionist actions, usually through the application of safeguard measures, these have tended to be across the board measures applied to all trade partners not specifically to CEFTA.[16] In 1997 Richter (1997, 4) wrote that of the various safeguard measures possible according to CEFTA rules just the 'structural adjustment' one has been applied in practice, and Hungary and Poland were the only parties that had made use of it up to then. More recently, the UNECE (1999,151) reported that despite the rise of 'trade frictions' among the CEFTA states in late 1998 (mainly to do with agricultural trade), there 'have been no major trade policy reversals in the east European and Baltic region ... Moreover, the general tendency remains for a further liberalisation of tariffs in 1999. Tariffs on the region's trade with the EU, as well as within CEFTA and BFTA, are expected to be reduced according to existing schedules'.[17]

Following the various amendments to the length of the original transition period, CEFTA producers receive preferential treatment *vis-à-vis* EU and EFTA producers. CEFTA has therefore gone beyond a mere levelling of the playing

Table 3.4 Liberalisation of industrial products in intra-CEFTA trade, 1993 and 1997 (% of imports by level of liberalisation according to customs rates)

	1993														
	Customs rate = 0					Customs rate < MFN					Customs rate = MFN				
CZ	HU 26.7	PL 51.9	SK 100	SL –	RO –	HU 0	PL 0	SK 0	SL –	RO –	HU 73.3	PL 48.1	SK 0	SL –	RO –
HU	CZ 50.0	PL 63.2	SK 63.7	SL –	RO –	CZ 0	PL 0	SK 0	SL –	RO –	CZ 50.0	PL 36.8	SK 36.3	SL –	RO –
PL	CZ n/a	HU n/a	SK n/a	SL –	RO –	CZ n/a	HU n/a	SK n/a	SL –	RO –	CZ n/a	HU n/a	SK n/a	SL –	RO –
SK	CZ 100	HU 53.7	PL 69.0	SL –	RO –	CZ 0	HU 0	PL 0	SL –	RO –	CZ 0	HU 46.3	PL 31.0	SL –	RO –
SL	CZ –	HU –	PL –	SK –	RO –	CZ –	HU –	PL –	SK –	RO –	CZ –	HU –	PL –	SK –	RO –
RO	CZ –	HU –	PL –	SK –	SL –	CZ –	HU –	PL –	SK –	SL –	CZ –	HU –	PL –	SK –	SL –

Table 3.4 continued

1997

	Customs rate = 0					Customs rate < MFN					Customs rate = MFN				
CZ	HU 94.4	PL 99.2	SK 100	SL 100	RO 98.1	HU 5.6	PL 0.8	SK 0	SL 0	RO 1.9	HU 0	PL 0	SK 0	SL 0	RO 0
HU	CZ 88.0	PL 95.4	SK 86.4	SL 89.9	RO 79.3	CZ 12	PL 4.6	SK 13.6	SL 10.1	RO 20.7	CZ 0	PL 0	SK 0	SL 0	RO 0
PL	CZ 90.5	HU 95.5	SK 74.8	SL 98.2	RO 3.6	CZ 9.5	HU 4.5	SK 25.2	SL 1.8	RO 96.4	CZ 0	HU 0	SK 0	SL 0	RO 0
SK	CZ 100	HU 95.6	PL 98.9	SL 100	RO 98.1	CZ 0	HU 4.4	PL 1.1	SL 0	RO 1.9	CZ 0	HU 0	PL 0	SL 0	RO 0
SL	CZ 100	HU 98.3	PL 98.1	SK 100	RO 96.0	CZ 0	HU 1.1	PL 1.9	SK 0	RO 4	CZ 0	HU 0	PL 0	SK 0	RO 0
RO	CZ 97.6	HU 74.5	PL 30.7	SK 100	SL 79.7	CZ 2.4	HU 25.2	PL 69.2	SK 0	SL 20.3	CZ 0	HU 0	PL 0	SK 0	SL 0

Source: CEFTA Joint Committee (1998).

field for regional producers. However, despite the overall record of substantial, on schedule, duty reductions achieved for intra-CEFTA trade, the lack of a genuine multilateral framework to ensure common treatment of all the member countries' intra-CEFTA imports has meant that the potential for some distortion of intra-CEFTA trade has characterised the transition period. Tables 3.4 and 3.5 illustrate the problem as far as industrial goods are concerned (Table 3.6 tells a similar story for agriculture). In the case of Hungary, for example, exports to the Czech and Slovak Republics, Slovenia and Romania are subject to less favourable treatment than those applying for producers from other CEFTA countries.

As far as agricultural trade is concerned, as a guide to the extent of liberalisation on the basis of changes in import duties Table 3.6 shows that levels of protectionism had been considerably reduced by 1997. It is, however, difficult to generate an overall picture of the progress in liberalisation for a number of reasons. First, as noted earlier in this chapter, trade in certain agricultural products is regulated by quotas as well as tariffs, so the data given in Table 3.6 is only a partial representation of the liberalisation progress. Second, some countries have negotiated exemptions from the obligations included in Additional Protocol 3, for example Slovenia, for which exchanges are subject to lists A1 and B1, which in the case of its imports only allow higher import duties for lists A and B goods until 2000; and Poland, which insisted (to the effect of complicating Bulgaria's accession negotiations) on retaining duties for a number of list A imports from Bulgaria. Third, since 1998 agricultural trade in CEFTA, particularly concerning strategic (and therefore deemed sensitive) lines such as dairy products, pork and wheat which also account for a high proportion of intra-CEFTA trade (Kiss, 1997), has been complicated by a mixture of problems. Some have been internal (overproduction, diverting of produce affected by loss of sales to Russia, re-exporting of produce imported from third parties, discrepancies in state support systems), others extraneous (increase of subsidised EU exports finding their way onto CEFTA markets). Faced with the political backlash of severe problems for sections of their farming communities, several CEFTA governments took a range of unilateral actions contravening both the spirit and rules of CEFTA[18] and following their meeting in Prague in August 1998 the CEFTA countries' agricultural ministers 'suspended liberalising their agricultural and food trade until a survey of the existing concessions and agricultural and trade policies has been made' (*Central European Business Weekly,* 28/8 – 3/9/98, 2).

The difficulties and disputes which have arisen in intra-CEFTA agricultural trade should certainly not be presented as a major failure of the CEFTA project. It must be remembered that trade in agricultural and food products represent only some 10 per cent of total intra-CEFTA exchanges and that the liberalisation has been maintained for most categories of products traded. Moreover, any assessment of this aspect of CEFTA has to be set against the fact that agricultural trade tends to be universally problematic. Bearing these points in mind, some earlier conclusions reached by analysts at the Warsaw-based World Economy Research Institute still seem like a reasonable assessment: '(a)lthough these decisions have run into technical problems, they have played a fundamental part in expediting liberalisation of the most heavily protected segment of international trade: agricultural products'(World Economy Research Institute, 1996, 188–9). The main issues to consider, therefore, are whether the success in the implementation of the tariff and quota dimensions of CEFTA cooperation, for industry and agriculture, has translated into an appropriate expansion of trade and market integration in CEFTA and whether there have been any significant non-economic outcomes of CEFTA cooperation so far. These questions are the topic of the next chapter.

Table 3.5   Industrial goods: numbers of tariff items included in 'Lists of Exceptions'

	Bulgaria	Czech/ Slovak R.	Hungary	Poland	Romania	Slovenia
Bulgaria	–	none	1592 items	27 items	8 items	1677 items
Czech/ Slovak R.	none	–	414 items	28 items	6 items	none
Hungary	1755 items	589 items	–	67 items	20 items	351 items
Poland	18 items	42 items	42 items	–	42 items	77 items
Romania	18 items	6 items	20 items	18 items	–	18 items
Slovenia	982 items	none	830 items	20 items	9 items	–

Notes:
Importing countries are in the vertical (far left) column; exporting countries in the horizontal (top) row.
In the cases of Bulgaria/Hungary and Bulgaria/Slovenia the number of items do not represent Lists of Exceptions as such but are the 'regular' sensitive items being liberalised according to the schedules agreed by particular groups of countries which can vary as long as the overall process of liberalisation is within the overall deadlines set for CEFTA.

Sources: Additional Protocols to CEFTA No. 5; Agreement on Accession of the Republic of Bulgaria to the Central European Free Trade Agreement; Agreement on Accession of Romania to the Central European Free Trade Agreement, Bucharest.

Table 3.6 Liberalisation of agricultural products in intra-CEFTA trade, 1993 and 1997 (% of imports by level of liberalisation according to customs rates)

1993

	Customs rate = 0					Customs rate < MFN					Customs rate = MFN				
CZ	HU 21.6	PL 32.5	SK 100	SL –	RO –	HU 16.8	PL 4.8	SK 0	SL –	RO –	HU 61.6	PL 62.7	SK 0	SL –	RO –
HU	CZ 0	PL 0	SK 0	SL –	RO –	CZ 17.5	PL 26.8	SK 20.5	SL –	RO –	CZ 82.5	PL 73.2	SK 79.5	SL –	RO –
PL	CZ n/a	HU n/a	SK n/a	SL –	RO –	CZ n/a	HU n/a	SK n/a	SL –	RO –	CZ n/a	HU n/a	SK n/a	SL –	RO –
SK	CZ 100	HU 19.2	PL 10.9	SL –	RO –	CZ 0	HU 16.3	PL 4.3	SL –	RO –	CZ 0	HU 64.5	PL 84.8	SL –	RO –
SL	CZ –	HU –	PL –	SK –	RO –	CZ –	HU –	PL –	SK –	RO –	CZ –	HU –	PL –	SK –	RO –
RO	CZ –	HU –	PL –	SK –	SL –	CZ –	HU –	PL –	SK –	SL –	CZ –	HU –	PL –	SK –	SL –

Table 3.6 continued

1997

	Customs rate = 0					Customs rate < MFN					Customs rate = MFN				
CZ	HU 28.1	PL 39.6	SK 100	SL 44.5	RO 22.2	HU 59	PL 59.4	SK 0	SL 8.3	RO 48.2	HU 12.9	PL 1.0	SK 0	SL 47.2	RO 29.6
HU	CZ 35.1	PL 28.7	SK 46	SL 6.4	RO 55.2	CZ 25.3	PL 58.4	SK 21.5	SL 19.9	RO 9.1	CZ 39.6	PL 12.9	SK 32.5	SL 73.7	RO 35.6
PL	CZ 22.5	HU 39.1	SK 35.1	SL 100	RO 86.9	CZ 77.4	HU 60.9	SK 64.9	SL 0	RO 11.7	CZ 0.1	HU 0	SK 0	SL 0	RO 0
SK	CZ 100	HU 67.3	PL 41.8	SL 10.1	RO 22.2	CZ 0	HU 23.5	PL 54.8	SL 0	RO 75.6	CZ 0	HU 9.2	PL 3.4	SL 89.9	RO 2.2
SL	CZ 0	HU 0	PL .0	SK 0	RO 0	CZ 82.2	HU 57.5	PL 44.2	SK 25.7	RO 90	CZ 17.8	HU 42.5	PL 55.8	SK 74.3	RO 10
RO	CZ 29.8	HU 11.6	PL 19.4	SK 1.9	SL 18.4	CZ 63.5	HU 62.4	PL 17.8	SK 84.7	SL 67.8	CZ 6.7	HU 26	PL 62.8	SK 13.4	SL 13.8

Source: CEFTA Joint Committee (1998)

58

NOTES

1. Which in turn was in line with the GATT–WTO regulations on the formation of regional free trade areas (Article XXIV) which stipulates that the transition period to free should be ten years.

2. It should be mentioned that CEFTA's similarity to the Europe Agreements applied only to the trade chapters of the latter. The Europe Agreements were, at least in principle, much broader and contained many elements of cooperation excluded from CEFTA. See Richter (1997).

3. Further clarification of some of the articles included in Chapter III is elaborated in the 'Record of Understanding', along with the provision to set up, if necessary, an arbitration procedure, and a declaration of the parties' 'readiness to examine in the Joint Committee the possibility of extending to each other any concessions they grant or will grant to third countries with which they concluded a Free Trade Agreement or other similar agreement to which Article XXIV of the General Agreement on Tariffs and Trade applies' (CEFTA, 21). The six annexes to the General Agreement cover: (I) goods defined as agricultural rather than industrial products for the purposes of the agreement; (II) timetable for elimination of import charges equivalent to duties; (III) details of goods covered by quantitative import restrictions and equivalent measures during the transition period and schedule for elimination of them; (IV) details of goods covered by quantitative export restrictions and equivalent measures during the transition period and schedule for elimination of them; (V) the procedure for the notification of draft technical regulations as required by Article 10; and finally (VI) the list of multilateral agreements applying as far as protection of intellectual property is concerned.

4. Full details of the products covered by each of the headings within Protocols 1 to 6 are given in their annexes.

5. Trade between the Czech Republic and Slovakia is governed by their mutual customs union (established upon the division of Czechoslovakia) rather than CEFTA. In their relations with the other CEFTA parties the Czech and Slovak Republics are treated as one entity.

6. Additional Protocol No. 6 was necessitated because of an intra-CEFTA dispute which arose in connection with the fact that though Slovenia's accession treaty had been signed in November 1995, her membership did not come on stream until January 1996. Thus Slovenia was not a signatory to Additional Protocol No. 3 which introduced important changes to the agricultural trade dimension of CEFTA. This was an important lesson for the CEFTA teams to make sure that this problem did not recur in subsequent enlargements.

7. During the Bulgarian accession talks the Polish side negotiated an exception to the provisions of Additional Protocol No. 3 by insisting on retaining import duties on imports of a few list A products from Bulgaria.

8. Some examples of goods (list A) which according to the provisions of Additional Protocol 3 became duty-free across CEFTA included: live horse, donkey, sheep, goat, poultry, fish, cattle and pig for breeding, sheep, goat, horse, donkey meat, fresh and frozen fish, some seafood, processed and preserved fish, animal hair and skin, and different non-edible animal products, live plants, bulbs, cut flowers, egg plant, mushroom, tomato, carrot, preserved and dehydrated vegetables, manioc, sweet potato, arrowroot, coconut, cashew nut, banana, dates, pineapple, avocado, mango, grape, papaya, pear, kiwi, preserved and dehydrated fruits, coffee, tea, pepper, vanilla, cinnamon, clove, ginger and other spices, hard wheat, seeding maize, rice, different oil seeds (rape, sunflower, cotton, sesame, mustard and so on) flour, soyabean, peanut, apricot, sugarcane, animal fats, vegetable fats, olive oil, palm oil, juice of tropical fruits, mineral water. Goods to which applied common tariff concessions across CEFTA (list B) included: cattle, pigs, chickens, turkeys, other poultry, beef, pork, poultry meat and liver, pig meat, pig and poultry fat, carp, milk, milk powder, cream, cabbage, lettuce, carrot, beans, spinach, asparagus, frozen vegetables, fresh melon and other fresh fruits, wheat, rye, oats, cereals, flour, barley, margarine, meat products, candy, cocopowder, chocolate, raw pastry, cucumber, onion, homogenised vegetables, grape juice, apple juice (Kiss, (1997, 7–8).

9. It should be noted that lists A1 and B1 operate in the case of Slovenia. As part of the compromise reached at Portoroz lists A1 and B1 set out lists A and B items for which Slovenia is applying quotas until 1 January 2000.

10. To make it clear, lists C and D are not general categories of goods receiving different treatment. In the Hungary–Czech/Slovak protocol, for example, list C covers the bilateral concessions given by the Czech/Slovak side to Hungary while list D covers the reciprocal bilateral concessions Hungary makes to the Czech Republic and Slovakia.

11. Calls to amend the CEFTA details, on grounds that the liberalisation schedules incorporated into the Cracow Treaty were not bold enough to generate a substantial early response in the volume of intra-CEFTA trade, were also emanating from the academic community. See, for example, Toth (1994).

12. Some recent statements by the top officials of the Czech Social Democratic Party indicate that the less zealous approach to trade reorientation and more positive attitude towards ex-CMEA markets has been a broader tendency among leftist political groups in CEE. Following his return from a visit with a trade delegation to central Asia in April 1999 Milos Zeman said that 'It's not a question of the abolition of the Comecon (Council for Mutual Economic Assistance) as an institution, it's the fact that we were dumb enough to abandon eastern markets, where the Americans, Germans, Japanese and a number of other producers promptly arrived in our place. It was simply economic stupidity, no more, no less'. The Trade and Industry Minister went slightly further: 'Miroslav Gregr, who was also on the trip, said during the visit that Comecon should not have been abolished and agreed with Mr Zeman that it was an error to leave the former Soviet markets in the 1990s' (*Central European Business Weekly*, 30/4–6/5/99, 4).

13. The present order of rotation of the CEFTA chair is as follows: 1. Bulgaria; 2. The Czech Republic; 3. Hungary; 4. Poland; 5. Romania; 6. Slovakia; 7. Slovenia.

14. The data on intra-CEFTA trade is, however, rudimentary, and covers only the US$ value of the mutual trade of each of the CEFTA countries.

15. This chapter's discussion of implementation is concerned with the core CEFTA objectives of CEFTA, the removal/reduction of tariffs and quantitative restrictions on trade. Articles of CEFTA dealing with other dimensions of liberalisation, including rules on state aids, public procurement, are dealt with in Chapter 5.

16. Actions which contravene the spirit of CEFTA are usually discussed at the various CEFTA meetings. For example the Portoroz agenda discussed the 7 per cent general import surcharge imposed by Slovakia in 1997, the import deposit schemes introduced by the Czech Republic and Slovakia in 1997, extraordinary customs duties on imports of petrol (13 per cent) and fuel oil (20 per cent) and metallurgical products (9 per cent) in the case of Poland. Extraordinary problems concerning Hungarian grain exports dominated the September 1998 Prague summit.

17. Though Hungary introduced a quota on Czech steel in January 1999 this was in response to Czech actions to restrict wheat imports from Hungary and thus was essentially a dispute based on problems of agricultural rather than industrial trade. Apart from this, intra-CEFTA trade was not included in the various protectionist measures for industrial products imposed by many CEFTA countries, particularly on the EU and producers from Russia and the Commonwealth of Independent States. See UNECE (1999, 151).

18. For example in August 1998 Slovakia introduced a 70 per cent tariff on wheat imports from Hungary – see the discussion of the 1998 CEFTA 'wheat wars' in Dunay (1998). Also, in August 1998 Polish farmers blocked roads in order to protest against what were seen as 'excessive' grain imports to Poland while losses accruing to the Polish state railway caused by Polish farmers spilling wheat onto railway tracks forced them to decide to limit the transport of grain coming from Hungary (BBC, EE/3298 C/5, 6/8/98). As a final example, in October 1998 the Czech government cut the amounts of sugar which can be imported from CEFTA countries in order to stave off farmers' threats to blockade all road and rail routes into Prague. The farmers were not only protesting about cheap sugar imports but also were 'against subsidised food imports from EU and CEFTA countries, notably dairy products and pigs'. (*Central European Business Weekly*, 30/10–5/11/98, 5).

4. CEFTA and Reintegration of Central and Eastern Europe

INTRODUCTION

This chapter discusses some of the results of CEFTA cooperation, focusing on both economic and political outcomes and taking into account two dimensions of reintegration which are firstly the contribution to the 'return to Europe' (primary integration strategy) and secondly the more immediate impact on subregional economic relations (secondary integration strategy). As far as the question of reintegration at the subregional level is concerned the main success indicator in this respect is trade. In the CEFTA case the baseline expectations should have been, first, that a 'normalisation' of trade would be achieved, based on resumption of exchange of those goods which are viable in the post-CMEA markets and, second, that fresh patterns of exchange would emerge on the back of transforming economic structures at the national level. The economic effects of CEFTA concern not only trade but also investment flows since the merging of national markets through trade liberalisation is usually regarded as a factor likely to further stimulate inflows of foreign direct investment (FDI). Since FDI inflows can influence the scale and structure of trade within the subregion as well as with other external markets, the relationship between CEFTA and FDI has to be investigated with this two-way process in mind.

The range of effects of CEFTA cooperation has not been confined to the strictly economic field, however. Recent work on the impact of subregional groupings (SRG) in the new Europe has revealed that political advantages of subregional cooperation can accrue even where the brief is formally restricted to the economic sphere. According to a major study carried out for the Institute for EastWest Studies (Cottey, 1996, 21) which covered the main SRG which have emerged in post-cold war Europe, the generic contributions of subregional cooperation include the following: 'they are a practical means of integration, creating interdependence and solidarity ... foster cooperative behaviour and reduced tensions (and) ... help create a political/economic continuum throughout Europe, warding off any new two way divide'.[1] The political dimension of CEFTA cooperation can be analysed at two levels. First, as Handl (1999, 7) reminds us

61

'the whole idea of CEFTA was highly political – to convince the EC partners of the ability of the CEFTA states to access the EC', so one important issue is the extent to which CEFTA cooperation has served the prime post-communist foreign policy objective. In other words, in what ways has CEFTA cooperation been an instrument for EU pre-accession, beyond facilitating preliminary mutual market integration of this particular cluster of future EU members? The second dimension of CEFTA's political role is the influence of the practical business of implementing subregional free trade arrangements on regional political relations and 'soft' security not only in CEFTA itself but in the wider CEE. The two dimensions of CEFTA's political role are the focus of the second part of this chapter.

4.1   SUBREGIONAL TRADE AND INTEGRATION

4.1.1   Developments in Overall Intra-CEFTA Trade

The CEFTA countries' own official evaluation of the performance of CEFTA over the first five years of its existence states that CEFTA had 'influenced significantly the development of mutual trade exchange and cooperation between the Parties. This is proved by official statistical data and by practical experience of companies'.[1] (CEFTA Joint Committee, 1998, 7) Table 4.1 provides data on the overall development of intra-CEFTA trade, in US$, between 1993 and 1998. The clear conclusion is that the mutual trade of the CEFTA countries did indeed grow rapidly during the five years since the formation of CEFTA with the expansion having continued into 1998.[2] The years to 1995 were essentially the period of recovery, with 1995 marking the point at which the net value of trade between the four original CEFTA members, the Visegrad four (V4), had regained 1989 levels.[3] An important point to stress here, of course, is that the expansion of intra-CEFTA trade was underwritten by the overall recovery of the V4 economies which more or less began around the same time as the entry into force of CEFTA. By the end of 1998 the US dollar value of exports of the V4 to CEFTA was three times the 1993 value in the cases of Poland and Slovakia, over three and a half times for the Czech Republic and almost four and a half times in the case of Hungary.[4] The rate of growth in the trade expansion (post–1995) period has been encouraging, ranging from an increase in exports of 60 per cent for 1998 over 1995 in the cases of Poland and Slovakia to 170 per cent for Hungary with the Czech Republic registering 180 per cent growth. Table 4.2 shows the positive movements in the shares of CEFTA trade in total trade since 1995 while Tables 4.3 and 4.4 demonstrate the tendency for growth in CEFTA trade to outpace total trade over the same period.

Table 4.1   Intra-CEFTA trade, 1993–1998 ($US million)

	1993	1994	1995	1996	1997	1998	Index 1998/93 1993 = 100
CZECH REPUBLIC							
Total CEFTA:							
Export	3488.9	3258.4	4348.3	4943.6	4815.8	5198.8	149.0
Import	2745.7	2718.1	3883.3	3886.3	3622.0	3656.7	133.2
Excluding Slovakia:							
Export	655.4	925.3	1343.2	1823.5	1927.3	2392.2	365.0
Import	497.3	594.3	900.0	1235.9	1368.8	1580.5	317.8
HUNGARY							
Export	461.6	565.2	757.4	1162.9	1387.2	2039.0	441.7
Import	655.3	900.3	982.3	1253.8	1377.7	1766.0	269.5
POLAND							
Export	680.4	823.0	1244.9	1480.8	1658.7	2026.0	297.8
Import	682.2	918.5	1624.0	2160.5	2585.0	2974.0	435.9
ROMANIA							
Export				293.6	341.8	369.0	125.7*
Import				540.9	641.6	1040.0	192.3*
SLOVAKIA							
Total CEFTA:							
Export	2716.0	3057.0	3778.0	3656.0	3357.0	3397.0	125.1
Import	2483.0	2226.0	2757.0	3225.0	2915.0	3122.0	125.7
Excluding Czech R.							
Export	406.0	555.0	767.0	918.0	999.0	1233.0	303.7
Import	208.0	268.0	424.0	543.0	563.0	732.0	351.9
SLOVENIA							
Export			403.2	450.7	479.8	588.0	145.8**
Import			633.7	615.8	688.4	725.0	114.4**

Notes:
* = Index 1998/1996.
** = Index 1998/1995.

Sources: Dangerfield (1999b); *CESTAT Statistical Bulletin.*

*Table 4.2   CEFTA states' mutual trade as a percentage of total trade,
1995–1998*

	Export 1995	Import 1995	Export 1996	Import 1996	Export 1997	Import 1997	Export 1998	Import 1998
Czech R.*	6.2	3.4	8.3	4.5	8.6	5.1	9.1	5.5
Hungary	5.9	6.4	7.4	6.9	7.3	6.5	8.9	6.9
Poland	5.4	5.6	6.1	5.8	6.4	6.1	7.2	6.3
Romania	–	–	–	–	4.1	5.7	4.4	8.8
Slovakia*	8.9	4.8	10.4	4.9	11.3	5.5	11.6	5.6
Slovenia			5.4	6.5	5.7	7.4	6.5	7.2

Note: * Excludes Czech–Slovak trade.

Source: CESTAT Statistical Bulletin.

*Table 4.3   CEFTA states' total exports and exports to CEFTA area, 1995–
1998 ($US values)*

	CEFTA 1995	Total 1995	CEFTA 1996	Total 1996	CEFTA 1997	Total 1997	CEFTA 1998	Total 1998
Czech R.*	145.2	110.3	135.8	101.2	105.7	101.0	124.1	115.7
Hungary	134.5	121.5	124.1	122.0	119.9	117.7	147.0	120.5
Poland	151.3	132.8	115.5	106.7	111.7	105.0	122.1	109.6
Romania	–	–	–	–	–	–	108.0	98.4
Slovakia*	138.2	119.0	119.7	102.3	108.8	102.2	123.4	129.3
Slovenia	–	–	117.7	99.9	103.9	99.1	122.6	108.1

Notes: * Excludes Czech/Slovak trade.
Previous year = 100.

Sources: CESTAT Statistical Bulletin; Dangerfield (1998b).

*Table 4.4   CEFTA states' total imports and imports from CEFTA area, 1995–
1998 ($US values)*

	CEFTA 1995	Total 1995	CEFTA 1996	Total 1996	CEFTA 1997	Total 1997	CEFTA 1998	Total 1998
Czech R.*	151.5	139.5	137.2	109.7	110.7	98.0	115.4	106.1
Hungary	109.1	106.3	127.6	117.3	109.8	117.0	128.2	121.1
Poland	176.9	134.7	133.0	127.8	119.7	113.9	115.0	111.2
Romania	–	–	–	–	118.5	98.6	162.9	104.8
Slovakia*	158.2	132.7	128.1	126.8	103.7	92.3	130.0	126.3
Slovenia	–	–	97.2	99.2	111.8	99.4	105.4	107.8

Notes: * Excludes Czech/Slovak trade.
Previous year = 100.

Sources: CESTAT Statistical Bulletin; Dangerfield (1998b)

Intra-CEFTA trade patterns have also been undergoing some realignment. Some changes have simply been the result of CEFTA enlargement and in this respect we need only note the most sizeable effects which included the impact of the accession of Romania upon the overall value and country distribution of Hungary's intra-CEFTA trade and changes to the country distribution of Romania's intra-CEFTA trade following the accession of Bulgaria. As far as changes which are more of a structural quality are concerned, the main event has been the weakening of the Czech and Slovak Republics' traditional dominance of intra-CEFTA trade.[5] The enlargement of CEFTA is only partially responsible for this, since the Czech–Slovak customs union has failed to stem negative trends in mutual trade (at the end of 1998 the US dollar value of Czech exports to Slovakia were more or less at 1993 levels while Slovak exports to the Czech Republic declined by around 10 per cent) and the share of intra-CEFTA exports and imports accounted for by each other has declined in favour of Poland and Hungary (see Table 4.5). This development is hardly surprising since the

Table 4.5 **Structure of CEFTA6 exports to and imports from CEFTA by countries, 1999 (% of total) exports**

	Bulgaria	Czech R.	Hungary	Poland	Romania	Slovenia	Slovakia
Czech R:							
Export	2.0	–	9.3	30.2	2.7	6.0	48.9
Import	0.6	–	12.2	24.8	0.5	4.4	44.9
Hungary:							
Export	3.1	20.5	–	25.6	22.7	12.7	15.4
Import	1.6	26.3	–	29.0	11.1	8.3	23.7
Poland:							
Export	2.7	47.1	23.9	–	5.0	4.6	16.7
Import	1.3	48.1	19.2	–	5.4	7.2	18.8
Romania:							
Export	19.7	2.5	45.0	24.3	–	6.5	2.0
Import	4.7	19.7	46.0	14.6	–	4.8	10.2
Slovenia:							
Export	3.5	25.5	21.8	32.6	6.2	–	10.4
Import	5.9	35.9	29.5	12.9	5.0	–	10.8
Slovakia:							
Export	0.9	61.1	15.2	17.3	2.3	3.2	–
Import	0.4	72.2	9.9	11.6	0.3	2.8	–

Notes:
CEFTA6 = Current CEFTA excluding Bulgaria.
Data is for the first half of 1999.

Source: CESTAT Statistical Bulletin.

formation of the customs union (which is usually an integration-strengthening development) in the Czech–Slovak context was, in effect, an expression of disintegration, and the implementation of CEFTA has gradually removed the bias the customs union offered to Czech and Slovak producers on each other's markets.

The CEFTA enlargement and changing patterns of intra-V4 trade have also been causing modifications to some of the asymmetries which have characterised intra-CEFTA trade. The Czech Republic and Slovakia have been the traditional surplus countries in CEFTA, Poland and Hungary the deficit countries. Taking the overall positions in intra-CEFTA trade first, by the end of 1998 the situation was as follows: the Czech Republic had consolidated its position with overall export/import coverage in CEFTA having risen from 119.9 per cent in 1994 to 142.2 per cent; Hungary had reversed its position with figures of 62.8 per cent and 115.5 per cent respectively, with the accession of Romania playing an important, but not exclusive, part in this turnaround; Poland's position had deteriorated with figures of 89.6 per cent and 68.1 per cent; Slovakia remained in surplus but considerably less so with figures of 137.3 per cent and 108.8 per cent. Some indication of the development of bilateral positions is given in Table 4.6 which compares country to country export/import coverage data for 1994 and 1998. From this we can see that Hungary has managed to strengthen its

Table 4.6   Trends in intra-CEFTA export/import coverage, CEFTA5, 1994–1998

	Czech R.	Hungary	Poland	Slovakia	Slovenia	CEFTA
Czech R.	–	0.53	1.18	1.23	0.98	1.19
Hungary	1.19	–	1.01	1.92	0.68	1.84
Poland	0.76	0.95	–	0.61	1.28	0.76
Slovakia	0.71	0.45	1.50	–	0.72	0.79
Slovenia	1.06	1.35	0.83	1.29	–	1.28

Notes:
Exporting countries are in the vertical (far left) column.
The numbers are arrived at by simply dividing export/import coverage value in 1998 by export/import coverage value in 1994. A figure greater than one indicates a positive trend for the exporting country (left-hand column) while a figure less than one means that the export/import coverage has deteriorated. The values in this table do not relate to the actual export/import coverage position. To illustrate this the trend in Hungary's export/import coverage with the Czech Republic, at 1.19, clearly indicates a positive change in favour of Hungary. This was, however, based on export/import coverage figures of 56.7 per cent in 1994 and 67.3 per cent in 1998 meaning Hungary remained a net importer in its trade relations with the Czech Republic.
All data for Slovenia cover 1995–1998.

Source: CESTAT Statistical Bulletin.

export/import coverage against each of the other V4, although only marginally with Poland, and the Czech gains have been based on net export growth with Poland and an improved trading position with Slovakia based on static exports and declining imports. The sustainability of the Czech position is of course questionable, given the stagnation in the Czech economy which set in after 1996 together with the role of currency depreciation rather than structural developments in 1998 export growth. On the other hand, while Poland has remained a major deficit country and has so far registered deficits with the CEFTA newcomers too, data for 1998 and 1999 show up some positive changes in the trade balance with CEFTA. Export coverage moved to 68.1 per cent in 1998 from 64.2 per cent in 1997 and had further advanced to 72.6 per cent in 1999.[6] Moreover, in recent years, imports from Poland have been accounting for growing percentages of total imports from CEFTA in the case of all CEFTA countries.[7]

Looking at the CEFTA newcomers, since their accessions both Slovenia and Romania have experienced expansion of their overall intra-CEFTA trade but have recorded opposite patterns for exports and imports. Since 1995, Slovenia's exports to CEFTA have grown at three times the rate of imports while Romania's first full year in CEFTA produced a 7.9 per cent increase in exports against a 62 per cent jump in imports from CEFTA.[8] Slovenia is a minor player in CEFTA, in line with its relatively tiny population and even taking into account the significantly higher GDP per capita (at US$12 341 in 1998 against an average of US$7405 average for the rest of CEFTA) has a low trade intensity with CEFTA.[9] Romania is a larger market but its intra-CEFTA trade is mainly centred on Hungary and it is a relatively poor country with GDP per capita of US$4990 in 1998. In addition, GDP contractions of 6.6 per cent and 7.3 per cent in 1997 and 1998 have meant that the main trade expansion opportunities in Romania have been based on possibilities for trade diversion or substitution for domestic production rather than an expanding economy. The latest entrant to CEFTA, Bulgaria, is in the smaller segment in terms of both population (eight million) and GDP per capita which, at US$4414 in 1998, is the lowest of all the CEFTA countries.[10] For these reasons, along with the fact that Bulgaria is an insignificant trade partner for all CEFTA countries apart from Romania (see Table 4.5), the accession of Bulgaria will not make any significant impact on the V4's dominance of intra-CEFTA trade.

4.1.2 Commodity Structure of Intra-CEFTA Trade

This section discusses commodity structure aspects of intra-CEFTA trade, which have to be seen in the context of the deep adjustments which followed the breakdown of the CMEA. The various analyses of the post-1990 mutual trade patterns of the former CMEA members tended to stress the steep deterioration in the position of final manufactures, in particular goods included in SITC7,

Table 4.7   Intra-CEFTA trade by commodity structure (SITC) of   V4, 1994 and 1997 (exports of CEFTA States, $US millions)

	0	1	2	3	4	5	6	7	8	9	Total
1994											
Czech R.	185.4	60.0	105.9	372.2	21.1	532.0	873.9	828.9	288.7	0.5	3268.6
Hungary	90.6	26.4	36.1	46.7	21.1	138.7	94.5	65.8	43.5	0.0	565.3
Poland	47.8	1.4	60.7	190.6	0.1	113.9	215.5	126.2	66.9	0.2	823.2
Slovakia	171.6	43.7	188.8	235.3	4.4	487.5	632.5	583.2	266.4	2.2	2615.6
Total	495.4	131.5	391.5	840.7	46.7	1272.1	1816.4	1604.1	665.5	2.9	7272.7
% of total exports	6.9	1.8	5.4	11.7	0.7	17.6	25.2	22.3	9.2	–	
1997											
Czech R.	274.2	95.6	135.2	330.4	19.5	700.2	1390.3	1482.6	432.6	4.5	4865.1
Hungary	323.6	17.9	66.3	86.8	41.7	279.4	254.0	221.7	95.4	0.0	1386.8
Poland	145.5	0.8	58.6	258.3	1.1	229.5	504.2	293.9	166.8	0.0	1658.7
Slovakia	144.9	45.0	167.0	339.5	8.5	532.3	1218.3	666.6	237.8	0.9	3360.8
Total	888.2	159.3	427.1	1015.0	70.8	1741.4	3366.8	2664.8	932.6	5.4	11271.4
% of total exports	7.8	1.4	3.8	9.0	0.6	15.4	29.7	23.5	8.2	–	

Index 1997/94

	0	1	2	3	4	5	6	7	8	Total
Czech R.	147.9	159.3	127.7	88.8	92.4	131.6	159.1	178.9	149.8	900.0
Hungary	357.3	67.8	183.7	178.6	197.6	201.4	268.8	336.9	219.3	0.0
Poland	304.4	57.1	96.5	135.5	1100.0	201.5	234.0	232.9	249.3	0.0
Slovakia	84.4	103.0	88.5	144.3	193.2	109.2	192.6	114.3	89.3	40.1
Total	179.3	121.2	109.1	119.9	151.8	136.9	185.4	166.1	140.2	186.2

Weighted index 1997/94

	0	1	2	3	4	5	6	7	8
Czech R.	8.3	3.1	3.6	6.0	0.4	18.9	45.5	54.5	13.3
Hungary	80.1	0.8	8.4	10.8	5.7	39.0	47.3	51.8	14.5
Poland	26.7	0.0	3.4	21.1	1.5	27.9	71.1	41.3	25.1
Slovakia	3.6	1.4	4.4	14.6	0.5	17.3	69.8	22.7	6.3
Total	4.1	1.7	4.1	10.7	1.0	21.1	55.1	39.1	11.54

Notes:

Formula for weighted average is as follows: Index 1994/97 × (per cent of total exports/100)

SITC9 excluded from weighted index.

Key to SITC codes:

0 = food and live animals; 1 = beverages and tobacco; 2 = crude materials, except fuels; 3 = mineral fuels, lubricants, related materials; 4 = animal and vegetable oils, fats, waxes; 5 = chemicals and related products; 6 = manufactured goods, classified chiefly by materials; 7 = machinery and transport equipment;

8 = miscellaneous manufactured items; 9 = others.

Source: Dangerfield (1999b).

which had accounted for more than half of intra-CMEA trade in 1989. Rudka and Mizsei (1995, 5) for example, wrote that the 'overwhelming trend in the trade structure in early 1990s was the dramatic decline in mutual trade of sophisticated products while the mutual trade of raw materials, foodstuffs, energy and chemical products strongly increased. Again, an especially sharp decline was noticed in the trade of machinery and industrial consumer goods'. Richter (1997, 17) put it this way: '(i)n the emerging post-transition intra-CEFTA structure inputs to production have gained in importance: energy sources, chemicals, and semi-finished products'. It is neither possible nor desirable for the distorted commodity structure of the CMEA period, which seriously flattered the CEE from the point of view of true levels of economic development and competitiveness, to be restored. At the same time, the question of whether there has been at least some modest reversal of the post-CMEA 'deterioration' noted above is worth pursuing since this would be indicative not only of some positive results of trade liberalisation but also of broader restructuring successes enabling CEFTA producers of 'sophisticated' products to find their way back onto the market on a competitive basis. With the aid of intra-CEFTA trade commodity structure data it is possible to investigate whether any such changes have occurred so far.[12] For obvious reasons, it is only possible to include the four founder members of CEFTA in this particular part of the analysis.

Beginning with a slightly more detailed look at the situation in 1994 (see Table 4.7), which represented the mutual trade picture in the very early phase of CEFTA, the following patterns were evident. First, trade was predominantly industrial and within that the most important product group was SITC6 (manufactured goods classified by materials – (including iron and steel, non-ferrous metals, rubber products), followed by SITC7 (machinery and transport equipment) and, in third place, SITC5 (chemicals). As far as the export profiles of the individual CEFTA countries were concerned, the Czech Republic and Slovakia followed the aggregate pattern, while in the case of Poland there was a slight difference with SITC3 – fuels and lubricants – ahead of SITC7 and SITC5. In Hungary's case, the most important group was SITC5, then SITC6 followed by SITC0 – food and live animals – in third place ahead of SITC7. Hungary therefore stood out as a country where food and agricultural products played a relatively more important role in its exports to CEFTA.

The patterns which had evolved by the end of 1997 were as follows. First, trade in CEFTA continued to be dominated by industrial products, heavily concentrated in manufactured goods classified by materials (SITC6), machinery and equipment (SITC7) and chemicals (SITC5). The main exception to the general pattern was Hungary, for which food and agricultural goods were revealed as the most important export category to CEFTA and which registered most growth (normal index 1997/1994 was 357.3). Poland, the other V4 country with a significant agricultural sector, also registered fast growth in agricultural exports to CEFTA over the period (normal index 1997/1994 was 304.4), thus indicating that it too experienced some positive results of the attempts to liberalise agricultural goods trade. For the record, in 1997 the exports of Slovenia to CEFTA followed the general pattern (SITC5 and SITC6 respectively were the most important categories).[13]

Second, a simple index of 1997 over 1994 shows that exports of all SITC categories had grown, with SITC9 and SITC6 having expanded most rapidly, followed by SITC7, SITC5 and SITC8. A more accurate and meaningful picture is obtained by using a weighted index of 1997 over 1994, which takes into account the relative importance of each commodity group in total trade. On this basis the most important gains revealed in exports of industrial goods were in categories SITC6 and SITC7, with all the other categories some way behind. Growth of exports of products in SITC7 was in first place for the Czech Republic and second place for Hungary, Poland and Slovakia according to the weighted index of 1997 over 1994. Exports of SITC8 also registered favourable aggregate growth. Therefore although exchanges of SITC6 products continued to play an important part in intra-CEFTA trade and showed strong dynamics, it has also been the case that exports of machinery and equipment had also shown significant growth, which may be taken as indicative of some positive movement in the overall commodity structure of intra-CEFTA trade.[14] The data also shows up some important differences within the CEFTA group, however. SITC7 grew most dynamically in Hungary (normal index 1997/1994 was 336.9) and Poland (normal index 1997/1994 was 232.9) with the Czech Republic (normal index 1997/1994 = 178.9) lagging somewhat in third place.[15] In the case of Slovakia, however, the normal index 1997/1994 was much lower at 114.3. Slovakia also lost ground in trade in exports of SITC8. Whereas (in this order) the Polish, Hungarian and Czech exports of SITC8 expanded reasonably impressively according to normal and weighted indices, Slovak exports actually contracted, largely due to substantial loss of position in the Czech market.[16]

The commodity structure trends of intra-CEFTA trade at the SITC single digit level suggest that the trade liberalisation process has enabled certain competitive advantages already evident from the early post-CMEA trade reconfigurations, particularly in SITC5 and SITC6, to further assert themselves, and the CEFTA countries have been able to access low unit labour cost inputs to production and that Hungary has also been able to regain its position as the pre-eminent intra-CEFTA agricultural goods exporter.[17] Also, insofar as above average increases in exports of SITC categories 7 and 8 are suitable evidence, intra-CEFTA trade has also been reflecting some modernisation of the export structure, though the CEFTA countries are clearly performing differently in this respect. Just as it was observed in the previous section that changes to the structural asymmetries of intra-CEFTA trade are a mirror for progress in supply-side transformations, particularly for the more trade-dependent countries, the same is true for commodity structure developments. In intra-CEFTA trade at least, Slovakia clearly stands out as the V4 country with the least progressive export structure, which is not only consistent with the lag in industrial restructuring and modernisation associated with the deficiencies of the mass privatisation strategy (which has also held back the Czech transformation) but also the relatively low involvement of foreign direct investment in the Slovak economy.

4.1.3 CEFTA and Foreign Direct Investment

The prospects for expanded FDI inflows have been stressed in many of the official endorsements of CEFTA, including those which have come from the EU. For example, former Commissioner Hans van den Broek, speaking in Sofia in 1997, said that '(t)he EU supports Bulgaria's application to join the Central European Free Trade Area which would boost trade, foreign investment and economic growth'[18] and European Commission officials Avery and Cameron (1998, 20), wrote that 'the Union strongly supports the Central European Free Trade Area (CEFTA) ... (a)s trade barriers fall, foreign direct investment should increase, with further gains to productivity and investment'. Spokesmen for the CEFTA candidate countries have also stressed their expectations in this respect. For example, when discussing the reasons why Croatian entry to CEFTA was seen as a 'strategic priority, the former Croatian Minister of Economic Affairs Nenad Porges explained that 'a small market such as ours cannot interest large American corporations. However, we have to bear in mind that Croatia's absolute priority is to join CEFTA, which means a wider Central European market, and that means that American arrival is more assured' (*Banka International*, 1997a). Finally, we should remember that the joint organisation of conferences and exhibitions on capital investment in the CEFTA countries is an official component of CEFTA cooperation, clearly demonstrating the member states' assumption about a positive relationship between CEFTA and FDI.[19] Before discussing whether the above statements have some empirical grounding, it is certainly the case that their intellectual foundations are well established. The argument that formation of regional economic associations will stimulate FDI inflows is standard in most textbooks on international economic integration and, with specific reference to CEE, it should be remembered that Richard Baldwin's (1994) well-known and influential argument about the damaging 'hub and spoke' consequences of failure to develop multilateral free trade arrangements in post-communist Europe had most resonance from the point of view of the consequences for inflows of FDI into CEE.

It is also commonly accepted that the FDI response varies with the type of regional/subregional economic cooperation. According to the *United Nations World Investment Report* 1998 the extent to which regional integration frameworks (RIFs) act as determinants of FDI depends on three factors: the scope and depth of integration foreseen by the specific project; the credibility of the RIF, meaning the extent to which the provisions are actually being implemented; and the extent of prior interdependence of the participants with RIFs which will create new rather than formalise existing interdependence equating with a stronger influence on FDI. According to these criteria, what could be predicted for CEFTA? On the scope of integration, the first point to make is that though CEFTA is formally at the more basic end of the integration spectrum the assumption is that even 'a shallow RIF that entails no more than tariff reductions among members and external tariffs on non-members can have an impact on FDI determinants through trade or strategic responses to competitors (static effects) and growth (dynamic effects)' (United Nations, 1998, 118). Added to this, the apparent 'shallowness' of CEFTA itself is also offset by the fact that it is a precursor for much deeper integration between the parties in the EU context. In other words, the longer-term integration aspirations are not confined to the parameters of the CEFTA treaty and its amendments. Moving on to the second criterion, the conditions for belonging to CEFTA (WTO membership, Europe Agreement or free trade arrangements with the EU and – in some cases – prior implementation of bilateral free trade agreements with the CEFTA states) mean that participation in CEFTA is restricted to countries that have already satisfied rather strict tests as far as commitment to liberal trade regimes and capacity to satisfactorily implement them are concerned. Furthermore, the record of implementation of the provisions of CEFTA, which has gone beyond merely adhering to original trade liberalising commitments to acceleration of the timetables for the reduction of barriers (see Chapter 3) has also been a strong positive signal to potential inward investors.[20] Factor three as identified by the World Investment Report also seems to work in CEFTA's favour. Due to the protectionist barriers which were implemented in the immediate post-communist period, not to mention the real lack of mutual openness which was a fact of economic life in the communist period, then the prior interdependence between the CEFTA countries was not considerable. Furthermore, the 'shortage economy' syndrome would have offset any worries about lack of complementarity. In fact, the prospect of unsaturated markets would have been a further motivation for foreign investors.

Turning now from the hypothetical influence of CEFTA upon FDI inflows to what has been discovered about the actual influence, some general observations from the secondary literature in which several authors have argued that CEFTA has indeed acted as an FDI determinant can be mentioned first. Rudka and Mizsei (1995) have noted that even before CEFTA was signed a number of large corporations, including ABB, Volvo, Philips and Procter & Gamble were interested in its prospects and concluded that the advent of CEFTA 'already played some role in a jump of foreign direct investment in Central Europe in 1992 and its continued flow in 1993 and 1994' (Rudka and Mizsei, 1995, 21).

According to Meier (cited in Handl, 1999, 9) investors' desire to obtain a share of the emerging market of Central Europe was a major reason for the concentration of FDI in the CEFTA states. For Inotai (1997a, 133) '(u)ntil now the main pattern of FDI in Central Europe seems to follow the "headquarters approach" ... It seems to strengthen the hypothesis that these countries are already playing a role in the strategic thinking of multinational companies as potential regional headquarters'.[21] Studies based on survey data about external investors' motivations, which provide more comprehensive and thorough evidence about FDI determinants, tend to confirm that inward investors have indeed been lured by or have upgraded their investments because of the potential of the subregional market. In their recent study of the motivation and behaviour of foreign investment into Hungary, which is a most appropriate country to focus on because of its pre-eminence as a venue for FDI and because the small market dictates export-oriented production (compared with, say, Poland where the domestic market is much bigger) Elteto and Sass (1998) found that the CEFTA agreement had indeed influenced FDI decisions. In the case of some companies which had started off with the intention to penetrate the local market (Elteto and Sass, 1998, 12) 'the main aim of the investment had become not simply to supply the local market (initially through imports and later through local production) but to supply the regional market as well. For some products, production capacity was established with the express purpose of producing for the regional (CEFTA) as well as the local market'. For export-oriented firms (Elteto and Sass, 1998, 20) '(t)he effect of the free trade agreements is apparent in the fact that "facilitation of access to foreign markets" was marked as important in mainly two directions: the EU (55 per cent important and very important) and CEFTA (49 per cent)'.

All the above suggest that the various inferences about the investment-inducing effect of CEFTA are indeed valid. Nevertheless, while regional free trade arrangements can only really serve to enhance FDI inflows, it is also necessary to stress that external trade arrangements of host countries are, of course, but one of the numerous influences on multinational corporations. Though the CEFTA countries are the leading recipients of FDI into post-communist Europe, the much lower level of FDI into Slovakia (see Table 4.8) shows that whereas multilateral free trade arrangements do influence FDI inflows into the subregion, they guarantee nothing as far as individual countries are concerned since the supplier to the subregional market will be more disposed to locations where the other FDI-relevant conditions are most favourable. There is one final point here which concerns Slovenia as well as any other potential CEFTA countries (for example, Croatia) without strong traditional trade links to the core CEFTA area. Countries which are in CEFTA but have a rather marginal position in the CEFTA market may also miss out on the CEFTA effect as far as FDI is concerned if firms associate them with a different geographic segment of the European economy. Bobek et al. (1996, 19) wrote that '(t)he main reason for the small inflow of FDI into Slovenia is the smallness of the domestic market. In the future, any larger FDI will use Slovenia as a base for covering the markets of former Yugoslavia'.

Table 4.8 **Foreign direct investment stock in CEFTA countries, 1998**

	$US billions	As % of 1998 GDP
Poland	29.1	19.4
Hungary	19.4	41.7
Czech Republic	8.7	15.3
Romania	3.7	10.1
Slovenia	2.6	13.7
Slovakia	1.7	8.0
Bulgaria	1.4	12.0

Sources: Business Central Europe, February 1999, June 1999, The Annual 2000.

As mentioned earlier, there is a symbiotic relationship between CEFTA and FDI, in that not only is CEFTA relevant in terms of inducing FDI but developments in intra-CEFTA trade (along with external trade in general) reflect a very important influence on the part of foreign-owned firms. Hungary's record of steadily reducing its passive trade balance in the V4 along with clear dynamic structural changes in its intra-CEFTA exports, and the comparatively high involvement of FDI in the Hungarian economy, are not merely coincidental. On the one hand, there is the strong positive relationship between FDI and export activity, which has been widely verified. The UNECE (1998, 132), for example, reported that '(f)or instance, in Hungary some two thirds of the increase in exports were generated by companies in industrial duty free zones – most of them in joint or foreign ownership – mainly on the basis of capacity improvements made in recent years'. On the other hand, there is the link between FDI and modernisation and diversification of the export structure. Once more we can refer to the UNECE (1998, 132):

> (a)nother important factor behind the accelerated growth of exports, and to a certain extent of imports of intermediate goods and other inputs, has been the starting up of new productive capacities in a number of sectors which came into operation as a result of 1991–1996 greenfield investments by multi-national companies. This was certainly the case with motor car and electronic industries in the CEFTA countries, and also with some engineering, chemical, food processing and tobacco production facilities throughout the east European and Baltic regions.

It is not only industrial exports that have been benefiting from significant FDI influence. Kiss (1997, 17), discussing intra-CEFTA agricultural trade specifically, wrote that the 'increase of the Hungarian agricultural and especially food exports can also be explained by the activity of foreign capital and MNCs in Hungary: as it is known, by now more than 50 % of the Hungarian food industry has been privatised by foreign capital and big international firms whose main purpose is to optimise their economic activity region-wide'.

Finally, though intra-CEFTA FDI is not yet a significant phenomenon according to the EBRD (1998, 80) some local companies in CEE countries are demonstrating a growing ability to develop new and rebuild former trade and investment links in the region and 'intra-regional foreign investors have typically acquired existing manufacturing plants and have concentrated on building regional supply and distribution networks'. The EBRD report also notes that of the CEFTA countries Hungary and Slovenia (along with Russia, Croatia and Estonia) are among the group of transition countries registering most outward investment.

4.2 THE POLITICAL ROLE OF CEFTA

4.2.1 CEFTA and the EU Pre-accession Process

As well as the direct effects of CEFTA integration discussed above, there is also the question of the contribution to the primary integration strategy of its member states which, as noted in the introduction to this chapter, is one of the main dimensions of CEFTA's political role. To what extent has CEFTA cooperation not only facilitated integration at the subregional level but also served the incorporation of the subregional unit into the EU? After all, it has often been stated in Central European circles that CEFTA was '(o)riginally designed as a "fitness centre" for candidates for future EU membership' (Kaczurba, 1997, 11). Officials from the various CEFTA aspirant countries have consistently made the connection between CEFTA membership and their own EU accession prospects. Following the signing of Bulgaria's CEFTA Accession Treaty on 18 July 1998, the Bulgarian Minister for Trade and Tourism Valentin Vassilev said, for example, that '(w)ith this accord, Bulgaria moves a step closer to membership in the EU' (*Warsaw Voice*, 26/7/98). Moreover, the official approach of the EU itself to subregional cooperation seems unambiguous. The EU gives its support (Cottey, 1996, 21) 'to subregional groups not primarily in the context of security but as part of its pre-accession strategy for the Central and East European states and partnership policy towards others'. While many of the statements about the contribution of CEFTA to EU membership tend to have a rhetorical feel to them, the link between EU integration and CEFTA cooperation does have substance and the accession process is served in a number of ways.

First, and related to the Visegrad group's willingness to form CEFTA against the background of early reluctance to participate in subregional initiatives, they were able to meet the EU requirement that future members should be taking steps to further their own integration. In this connection, Lavigne (1995, 199) noted that 'the pressure from the Central European countries on the EC mounted following the signature of the CEFTA agreement, as if to stress that the CEFTA countries had fulfilled a precondition'. In addition to their mutual cooperation the willingness of the V4 to expand CEFTA is also relevant in this respect, having noted that the European Union (Avery and Cameron, 1998, 20) 'strongly supports the Central European Free Trade Area (CEFTA) and its extension to all the associated states'. [22]

Second, demonstrating that the EU's insistence on subregional economic cooperation had a practical dimension, CEFTA has advanced the process of putting in place the market integration which the CEE would have to practise anyway once they were together in the EU. This was emphasised at the 1997 Portoroz summit by Slovenian Premier Drnovsek who stated that: 'our continuous cooperation not only leads to strengthened trade links in Central Europe but also contributes to greater efficiency of our economies and their readiness to join a larger, more complex economic area, the European Union' (Ministry of Economic Relations and Development, 1997, 1). The verification of whether CEFTA cooperation really offers any advantages in terms of 'hardening' the CEFTA markets in advance of the fresh competitive challenges full membership of the EU will bring is really beyond the agenda of this study, but it could just be mentioned that according to integration theory the 'insufficient commodity differentiation of production or export specialisation profile among the individual CEFTA countries' (Outrata, 1999, 145) ought to mean that trade liberalisation in CEFTA is at least a source of efficiency gains in the sectors which are competitive (SITC5 and SITC6) in the CEFTA context. [23]

Third, the implementation of CEFTA has also yielded 'practical experience of the modalities of voluntary multilateral cooperation' (Cottey, 1996, 21) which helps prepare for operating in organisations with bigger and more complicated agendas and demonstrates suitability to join those organisations on the assumption that 'a good record of cooperation at subregional level will help, not handicap, states which otherwise meet the conditions for membership, reflecting as it does the qualities of maturity, stability and good-neighbourliness which are central to the NATO and EU acquis' (Bailes, 1997, 30). This third factor can be seen as a potential product of all SRG, though it might be the case that CEFTA has a higher grading in this respect due to its focused agenda, shaky early foundations and potential to generate really testing problems (namely the 1998 agricultural trade disputes) which, it is important to stress, the CEFTA team has to confront as *policy-makers* thus giving CEFTA cooperation clear value added in terms of this particular function.

Fourth, as will be discussed in more detail in Chapters 5 and 6, CEFTA has been serving the more mature stages of the EU pre-accession process by providing a forum for discussing EU-compatible cooperation at the subregional level. Free movement of capital, liberalisation of trade in services, opening public procurement to intra-CEFTA competition and common actions to combat organised crime have all already featured on the agenda. Even where it has been difficult to expedite concrete progress in new areas of cooperation, the exercise of exploring the possibilities and problems is extremely useful for when much deeper mutual integration comes back on the agenda in the context of the CEFTA states' obligations to each other as full EU members. It may even be that early discussions of implementing these requirements of the *acquis* with each other can highlight issues and problems which inform the negotiations on the relevant chapters of the *acquis* (agriculture, and free trade arrangements with non (EU) associated countries, for example).

Though CEFTA's part in the EU pre-accession process has not extended to any formal coordination of its members' approaches to the EU, it is worth noting that this dimension of CEFTA cooperation has been subject to a number of different interpretations by the various actors in the CEFTA states. During the early phase of CEFTA the Hungarian and Polish sides persisted with the argument that CEFTA could play more of an active role. At the first CEFTA summit in Poznan in November 1994, for example, though there was approval of 'a declaration calling for "consultations" on joining the European Union' (*RFE/ RL Daily Report Slovak Selection*, 28/11/94), it was the case that '(p)leas for close coordination of these efforts, made repeatedly by Hungarian Premier Gyula Horn, went unheeded by the Czech prime Minister Vaclav Klaus, who is in favour of each country entering the union separately'. During the 1995 CEFTA summit which met in the context of importance advances in the EU eastward enlargement process, the Polish side in particular pushed hard for various new cooperation initiatives in the economic sphere (see Chapter 5) and for a revival of formal political cooperation. It was reported that (BBC, 13/9/95, A/1) '(w)ith regard to West European institutions, Warsaw arrived here with the proposal to co-ordinate the activities of the countries of Central and East Europe in their contacts with the European Union, NATO, the Organisation for Economic and Cooperation and Development as well as other international institutions'. Not surprisingly, given the rule of unanimity that applies in CEFTA and since the main antagonist of political cooperation was in the CEFTA chair that year, there was no mention of this Polish preference in the final declaration of the 1995 summit. A year later, in Jasna, while the Polish and Hungarian premiers once again stated that (BBC, 16/9/96, C/3) they 'favoured the continuation of political cooperation within the Visegrad Group', Klaus made it clear that 'his country was only interested in economic cooperation in the region'(BBC, 16/9/96, C/3). Throughout this period, the Slovak side's main priority was to push for upgrading of CEFTA cooperation and expanding the organisation as a counterbalance to Slovakia's diminishing EU prospects. At the 1997 summit, in response to the *AGENDA 2000* proposals, former Slovak Premier Meciar sought more actively to disentangle CEFTA cooperation and EU enlargement and stated that 'CEFTA should not be a back door for EU membership' (BBC, 16/9/97, C/1) yet still attempted to use CEFTA in this respect by proposing that the Portoroz summit declaration should include a clause which committed the CEFTA members to pledge support for each other's EU application. The Hungarian side demanded that the clause be omitted. Even before the *AGENDA 2000* proposals divided CEFTA into *ins* and *pre-ins* and rendered CEFTA a less appropriate forum for coordinating CEE approaches to the EU, the long-standing differences in attitudes to subregional political cooperation, difficulties of bilateral political relations and a general tendency to compete rather than cooperate in the race to the EU were decisive in CEFTA's prospects for playing a more active role in this respect.

4.2.2 'Soft Security' and Subregional Political Relations

The second dimension of the political role of CEFTA concerns the impact on the member states' mutual political relations. Though CEFTA has had no openly stated or consciously planned political agenda in this respect, it is commonly accepted that voluntary economic integration generates spin-offs for the regional/ subregional political relations by, for example, increasing the potential costs of conflict and expanding the range of stakeholders in the integration process. Even where the ambitions of the integration project are modest, which is how free trade areas are usually interpreted, they are usually vehicles for the necessary interdependence. Beyond these standard non-economic by-products, the political role of CEFTA and other SRG has been discussed in terms of contributions to the various layers of the new system of security governance which has emerged in post cold-war Europe. Even though the various SRG which have emerged since 1990 tend to have no explicit security agenda and clearly are not concerned with conventional or 'hard' security,[24] the enthusiastic school (Cottey, 1996, 1999; Bremner and Bailes, 1998) in the debate on the significance of SRG stress their inputs to European security as follows: first, in terms of so-called 'soft' security issues (economics, organised crime, environment); second an (often subconscious) contribution to alleviating the various stresses and strains created by divisive patterns of EU and NATO enlargement. Since CEFTA is somewhat more homogeneous (that is, it is an exclusively post-communist entity restricted to Europe Agreement countries) with a specifically (macro) economic function, its contributions would seem to be mainly to do with the economic interdependence dimension of 'soft' security. The four more pan-European SRG appear to be the more suitable vehicles for the other aspects of the subregional cooperation agenda which include (Bailes, 1997, 30):

to complement and cushion the integration process, absorbing some of the inevitable strains. At the very least, these groups will allow NATO/EU members, first and second wave candidates, neutrals and non-candidates like Russia to continue meeting and talking to each other ... (t)he integrated members could brief on developments in the EU and NATO, they could feed back their neighbours' concerns to these institutions, and they should be able to devise schemes to benefit all members of the grouping which they can recommend for NATO's or EU's support.

Nevertheless CEFTA has made some security-related input beyond generating interdependence, usually related to regional problems or tensions not necessarily linked to the issues generated by the mode of EU and NATO expansion. In this connection, we can point to the following contributions.

First, CEFTA has acted as an important forum for top-level political dialogue between the member states' officials. The annual summits are attended by the CEFTA states' Prime Ministers as well as other senior government figures and time is set aside for bilateral meetings (including, until 1997 at least, meetings with the leaders of the guest countries). For those CEFTA states whose bilateral political relations have been somewhat strained, but without the advantage of special bilateral arrangements (that is, Slovak–Hungary treaty, the Romanian–Hungary treaty), this special opportunity for the political leaders to meet took on extra significance. The case of Czech–Slovak relations is a good example. According to one report on the 1995 summit: 'Brno, 11th September: Czech and Slovak premiers Vaclav Klaus and Vladimir Meciar said today that the main result of their first meeting in 21 months was the resumption of mutual communication' (BBC, EE/2407 A/3, 13/9/95). A few years later, the 1998 CEFTA summit (Prague, 11–12 September), gave Milos Zeman and Vladimir Meciar the chance to discuss some aspects of Czech–Slovak affairs and reach an agreement that the two would aim to meet at least twice a year, a development which never materialised of course but which could have been useful if the outcome of the September 1998 Slovak parliamentary elections had been different. Even where relations are not particularly problematic CEFTA has acted as a vehicle for reactivating diplomatic activity between the former CMEA partners (as a result of the various CEFTA accession negotiations for example).

The second contribution is really more an extension of point one above, and this is that CEFTA clearly served as a 'holding operation' for political cooperation during the dormant phase of the 'Visegrad group'. In this respect Handl (1999) has noted that 'some Polish experts argue that CEFTA – a product of Visegrad co-operation – contributed to increased political understanding during the years of "separatist policy" pursued by the Czech government of Vaclav Klaus during the period 1992–1994'. Certainly, until CEFTA's first expansion in 1996 the series of annual summits, which began in Poznan in November 1994, were Visegrad group meetings in all but name. Though the agenda was formally fixed to pure CEFTA business the discussion often extended into other spheres, as the various references to the CEFTA summits contained in this book have shown. In fact, the CEFTA meetings were an important factor in achieving the reconvening of the Visegrad group. As noted above, the desire of some parties to resume political cooperation was often expressed at CEFTA summits and the 1998 summit in Prague (see Chapter 6) was a clear breakthrough in this respect.

Third, the CEFTA factor has also made contributions to the resolution of complications in relations between the CEFTA states and those countries which were or still are potential future members of CEFTA. Ukraine and Lithuania, for example, have had strong incentives for consolidating their relationship with Poland, their 'sponsor' in CEFTA. Romania could also have listed its desire to enter CEFTA as another reason to secure and consolidate improved bilateral relations with Hungary, the CEFTA member which had most interest in securing Romanian accession.[25] Linked to this, it is the case that matters such as debts remaining from the break-up of the CMEA have had to be resolved so as to obtain the necessary unanimous approval needed to enlarge CEFTA. For example, Bulgaria's accession to CEFTA necessitated reaching agreement on its transferable rouble-denominated debts to certain of the CEFTA states. On 17 September 1998, Poland and Bulgaria reached agreement on a payments, timetable for Bulgaria's DEM 123.6 billion to Poland and it was also confirmed that 'settlement of this debt to Poland was part of Bulgaria's preliminary agreement for Central European Free Trade Agreement membership' (*Central European Business Weekly*, 25/9–1/10/98, 11). It was also necessary to clear 'the obstacles to settle a similar type of debt with Hungary in order to Bulgaria's access to the Central European Free Trade Agreement (CEFTA)' (*Central European Express,* July 1997, 4).

Stability and security within CEE is also likely to be enhanced by any practical cooperation initiatives which foster 'region-building' and have the effect of forging some kind of collective identity. Clearly the idea of a sense of community in the CEFTA area can only be postulated rather than proved and the steadfast refusal of certain of the CEE countries to formally identify with or see themselves as part of anything other than the mainstream European structures, the divisive effects of serious bilateral disputes (where the situation of ethnic groups is often the issue) and the complication of attitudes which change when particular governments are replaced all provide credible reasons to be sceptical about subregional affiliations. However, it can be noted that as far as CEFTA as a source of a 'Central European' identity is concerned, this idea seems to have been relevant for countries outside the V4 which sensed a 'clubbish' character of CEFTA and have viewed CEFTA membership as a chance to join the 'avant-garde' group of post-communist countries and in certain cases (Lithuania, Croatia, Ukraine – see Chapter 5) to attempt to reinforce a preferred geopolitical identity. Furthermore, collective involvement in a successful subregional project promotes bonding and confidence-building at least among sections of the government machinery of the member states. Even the top officials of the CEFTA countries have put CEFTA cooperation forward as one successful area of transformation which represents the member countries' own efforts and not just another result of external assistance.[26] Certain of the more Euro-sceptic personalities have even drawn favourable comparisons between the *modus operandi* of CEFTA and that of the EU![27]

It seems that there is sufficient evidence to suggest that the results of CEFTA in both the economic and political realms have been genuine and worthwhile. Once the implementation of a given regional economic cooperation schedule has been accomplished, the desire to move on to more advanced areas of cooperation often comes onto the agenda and outsider countries tend to become increasingly interested in accession. Aspects of the further development of CEFTA are discussed in the next chapter.

NOTES

1. The Institute for EastWest Studies conducted the first major comparative study (see Cottey, 1996) of the various subregional organisations which emerged following the fall of communism. Of the six groupings covered, CEFTA and the Visegrad group were the only exclusively post-communist ones, while the Barents Euro–Arctic Council (BEAC), Council of Baltic Sea States (CBSS), Central European Initiative (CEI) and Black Sea Economic Cooperation (BSEC) created 'quite large networks of NATO states, Western neutrals and states of Central and Eastern Europe, exploiting the collapse of Cold War barriers to reunite natural regional families' (Bailes, 1997,1).

2. Some of the data cited in this chapter is contained in the composite tables included in the chapter and referred to in the text. For more detailed trade statistics, readers should consult the detailed information contained in Appendix Five which gives a comprehensive picture of the intra-CEFTA trade of the Czech Republic, Hungary, Poland, Slovakia and Slovenia. Romania is also included though less comprehensively detailed due to the relatively short time in CEFTA.

3. The reliability of data is of course a well-known problem as far as this kind of comparison is concerned. Bearing that in mind, data provided by Richter (1997) shows that the value of the mutual trade of Czechoslovakia, Hungary and Poland amounted to some $US3412 million in 1989. According to national statistics, the mutual trade of the V4 (excluding Czech/Slovak mutual trade) amounted to $US4111 million at end 1995. Only Hungary had failed to reach its 1989 value of exports to the other V4, a situation which became rectified over 1996.

4. Excluding Czech–Slovak trade in this case.

5. As well as the enormous influence of their mutual trade on CEFTA aggregates, the relatively strong position of the Czech and Slovak Republics vis-à-vis Hungary and Poland has stemmed from various factors including geographic position at the centre of the original CEFTA area, the inherited situation of the former Czechoslovakia which was a relatively more important supplier of industrial goods in the former CMEA for which trade was relatively less oriented to Western markets before 1989. There was also of course the comparatively deep devaluation of the Czechoslovak koruna in 1991.

6. Based on the first half of 1999 only.

7. In 1996 the Czech Republic took 19.9 per cent of its total CEFTA imports from Poland; in 1999 (first half only) the figure was 24.8 per cent. The respective changes for the other CEFTA countries were as follows: Hungary 23 per cent and 29 per cent; Romania 14.0 per cent and 14.6 per cent; Slovenia; 7.9 per cent and 12.9 per cent; Slovakia 8.2 per cent and 11.6 per cent. (The source of this data is *CESTAT Statistical Bulletin*, 1999/2.)

8. At the CEFTA Joint Committee meeting held in Budapest in June 1999 the Romanian Minister

for Industry and Trade drew attention to the problem of 'deepening of trade imbalances between Parties' (source: Slovak Ministry of Economy).

9. On the CEFTA trade intensity of Slovenia see Dangerfield (1999a).

10. Source of data on Slovenian, Romanian and Bulgarian GDP per capita and changes in GDP is *Business Central Europe*, June 1999.

11. In crude terms the adjustments which followed the end of the socialist-era trade arrangements can be seen as the logical and necessary decline in the exchanges in products which would have come under the category of 'soft' goods in the CMEA context and market-driven expansion of what were 'hard' goods. There is a consensus among specialists on intra-CEE trade that the exchange of SITC7 products will never return to the kind of pre-eminent position that it held during the CMEA times. This is fair enough but it also needs to be stated that this is not a criteria for the success of CEFTA cooperation since the objective is not to regain the past but to make the most for genuine opportunities for trade in the region. The post-CMEA trade regime needed to ensure that 'soft' goods received no further protection but also to ensure that 'hard' goods and any manufactures which might turn out to be viable were not subject to unjustified discrimination.

12. Data covering the years 1994 to 1997 was available for this purpose and is contained in Appendix Four and the composite table (Table 4.7) included in this chapter. The comprehensive statistical collection provided in Appendix Five gives a detailed breakdown of the commodity structures of the CEFTA countries' (excluding Romania and Bulgaria) exports to and from the CEFTA area. The data includes a breakdown, at Standard Industrial Trade Classification (SITC) single-digit level, of the product comparisons between each country's exports to and imports from CEFTA for each year between 1994 and 1997, the balance of trade in each single-digit SITC group in 1997 and ratios of CEFTA exports/imports to total exports/imports for each commodity group in 1997. Because we are restricted to single-digit data, there is no discussion of patterns for intra-industry trade in CEFTA.

13. In a footnote to their own table (see UNECE, 1998, 79) on changes in the commodity structure of the *overall* trade of the CEFTA countries, the UNECE note that the data should be treated with a measure of caution due to amendments in the foreign trade reporting systems introduced by the Czech Republic in 1996, Hungary in 1997 and Slovakia in 1998. This may affect the exact precision of the data but not the reliability of the broad trends identified, however.

14. Some surveys from within the CEFTA countries have also highlighted these trends. In the case of the Czech Republic, analysts at CzechTrade (Prague) observed that during 1997 Czech exports to CEFTA were characterised by (CzechTrade, 2/1998, 75) 'a strengthening of even so already significant position of machinery and transport equipment (SITC7) which moved to the foremost place in the export structure' while Polish analysts observed (WERI, 1996, 191–2) that 'the primitive model of trade typical of the early nineties was put further behind. One of the most notable developments in this sphere was the fact that electro-engineering exports grew faster than exports in general ... Similar improvements were recorded in exports of the chemical, wood and paper and light industries, that is branches characterised by high value-added ... there was a marked decline in the share of the metallurgical and mineral industries, that is, ones with the highest percentages of raw materials and low value-added products'.

15. The Czech position is somewhat flattered by the huge contribution of the exports of the Volkswagen-owned Skoda automobile plant.

16. Slovak exports of SITC8 products to CEFTA were rather seriously affected by ongoing losses of sales to the Czech Republic. In 1997, for example, the reduction in the value of Czech SITC8 imports was, at Czech Koruna (CZK) 1131 million, over three times the total decline in Czech imports from Slovakia (see CzechTrade, 2/1997, 79).

17. Agricultural trade became increasingly complicated in 1998, as already noted and Hungary's overall CEFTA exports are affected more than most by any tendencies for agricultural trade to fluctuate. Any changes in Hungary's position vis-à-vis other CEFTA countries should be analysed with this in mind.

18. Taken from *EU Support for Reform in Bulgaria*, a transcript of a speech the Commissioner gave at Sofia University, 18 March 1997.

19. The first joint conference on investment opportunities in CEFTA, which targeted potential

US investors, was held in New York city on 5–9 May 1997. The conference was organised jointly by the CEFTA members and the Business Council for International Understanding (BCIU) in New York. The CEFTA delegates addressed over 200 people from the US business community and representatives of US companies active in the CEFTA market, including Procter & Gamble, for example, gave presentations on their successful investments. According to the report in *Warsaw Voice* (18/5/97, no. 20 – online version) 'the conference clearly rekindled the interest of American companies in Poland and other CEFTA countries'. The second CEFTA investment conference was held in Tokyo in October 1997.

20. Notwithstanding the problems of implementing the agricultural trade liberalisation agreements, of course.

21. Firms following 'headquarters' approach locate in one country in the region and use this facility to supply the whole region. The 'landlocked' approach is based on a desire to serve the protected domestic market.

22. There was a feeling in CEE that the stance of the EU concerning the need to engage in subregional economic cooperation was aimed at the creation of a new 'bloc' in CEE and was therefore a device to forestall EU enlargement but in fact it has been a long-standing element of the EC/EU enlargement process, as Preston (1997) has informed us.

23. Outrata also notes, as has been suggested by the commodity structure developments noted in section 1.2, some of the CEFTA countries are making faster progress in closing the gaps in commodity structure competitiveness on the global economy.

24. Meaning collective defence, arms control, and so on.

25. See comments by Gyula Horn, at the 1995 Brno summit, concerning Hungary's 'high interest' (BBC, 13/9/95) in Romania's membership of CEFTA. Hungary had in fact proposed Romania as a candidate during the previous year's summit in Poznan.

26. Former Hungarian Premier Gyula Horn stated that the 'fact that this Central European free trade zone – for after all this is what CEFTA represents – has become an enormously dynamic market and that trade among members has continued to grow is a great achievement in itself' (BBC, EE/3025 C/2, 16/9/97). See Chapter 6 for further examples of official endorsements of the success of CEFTA.

27. At the Portoroz summit former Czech premier Klaus 'held up the Central European Free Trade Agreement (CEFTA) today as a model of a non-bureaucratic organisation functioning on the basis of consensus, contrasting it with the EU and its large Brussels apparatus and tendency towards majority decisions' (BBC, EE/3024 C/2, 15/9/97).

5. Issues and Controversies in CEFTA Cooperation

INTRODUCTION

The previous chapter argued that CEFTA cooperation has proved to be a valuable exercise in terms of reconstructing the trade and economies ties of the member countries, assisting the process of maintaining stable political relations and supporting the EU pre-accession strategy to an extent that should perhaps have gained greater recognition than it has so far in the main literature on the EU's eastward enlargement. This chapter is concerned with the evolution of CEFTA cooperation over its relatively short period of existence. The focus is on developments and debates in three particular themes which usually arise in analyses of integration projects and which have been relevant for CEFTA too: deepening, widening and insitutionalisation.[1] Two of these matters – deepening and widening – are revisited in Chapter 6, which concentrates on the implications for CEFTA of the AGENDA 2000 provisions and subsequent activation of EU accession negotiations. Though there is some inevitable overlap, the main task of this chapter is to cover the various developments in and influences on the evolution of CEFTA during the period leading up to these events when CEFTA cooperation was still maturing and impact of the EU accession somewhat less immediate as the scope and strategy for EU enlargement was still crystallising.

The question of whether CEFTA has experienced any integration- 'deepening' is covered first. According to some analyses of economic integration processes (for example, Hitiris, 1998) the free trade area tends to be the only form other than 'complete economic integration' which is stable, that is, does not automatically generate pressures to 'deepen'. These days, as the CEFTA experience shows, the stability hypothesis seems worth discussing only in the case of the 'classical' concept of free trade which stresses border controls (tariffs, quotas) only. It is less relevant for a present-day context when even the global layer of trade liberalisation within which regional and subregional trade arrangements operate is increasingly addressing the array of non-tariff barriers which further distort competition between national and overseas producers. As was noted in Chapter 3, the CEFTA agreement, duplicating the trade chapters of the Europe Agreement, has provisions which align it with the present day rather than the 'classical' concept of free trade, and rather than 'stability' there is a continuing programme of harmonisation tackling non-tariff barriers.[2] In addition, the stability of even the classic free trade area may be compromised by an external influence, in particular the spillover effects from one regional economic association to another. Countries may be induced to transfer to the dominant regional association, and unless the free trade area is somehow deliberately insulated from other (regional and/or global) integration and trade liberalisation frameworks, the latter will usually impart an integration-deepening effect on the former. The CEFTA countries' intentions to join the EU have always been given, leaving the question of how CEFTA cooperation and engagement with the EU would interact in the meantime.

As far as the second topic – the enlargement of CEFTA – is concerned, integration theory, as noted above, has most to say about the effects of the existence of parallel regional economic associations and the tendency of the subordinate associations to converge on the dominant integration project. Baldwin's (1994) well-known analysis of the political economy factors (the influence of lobbies of producer groups who lose market shares through being excluded from regional economic associations) which caused many EFTA states to develop increasingly close relations with the EC/EU may have some relevance for the CEFTA case. However, the analysis of CEFTA enlargement has to take into account the fact that incumbent, acceded and aspirant CEFTA members have identified CEFTA as an instrument to facilitate the transition to EU membership. Thus, from the point of view of aspirant CEFTA members, interest in acceding has been strong even when the potential economic gains are not so large. Furthermore, the link between CEFTA membership and the EU enlargement process is problematic to the extent that it interferes with the current CEFTA members' inclinations, based on a mix of political and economic motives, to extend the CEE free trade complex and the ability of CEE currently without Europe Agreements to join it. For the latter, an important lifeline to the European integration process may be at stake, giving the issue of CEFTA enlargement even broader implications.

The third matter to be discussed, the question of permanent institutions for CEFTA, is a topic which has come up for regular debate in CEFTA meetings. Even in the case of a classic free trade area, such as the original EFTA was, a secretariat performs some useful coordinating and organisational functions. Given that the CEFTA concept of free trade is the present-day one and the fact that its role as an EU pre-accession instrument might at least suppose some extra coordination, some modest institutionalisation might have been justified. The Slovaks have been persistent advocates of creating institutions for CEFTA, though their agenda also reflected the desire to upgrade CEFTA in order to compensate for falling behind in relations with the EU. That, along with the negative influence of the recent experiences with the vastly over-bureaucratised CMEA and the strong neo-liberal and anti-institutionalist inclinations of the Czechs in particular, meant that the policy on institutions for CEFTA would not be decided according to practical questions alone.

5.1 PRESSURES FOR 'DEEPENING' INTEGRATION IN CEFTA

Article 33 of the CEFTA treaty is the 'Evolutionary clause'. It states (CEFTA, 17) that

> '(w)here a Party considers that it would be useful in the interests of the economies of the Parties to develop and deepen the relations established by the Agreement by extending them to fields not covered thereby, it shall submit a reasoned request to the other Party. The Parties may instruct the Joint Committee to examine such a request and, where appropriate, to make recommendations, particularly with a view to opening negotiations.

Article 33 clearly provides for the CEFTA parties to discuss further development of their cooperation and the use of the term 'deepening' implies that moves to go beyond the basic free trade area can at least be discussed. Though it may well have been the case that Article 33 was originally included as a token gesture and seemed to go against the prevailing sentiments, the issue of further development has nevertheless been a regular item on the CEFTA agenda. The pressure has come from three main sources: first, the desire to make the basic tariff and quota removal process work more efficiently and put agricultural trade liberalisation on the same level as industrial goods liberalisation; second, the activation of 'single market' type features of CEFTA cooperation which were built into the original CEFTA treaty and which have represented a commitment to policy harmonisation probably not appreciated/anticipated when the treaty was signed; third, overspill from the EU pre-accession process which has led to proposals to extend CEFTA cooperation beyond the scope of the current treaty and which represented a genuine use of Article 33.

5.1.1 Enhancing the Trade Liberalisation Process

Several CEE countries committed themselves to international free trade agreements at a very early stage in the overall economic transformation process and this has meant that the implementation of these agreements has very much been a learning process. This was especially true of CEFTA, where other treaties could be used in the design stage but there was no experienced external partner to look to when it came to finding ways of enhancing and improving the functioning of the trade liberalisation process. The various initiatives which emerged in the first phase of implementation reflected the differences in the national approaches to subregional cooperation in CEFTA. In line with the prevailing neo-liberal principles and their more open economy the Czechs in particular were eager advocates of the acceleration of the trade liberalisation programme and its extension to the agricultural field. The Czech side also initiated a debate, in 1996, about whether CEFTA should develop procedures for settling disputes by arbitration. The latter was rejected because (Joint Committee, 6) certain of the CEFTA countries deemed 'it would not be in harmony with the spirit of the agreement' though 'taking into account the need to improve the functioning of CEFTA and with the aim to avoid any possible disputes, the Parties agreed to begin work on a draft concerning common interpretation of certain Articles of the Agreement'.[3] While these developments, together with certain other relatively uncontentious initiatives (joint investment conferences, coordinated positions at WTO meetings[4]), should be seen as natural outcomes connected to the implementation of a duty-free trade zone, the Polish side's proposals to enhance trade growth through the development of common financial institutions were a different matter. At the Brno summit former Polish Premier Oleksy suggested that the CEFTA states should establish (BBC, 13/9/95, A/2) 'a Central European bank which would deal not only with accounting in mutual trade but also joint investment. I have the impression that we have given up too quickly the earlier created instruments of economic cooperation without substituting for them'. This idea failed to attract any support, as did a follow-up proposal tabled at Jasna by Oleksy's successor, former Premier Cimoszewicz, for a meeting of representatives of the CEFTA states' major commercial banks, to be attended also by central bank officials, to discuss mutual payment issues and capital mobility.[5] Advising against such initiatives, Vaclav Klaus said (BBC, 16/9/96, C/4): 'We cannot imagine why we should add another one to the existing system of banks – a new Comecon bank. We cannot order commercial banks to meet. It is their own business'. The Slovak contributions included the recommendation that CEFTA would work better with its own institutions (see Section 5.3 below), but even the relatively modest idea of a secretariat was too reminiscent of the top-down, institutionalised methods of the past, especially for the Czechs. It should be noted too that the Czechs and the Slovaks were both selectively drawing on their own experiences in the Czech–Slovak customs union, which for the Czechs suggested the usefulness of an arbitration panel while the Slovaks were influenced by the existence of the customs union secretariat.

5.1.2   Towards a Single Market in CEFTA?

The discussions about creating and developing cooperation between financial institutions were not only linked to ideas about how to remove some of the impediments to full utilisation of market opportunities created by trade liberalisation but were also connected to important 'deepening' impulses emanating from the outside. While the Brno summit confirmed that CEFTA-'deepening' would not be based on dirigistic approaches, the outcomes of that meeting nevertheless marked some important steps forward in the concept of CEFTA cooperation which implied a shift in the direction of a single/common market. The main development in this sense was the agreement to implement a (Czech) proposal to set up working parties to examine ways of liberalising capital flows and trade in services. The former was led by Poland (which may have been connected to the subsequent suggestion that the CEFTA countries' central banks should hold coordination meetings) and the latter by the Czech Republic.

Developments in the EU pre-accession strategy and impending accession to the OECD (especially of the proposer of these measures, the Czech Republic) were important influences in bringing these issues onto the CEFTA agenda.[6] The European Commission's White Paper of May 1995 (Preparation of the Associated Countries of Central and Eastern Europe for Integration into the Internal Market of the Union) marked a new phase in the pre-accession process. Accordingly it both broadened the potential boundaries of CEFTA cooperation and set a new challenge of incorporating the 'four freedoms' into their own relations, or at least be seen to be considering so doing in order to support the EU accession drive. In their joint statement from the Brno summit the CEFTA Prime Ministers confirmed 'the intention of their governments to develop mutually advantageous economic and trade cooperation, to extend the areas of liberalisation and to remove trade barriers. They are convinced that such an approach will have a positive effect on the preparation of their countries for entrance into the European Union'. (BBC, 14/9/95, A/1) The spillover from EU pre-accession to subregional cooperation was further illustrated by the fact that the Brno summit also discussed the possibility of introducing free movement of labour into the CEFTA area. The other parties were not prepared to endorse the proposal, leaving labour mobility the only one of the 'four freedoms' not within the potential coverage of CEFTA cooperation.[7]

In common with other integration antecedents, however, the CEFTA experience demonstrates that the emergence of a pressure or a rationale to intensify the integration process may not result in actual moves forward if either the political will is lacking or other necessary prerequisites are not in place or (as in the case for CEFTA countries) the intensification will in any case occur at a future point in the framework of the regional (that is EU) integration. An additional complication is that CEFTA enlargement has also further differentiated the group in terms of progress towards integration into the broader trading and regulatory frameworks (for example, OECD membership, 'in' or 'pre-in' status in the EU enlargement). So far, concrete progress in liberalising flows of capital and services has been slow to materialise. In fact the matters have not been discussed seriously since the 1997 meetings of the CEFTA summit and Joint

Committee, indicating that they have been put to one side for now or are off the CEFTA agenda indefinitely.[8]

A further and more active way in which CEFTA cooperation may be on course to move beyond the free trade area is through the official policy of the CEFTA countries to take free movement of goods to a qualitatively higher stage. As Tsoukalis (1997, 67) wrote in connection with the move to create the EU's single market, 'the most effective barriers were not to be found at the border; they were, instead, the result of different regulatory frameworks which created the notorious NTBs'. The articles of the CEFTA treaty aim to tackle important non-tariff distortions to fair competition including, for example, the need to ensure the parties are informed of draft technical regulations and amendments (Article 10), use of state aids (Article 23) and discriminatory public procurement practices (Article 24). The CEFTA countries' five-year review of the operation of CEFTA (Joint Committee, 1998, 4) concluded that while Article 10 was now covered by the relevant WTO agreement, insufficient progress had been made with Article 23 and recommended the establishment of a working group to ensure its implementation. The Joint Committee meeting held in Prague on 3 July 1998 decided to set up the relevant working group, which was led by Slovenia. Its conclusions, accepted by the CEFTA Joint Committee in 1999, were that it was not necessary to prepare special CEFTA criteria for assessment of state aids because of the results of negotiations with the EU on state aids in the framework of the Europe Agreement. Instead, it was agreed that the relevant criteria established with the EU will apply to CEFTA as well.[9] The 1999 Joint Committee session also agreed that progress on the level of liberalisation of public procurement would be examined over the course of the next year.[10] Finally, notwithstanding the numerous factors which have complicated the liberalisation of agricultural trade, the parties have nevertheless been acting to remove veterinary and phytosanitary obstacles to trade in farm products. In this connection the CEFTA Prime Ministers agreed, at the 1998 summit (Declaration of the Prime Ministers of the CEFTA Countries, Prague, 1998, 2) 'to intensify bilateral negotiations concerning the certification of industrial and agricultural products, including mutual recognition of test results and certificates with the aim to conclude bilateral agreements, if possible until the end of 1999'.

5.2   ENLARGING CEFTA

5.2.1   Article 39A

Though the Cracow treaty did not envisage or contain provision for enlargement, it was not long before strong pressures to include other CEE states in CEFTA asserted themselves. As soon as the EU signed or opened negotiations for Europe

Agreements elsewhere in the region the main basis for CEFTA states to differentiate themselves had become eroded. In any case, the bilateral free trade agreements which began to spread through the region, starting with the signing of the Czech–Slovenia agreement on 4 December 1993 (Brinar, 1999, 251) served as important pathways to CEFTA and showed that the CEFTA states were not inclined to maintain an exclusive group.[11] The green light for CEFTA enlargement came at the Poznan summit in November 1994 which recognised Slovenia's candidacy and established the CEFTA accession conditions. It was decided that in order to be eligible for CEFTA candidates must (a) be members of the World Trade Organisation (WTO), (b) have signed (though not necessarily have had ratified) 'Europe Agreements' with the EU, (c) have bilateral free trade agreements with the existing members, and (d) have the approval of all of the existing CEFTA members. The next step was to make the necessary amendments to the CEFTA treaty and, following (all in July 1995) Slovenia's entry into the WTO, conclusion of the outstanding bilateral free trade agreement with Poland and lodging of its formal application to join CEFTA, this was duly carried out at the Brno summit. The 'Supplementary Agreement to CEFTA' added Article 39a which confirmed that CEFTA membership was open to any European country that met the Poznan criteria.

5.2.2 The CEFTA Enlargement Process

As far as the accession criteria are concerned, the WTO condition reflects that CEFTA was created and operates in the framework of Article 24 of the GATT which covers regional economic associations, and at the same time WTO membership is assumed to guarantee that prospective members have reached a mature enough stage in their economic transformation to ensure that free trade arrangements can work fairly and efficiently. The Europe Agreement condition reflects CEFTA's role as an instrument to serve the EU accession process and demonstrates that CEFTA membership is restricted to countries which are fully committed to gaining full EU membership.[12] The third condition relates to the fact that the discussions to conclude the trade liberalisation schedules are at the same time the 'nitty-gritty' of accession negotiations. The requirement for bilateral free trade agreements to be in force prior to accession was an obvious necessity in the first phase of CEFTA, though it has become less important with time (see below) since the necessary detail can be included in the annexes to accession treaties.[13] Finally the enlargement by consensus rule is (Winkler, 1997, 81) 'to guarantee that changes to CEFTA will not happen at the expense of any of the participating countries or contrary to its interests'.

Of the three accessions which have taken place so far, it is worth mentioning first that the Slovenian accession differed from the Romanian and Bulgarian cases in several ways. For example, both Bulgaria and Romania had signed

Table 5.1 Past and possible future enlargements of CEFTA

Country (years invited as guest at CEFTA summit)	Date of formal application to join CEFTA	Date of accession to CEFTA	Date of WTO accession	Date of signing of Europe Agreement	Bilateral free trade agreements with CEFTA states?
Slovenia (1994)	17/7/95	1/1/96	30/7/95	10/6/96	Czech Republic (4/12/93), Slovakia (22/12/93), Hungary (6/4/94), Poland (17/7/95)
Romania (1995, 1996)	10/4/96	1/7/97	1/1/95	4/10/93	Czech Republic (24/10/94), Slovakia (11/11/94)
Bulgaria (1995, 1996, 1997)	30/5/96	1/1/99	1/12/96	4/10/93	Czech Republic (15/12/95), Slovakia (8/12/95), Slovenia (22/11/96)
Lithuania (1995, 1996, 1997)	3/7/97		*	15/6/95	Slovenia (4/10/96), Czech Republic (14/10/96), Poland (27/5/96), Slovakia (27/11/96)

Table 5.1 continued

				Bilateral Free Trade Agreements
Latvia (1996, 1997)		18/10/98	15/6/96	Czech Republic (1/4/96) Slovenia (22/4/96) Slovakia (19/4/96)
Croatia (1997)		*		Slovenia (1/1/97)
FYR Macedonia (1997)	21/12/95	*	**	Slovenia (1/7/96)
Ukraine (1996, 1997)	3/7/97	*	***	
Moldova (none)		*	***	Romania (15/2/95)

Notes:

In the Bilateral Free Trade Agreements column, the dates in brackets refer to the entry into force of the particular agreement.

*WTO applications currently being considered by accession working parties.

** FYR Macedonia's 'Trade and Cooperation Agreement' with the EU entered into force on 1 January 1998.

*** EU relations are on basis of 'Partnership and Cooperation' agreements which contain a provision for the two parties to discuss the establishment of a free trade area. So far this is not on the agenda.

For the column 'Date of formal application to join CEFTA', in the cases of FYR Macedonia, Lithuania and Ukraine, the dates given are the days on which the CEFTA Joint Committee discussed those countries' formal requests to accede to CEFTA.

Sources: Brinar (1999); WTO Database on Regional Trade Agreements.

their Europe Agreements when they acceded to CEFTA whereas Slovenia had not. This was not so important, however, since there were no immediate practical implications and preparation of Slovenia's Europe Agreement was at an advanced stage to the effect that its EU Associate status was as good as confirmed. The CEFTA four were therefore happy to let the accession of Slovenia go through at that particular time. Another aspect of Slovenia's accession did however offer some important lessons for subsequent enlargements. Slovenia signed up for CEFTA as it stood at 25 November 1996. By the time Slovenia's entry took force just over one month later the CEFTA four had signed, on 21 December 1995, Additional Protocol 3 which made important changes to rules for agricultural trade to which Slovenia was not legally obliged to follow. Over a year and a half of dispute over the extent of access to Slovenia's agricultural goods market followed until the agreement signed in Portoroz settled the matter. Future accessions would not permit any such unforeseen 'derogations'.[14] Finally, as Table 5.1 shows, the rule about prior bilateral free trade agreements with all current CEFTA members was not applied in the cases of Romania and Bulgaria. Since they both joined after 1 January 1997 when most industrial goods trade became duty- and tariff- free, the only relevant negotiations concerned the lists of exceptions for industrial products and details of the agricultural concessions. These were taken care of in the protocols of the accession treaties removing the need for any separate bilateral free trade agreements. Thus, whereas CEFTA membership for Slovenia was more or less a case of rubber-stamping a *de facto* membership of CEFTA into a formal full membership, the Romanian and Bulgarian accessions were really negotiated ones because they involved planning for a rapid transition to free trade between the applicants and those incumbent CEFTA with which trade liberalisation had not yet started. One consequence of this was that the accession negotiations themselves took longer to complete (see also Table 5.1).[15] So far, the need for prior bilateral free trade agreements has therefore reflected the stage of CEFTA liberalisation and the state of readiness of the candidates. They do, however, remain relevant for CEFTA aspirants still outside the WTO and without EAs because they can serve as a kind of CEFTA 'pre-accession' and enable the countries concerned to get on with some real integration with the CEFTA area.

The usual procedure for states wishing to join CEFTA is to send a formal letter of application or expression of interest to the Foreign Ministry of the CEFTA chair country. The request is then placed on the agenda of the next meeting of the CEFTA Joint Committee. For certain countries the formal approach had been preceded by informal discussions with officials of individual CEFTA members in the framework of bilateral trade talks or general state visits. In most cases the result of the application has been to go on the 'waiting list' for CEFTA accession pending fulfilment of the membership conditions or completion of ongoing negotiations (CEFTA absorbs countries individually rather than in groups). Until recently at least, it has been possible to identify the potential future members of CEFTA by checking out the list of guest countries invited to the CEFTA summits (Table 5.1). Slovenian representatives, for example, attended the 1994 (Poznan) summit indicating their country's impending accession and Bulgaria and Romania, together with Lithuania, were represented at the 1995 summit. The CEFTA chair, having responsibility for all arrangements for the main CEFTA meetings including invitations to guest countries, can clearly influence the list of observers, hence the attendance of Macedonia and Croatia at the 1997 summit organised by Slovenia. The list of invited countries must, however, have collective approval. The 1998 summit was notable in that no CEFTA candidate countries were in attendance. Though the reasons for this were mainly to do with the feeling that there was a need to maximise the time available for 'private' discussions of CEFTA business, particularly with the crisis situation in agricultural trade, the aspirant members may have drawn certain conclusions as regards the sensitivity of this move. For the non-CEE10 candidates in particular, attendance at the CEFTA summit has also been a counterpoise, modest but symbolically important, to their general feeling of estrangement from the European integration process.

So far the order of accession has been determined by the date of application in the first instance and then according to which applicants have met the WTO and Europe Agreement conditions. FYR Macedonia, for example, applied at the same time as Slovenia and therefore before most other candidates, but there have been no moves towards opening negotiations. As we have already noted, however, in the cases of states such as FYR Macedonia, Ukraine, Croatia and Moldova (the newest CEFTA aspirant[16]) bilateral discussions concerning free trade agreements are of course part of the preparations for CEFTA membership. As far as the unanimity principle is concerned, potentially there could be alternative preferences according to different national interests (Poland, for example, has been more interested in the accession of the Ukraine and the Baltic countries, while Slovenia and Bulgaria have more direct interest in the cases of Balkan countries and Romania is the main link to Moldova) though the nature of the accession criteria seems to have so far avoided any serious disagreement about which countries should be admitted and the timings. Taking the existing and candidate members together, depending on how far enlargement can go, CEFTA could reach a combined market of 164 million people. The factors which will determine the future path of CEFTA enlargement, particularly as far as non-CEE10 candidates are concerned, will be discussed in Chapter 6 in the context of the impact of the current phase of the EU enlargement process.

5.2.3 Dynamics of CEFTA Enlargement

All past and present CEFTA candidates have stressed the importance of economic benefits. Slovenia's membership was, for example, 'primarily a consequence of market interest' (Bobek et al., 1996, 82) which reflected the need to reorient from the former Yugoslav market which (due to the simultaneous shocks of transformational adjustment and war) contracted rapidly following Slovenia's independence. For Slovenian analysts (Bobek et al., 1996, 83) the 'largest increases in trade between CEFTA countries are expected in the sectors which are not highly protected, but are protected in the EU, which prevents them from directing their trade to this otherwise most important market'. Notwithstanding the possibilities for modest but useful expansion of subregional trade through CEFTA and the strategic value of gaining a key presence in markets that should be strong growth centres in the future EU, it seems the economic motivations for placing great stress on CEFTA membership could be overstated. In the case of Slovenia, for example, CEFTA still accounts for a small proportion of exports (5.7 per cent in 1997) with imports remaining more important (7.4 per cent) reflecting growth, particularly from Hungary and the Czech Republic, of 'raw materials and agricultural produce which had formerly been "imported" from other parts of Yugoslavia' (Brinar, 1999, 257). Moreover, Slovenia's official 'international economic strategy' places at least equivalent (to that placed on CEFTA markets) stress on its main pre-1990 markets and assumes that while past levels of trade are unlikely to be attained there 'is no doubt that the re-establishment of ties with *the markets of former Yugoslavia* is wanted and needed' (Bobek et al,, 1996, 95).

Table 5.2   CEE countries' trade with CEFTA, 1997 (as % of total trade)

Country	Exports to CEFTA	Imports from CEFTA
Bulgaria	1.8	4.0
Croatia	16.3	15.0
Latvia	2.1	5.6
Lithuania	3.2	8.8
Ukraine	8.1	6.9

Sources: CESTAT Statistical Bulletin, 1997/4; DIW (1998).

As Table 5.2 shows, the value of trade with CEFTA tends to be relatively small in the cases of Latvia, Lithuania and Ukraine.[17] The position of Croatia looks rather different according to this data and seems to provide economic justification for Croatian officials' repeated stress that 'Croatia's absolute priority is to gain entry into CEFTA'.[18] Yet Slovenia accounts for the majority of Croatia's trade with CEFTA and these two countries are already implementing a bilateral free trade agreement. Meanwhile, FYR Macedonia also has a free trade agreement with Slovenia and impending free trade arrangements (see Chapter 6) with Bulgaria will open the other significant CEFTA market. This begs the question of what exactly does *full* membership of CEFTA contribute in the economic sense, in that any country which signs and begins implementing a free trade agreement with one or more of the CEFTA states has *de facto* become part of CEFTA in that it is incorporated either fully or partially into the tariff- and quota-free zone? One answer might be to do with anticipated positive effects on inward investment. There is, however, no substantial evidence that CEFTA membership *by itself* has had any significant impact on inward investments to individual countries (see Chapter 4). This means that though the potential economic advantages will have been noted they will not be the only incentives and not necessarily the most important. As Grela (1997, 142) wrote: '(i)interest in CEFTA springs from both political and economic sources. First, there is fear of marginalisation and a new division in Europe. Secondly, there are financial and trade considerations'.[19]

It is important therefore to distinguish between the idea of CEFTA as a trade liberalisation zone and CEFTA as a 'club', which, as such, has attractions for non-members over and above the free trade aspect which, after all, can be realised without formal membership of the grouping. The range of perspectives on CEFTA can be listed as follows. First, CEE states (and especially the newly independent 'state-building' ones) regard accession to international organisations as confirmation that they are making their mark on the international stage. CEFTA has gradually emerged as a successful subregional organisation, in some perceptions a club of the 'avant-garde' post-communist countries in the best position as far as the main goal of admittance to the EU is concerned.[20] Calin Tariceanu (Romanian Minister for Industry and Trade at the time) said the following about Romania's accession to CEFTA: 'politically speaking, CEFTA is a good training school with a view to adherence to the European Union, as well as a signal for NATO' (Romanian News Agency, April 1997). Similarly, prior to Bulgaria's accession, Zhan Videnov, the former Bulgarian Prime Minister, stated in Jasna that 'Bulgaria's membership in CEFTA and the expansion of the CEFTA market would be a logical development and would undoubtedly reflect on trade relations, strengthening Bulgaria's position in the European integration process'(BBC, EE/2718 C/2, 16/9/96).

Second, the idea that CEFTA membership enhances prospects for EU accession has an additional dimension in that CEFTA membership has been viewed as a means to lend support to certain states' aspirations as far as regional identity is concerned. The desire to be part of 'central Europe' has to some extent been connected to the wish to be placed in the right basket of CEE countries as far as relations with the European Union are concerned. Lithuanian and Croatian officials have stated that, as well as economic motives, their interest in joining CEFTA has reflected a wish to confirm their central European identities, though the labels/identities these countries wish to discard (former Soviet Republic and post-Yugoslav/Balkan state respectively) must be equally relevant. In 1997 the Lithuanian position was described as follows: 'At present accession to CEFTA is one of the priorities of Lithuanian foreign policy. CEFTA is valued as a good practical preparation for membership in the European Union. Lithuania's accession to CEFTA will once again confirm Lithuania's Central European identity and will pave the way for the rapprochement of the other two Baltic states with Central Europe' (Paleckis, 1997, 1). As for Croatia, describing the official approach towards the South-east European Cooperation Initiative (SECI), the Minister for Foreign Affairs Mate Granic stated the following (Croatian Investment Promotion Agency, 1998) 'SECI ... is an initiative ... which has not yet produced any results in the form of specific projects. Croatia remains open towards this – ostensibly economic – initiative, but only to the extent that it corresponds with our national interests ... we do not wish – in accordance with our priorities – to participate in any association which would tie us to the Balkans'.[21]

Third, for those CEE countries currently on the sidelines of the expansion of the Euro–Atlantic organisations (that is, NATO, EU) membership of subregional initiatives such as CEFTA can help reduce the sense of isolation and thus offset what Madej (1997, 100) calls the 'syndrome of the deserted'.[22] In this connection Madej (1997, 91) also noted that the 'Ukraine authorities have been displaying an interest in CEFTA for some time now. Incidentally, they combine this with broader political suggestions, for example, for making East-Central Europe a nuclear-free zone and making the region engage in constructive action to promote peace and good-neighbourly relations throughout the Eurasian continent'.[23] Finally, it should be remembered that as well as the key to joining CEFTA, the CEFTA accession criteria are vital strategic objectives and are arguably more important in themselves. Engagement with CEFTA cannot guarantee WTO membership and Associate membership of the EU, but it can only assist the process of attaining these objectives as it brings pressure on the target organisations, especially in cases where the current CEFTA members act as sponsors (for example, the country which has acted as Ukraine's sponsor with respect to CEFTA, Poland, has also voiced support for Ukraine's case for acceptance into the WTO and for the granting of a Europe Agreement). Clearly the aspirant countries were linking the process of attaining CEFTA membership with their broader strategic aims.

What about the existing member states' motives for expanding CEFTA? The absence of any provision for expansion of CEFTA in its original formulation seems explicable in terms of the initial hesitance towards the subregional economic association and the idea that the V4 were not only an avant-garde group of transforming countries but would continue to have a privileged relationship with the EU. Even when the latter idea was dissolved with the signing of the EU Association Accords for Bulgaria and Romania in 1993 and the emergence of an increasingly globalised EU approach to CEE countries, the fact that actors in the Czech Republic, Hungary and Poland at least were prone to believe that (for different regions) their country was the number one CEE candidate for early EU membership, engagement with non-Visegrad countries was therefore perceived as risky if the EU proceeded with a bloc enlargement. While these factors were no doubt important impediments as far as the further development (indeed continuation) of the 'Visegrad group' were concerned, if there was indeed any tendency for this to spill over into CEFTA and restrict its expansion it was short-lived.[24] Various factors gave the CEFTA countries a stake in enlargement.

First, welcoming other CEE states into CEFTA was a useful way for the CEFTA countries to support their EU candidacy by demonstrating that they were responsible subregional players. The nature of the CEFTA accession would ensure that the organisation would not spread beyond the 'inner circle' of Europe Agreement countries. Second, moves to enlarge CEFTA have been influenced by broader foreign policy and strategic objectives of certain CEFTA states. In this connection, Hudak (in Cottey, 1996, 13) has argued that 'within CEFTA the initiative belongs primarily to Poland and Slovakia. Slovakia is interested in CEFTA for economic reasons and also because, should it be excluded from the first wave of NATO and EU enlargement, CEFTA could offer a transitional alternative. The Polish interest in developing subregional cooperation stems largely from the fact that Poland is a (sub-) regional power. As such, Poland has a more active, "Eastern policy" which envisages the admission of Ukraine and the Baltic States to CEFTA'. These views were often juxtaposed with the image of the Czech Republic as the main go-it-alone CEE state. Yet while this may have been true for the Klaus team as far as subregional political cooperation in the Visegrad group was concerned, if anything the opposite was true for CEFTA and subregional economic cooperation (conducted of course within the parameters of the pluralist/neo-liberal approach to economic integration). We have already noted the central role played by the Czech party concerning deepening of CEFTA cooperation and Czechs have also been prime movers in opening CEFTA. In this respect we should note some official statements such as the one by the former Bulgarian premier, Zhan Videnov, who, during the Jasna CEFTA summit, described Vaclav Klaus as one of the 'staunchest supporters of expanding CEFTA' and, at the same occasion, the former Czech leader himself said that (BBC, C/1, 16/9/96) 'CEFTA must not be an exclusive organisation, a club of the chosen, which doesn't want new members. We will certainly push in this direction' (BBC, C/6, 16/9/96). Together with their role in courting Slovenia for CEFTA membership (Kolankiewicz, 1994), the fact that the Czechs, together with the Slovaks, set the pace in concluding free trade agreements not only with Slovenia but with Bulgaria and Romania also represents an altogether more substantial reason for arguing that the Czech side has been a proactive element in the enlargement of CEFTA.[25]

Third, there were clear economic interests at work. The external imbalances which returned after 1993 not only created a logic for faster liberalisation of the CEFTA market, especially on the part of those countries – again the Czech and Slovak Republics – which had big surpluses in their intra-CEFTA trade, but also for the expansion of the CEFTA market. At a time when the CEFTA states were struggling to maintain dynamism in their exports to the EU (external disequilibrium remains a constant threat to economic growth), the expansion of the subregional free trade complex through CEFTA enlargement was important so as to ease access to other CEE markets and reduce the discrimination CEFTA producers were facing vis-à-vis EU producers. Especially important was the fact that the CEFTA countries could expect to experience trade growth in their favour. With the exception of Poland, the original CEFTA countries experienced net export growth with Slovenia, and the subsequent enlargements to Romania and Bulgaria took in slower reforming, less developed, less restructured countries with less FDI whose markets the CEFTA industrial (and in the case of Hungary, agricultural) producers could expect to do well in.[26] In the case of the Ukraine (still on the fringes of CEFTA), for example, trade liberalisation with CEFTA would, according to Madej (1997, 97), give the CEFTA producers preferential access to markets that are still engaged in crisis imports, to be followed by mass consumption then 'after 2000 a huge modernisation of Ukrainian industry will get under way. Domestic producers will be involved in it but there will be vast opportunities for enterprises from CEFTA countries and from all over the world'. Thus CEFTA countries seemed to have the prospect of preferential market access to a country which is big, a market they already have good knowledge of, and where a reasonable prognosis is net export growth in favour of the CEFTA states.[27]

Finally, it should be mentioned here that the period in which the deterioration in the external trade situation became clear (1993/4) corresponded with a temporary political sea-change in certain of the Visegrad countries. Because officials in those (sic) new governments in Poland and Hungary were essentially reform communists making a comeback, they had strong links with the previous regime and this was consistent with the diminution of the CMEA syndrome and a more pragmatic view of subregional economic cooperation. Even though the political economy forces would have mainly stressed the former Soviet market this was able to spill over into the CEFTA dimension, especially as intra-CEFTA trade was expanding rapidly. These days the CEFTA countries' attitudes towards the openness of CEFTA remains positive, though the proximity of certain of them to EU membership has introduced new factors into the CEFTA enlargement calculations. The question of the further enlargement of CEFTA is taken up in Chapter 6.

5.2.4   CEFTA and Russia

Finally, on enlargement, some mention should be made of the geopolitical context of CEFTA expansion and the question of relations with Russia in particular. While Russian policy-makers were never likely to be preoccupied with CEFTA, at the same time it has not been completely ignored. In September 1996 the Russian Prime Minister wrote to the Jasna summit expressing Russia's view of CEFTA as a model for developing its 'traditional relations with our partners in Central and Eastern Europe on a new basis' (Dangerfield, 1997, 13). Yet shortly afterwards contradictory messages came from other Russian officials. In October 1996 it was reported that Deputy Premier, Oleg Davydov (RFE/RL, 11/11/96, 2) 'repeated and publicly argues that this economic "buffer" zone harms Russia's political and economic interests ... (and) warned that Russia "cannot stand by and watch the emergence of a potential opportunity for infringing upon Russian interests". And he has told the East Europeans that Moscow will soon deploy its economic muscle against this group unless it takes into account Russian concerns'.

According to Zagorski (1997, 538–9) the Russian attitude to subregional cooperation depends on whether it is included in particular initiatives and 'the Central European Initiative and the Visegrad Group are generally viewed with greater mistrust, especially by the military establishment ... Approaches towards subregional organisation may thus be only one example of the stereotyped, almost paranoid Russian geopolitical thinking which is obsessed with the idea of hostile encirclement by any coalitions of which Russia is not a member'. Thus the tendency for CEFTA to have been both courted and cautioned by various Russian spokesmen may simply have represented different approaches to dealing with organisations in the geographic vicinity. The accession of Ukraine, were it to come about, would probably raise the profile of CEFTA in Russian policy circles and cause CEFTA generally to acquire much more of a political dimension. As Cottey (1996, 14) wrote: 'Ukrainian membership and economic ties with Russia cannot be separated from politics and wider regional relations'.

5.3   INSTITUTIONALISATION

During the Jasna summit former Czech premier Klaus said that 'the Czech Republic was happy that CEFTA was unique among world organisations in that it did not have a single paid employee, did not have a budget, a building, bureaucrats and so on' (BBC, 16/9/96, C/1). It is possible to see several reasons why there was no great urgency to set up institutions for CEFTA. For example, the CMEA experience, which had involved an overly extensive and, even by Soviet bloc standards, exceptionally ineffective bureaucracy, was still a recent memory. There was also the worry, at least in the early years, that to create institutions would serve to perpetuate the outmoded idea of a CEE 'bloc'. On the practical level, why allocate resources in this way to a temporary economic association? Opposition to all forms of economic bureaucracy was also, of course, part of the neo-liberal rhetoric of certain CEFTA country policy-makers, especially in the Czech Republic. Another way of thinking about the opposition to institutionalisation in CEFTA is to see it as the reverse situation to 'regionalist entrapment'. Instead of *creating* regional institutions in order to 'restrict the free exercise of hegemonic power' (Hurrell, 1995, 342), the idea was not to entrap any larger subregional power but to ensure that there was no institutional arena for any party (in the Visegrad case the country under suspicion was Poland) to forward a subregional/regional rather than Euro–Atlantic integration and security agenda.

Anti-institutional sentiments have prevailed to such an extent that even the seemingly innocuous step of setting up a CEFTA secretariat to deal with the organisation of the various official meetings, to disseminate information and so on, has so far not proved possible. The need for a permanent secretariat was first raised by the Slovak side at the 1995 (Brno) summit. On that occasion the Czech contribution was to stress that there were far more urgent matters to attend to. Vladimir Dlouhy, at that time the Czech Minister for Industry and Trade, remarked that (BBC, 13/9/95, A/1)

> the Czech Republic believes that the creation of a secretariat is not the main problem, we should rather complete liberalisation in agriculture, try to expand it to the sphere of services and see to the well-considered expansion of CEFTA by addition of other countries. From this point of view I would prefer liberalisation of systemic conditions to institutionalisation.

The summit agreed that Slovakia would 'draw up proposals for CEFTA's organisation structure ... in time for the next meeting of premiers in autumn 1996' (BBC, 13/9/95, A/2).

The Slovak government proceeded to develop a more concrete plan to put to the other CEFTA parties according to the schedule agreed, which also coincided with its own presidency of CEFTA. In March 1996 the Slovak Information Agency reported that the Slovak cabinet had approved a project to establish the 'CEFTA Central Offices' in Bratislava to carry out 'the coordination of the administrative and commercial relations of the member countries. These activities would be carried out by a team of about fifteen representatives. The planned costs for the first year of its existence go up to $US 1.3 billion. The financial contribution of each one of the member countries is to be decided between either equal contributions or according to the country's population' (*Slovakia Today*, March 1996). The proposal was firmly rejected by the Jasna summit and the matter seemingly put to rest with the agreement that from then on CEFTA would have a kind of quasi-secretariat consisting of civil servants of the chair country assisted by embassy (commercial attaché) staff of the other parties. The fact that the idea for a permanent secretariat was a Slovak project gave the issue far more significance than it really merited of itself. The apparent largesse of the 1996 proposal and the preferred location were taken to be indicative of a broader Slovak agenda for CEFTA which was out of line with the other parties, and the Czech side in particular. In late 1995 former Slovak premier Meciar clearly politicised the issue. He was reported (*OMRI Daily Digest, Slovak Selection*, 13/11/95) as saying that 'it would be a great result if he managed to make Bratislava the CEFTA's residence. "It would certainly help to form the political position of Slovakia in Europe", said V. Meciar'.[28]

A further twist in September 1998 illustrated the fluidity of the situation. The Czech side, now represented by a team whose attitude to subregional cooperation was considerably more enthusiastic than their predecessors, not only at last agreed to the creation of a CEFTA regional office but also suggested that CEFTA could be given 'a political dimension along the lines of the Visegrad accords' (RFE/RL Newsline, 14/9/98). This time it was the Hungarian delegation which refused to sanction a secretariat. Victor Urban (BBC, 14/9/98, C/5) stated that he advocated

> developing more profound and more sincere cooperation between the Czech Republic, Hungary, Poland and Slovakia. In turn, I oppose institutionalisation, for instance the Slovak proposal for setting up a regional coordination office of CEFTA in Bratislava. CEFTA is in fact a free trade agreement, not a system of institutions. The Hungarian government would oppose the shifting of free trade cooperation towards bureaucracy.

Meanwhile, the Slovak side opposed any moves to 'have CEFTA discuss political matters in 1999, when the organisation's presidency is taken over by Hungary' (RFE/RL Newsline, 14/9/98). Some serious problems involving wheat trade between Hungary and Slovakia, together with the further deterioration of the two countries' political relations which followed the 1998 Hungarian elections, were key factors. This spat, however, marked the end of a period in which CEFTA and broader subregional cooperation was compromised by bilateral tensions involving Slovakia. The ousting of the Meciar government, together with the earlier change of government in the Czech Republic, not only contributed to an easing of bilateral tensions but also enabled the Visegrad group to convene.[29] As for the secretariat question, it should at last retreat to the relatively minor, neutral issue it really ought to be and no moves to change the status quo arrangements are now likely.

NOTES

1. Most evaluations of CEFTA have included the agricultural trade difficulties in the list of the main problem areas of CEFTA. Since developments in intra-CEFTA agricultural trade are covered in Chapters 3 and 4 they are not raised again here. In any case the idea of this chapter is to discuss broader aspects of the development of CEFTA rather than specific details of trade liberalisation.

2. Integration-deepening is usually equated with moves to further enmesh national economies into the regional economic complex, usually entailing a key shift from 'negative' (market) to 'positive' (policy) integration. According to first generation theories of integration (that is, the classic Balassa framework) this involves progression through the various 'stages' of integration, that is from a free trade area to a customs union to a common market and so on. In CEFTA circles this has sometimes been referred to as deepening in the 'EU meaning of the word' (Winkler, 1997, 78). Since El-Agraa (1998, 2) asserts that 'each of these forms of integration can be introduced in its own right', the shift from one stage to the next may be presented in terms of an economic rationale but depends on a political process due to the fact that progressive transfers of sovereignty are involved. According to this framework, integration-deepening for CEFTA would not be predicted. For one thing, all the CEFTA parties have been resolutely determined to avoid transferring any sovereignty to subregional organisations and in any case there has been the assumption that the more mature phases of integration are scheduled to occur in the context of EU membership. Any explicit moves to emulate the evolution of the EU would contradict the baseline assumption that CEFTA was not conceived of, or planned to develop into, an alternative to the EU. Moreover, the Czech side was for a long time (that is, the Klaus era) strongly committed to the neo-liberal approach to integration and even applied this in its rhetoric towards the EU. No CEFTA policy statement has expressed the intention to emulate the EU development model. Alternatives to the traditional approaches to integration-deepening are however more useful for explaining the nature of the deepening process in the CEFTA setting and understanding its dynamics. Tsoukalis (1997, 62) has argued that the integration experience of the EU has shown the textbook model of deepening to be invalid: '(t)he different stages are usually presented in the form of a ladder which can be climbed one step at a time ... However this categorisation, together with the traditional theory of international trade, has been shown to be very misleading because both basically ignore the reality of mixed economies where state intervention is not limited to border controls or macroeconomic policy ... In the context of such economies, a complete customs union or a common market can be nothing short of total economic integration'. This approach depicts a more seamless integration process moved by 'spillover' effects which are equivalent to inbuilt pressures to move the project forward.

3. The initial move to create a mechanism for solving disputes within CEFTA was essentially 'a result of a "big dispute behind closed doors" over Slovenia's failure to fulfil some agricultural trade agreements' (BBC, 19/9/96, C2).

4. The Jasna summit approved a joint strategy to further attract inward investment through joint conferences to advertise investment opportunities in CEFTA as a defined region (see Chapter 4). At the same time it was agreed that the CEFTA states would coordinate their positions in the World Trade Organisation (WTO), starting with the WTO meeting scheduled for the end of 1996.

5. Part of the context of this was the role of Western intermediaries in intra-CEFTA trade who were able to profit from the lack of a reliable and fast payments systems and credit lines within CEFTA. German and Austrian companies in particular made large-scale purchases from CEFTA suppliers for resale to purchasers in other CEFTA countries, thereby either reducing the profits of the CEFTA seller or increasing the costs of the CEFTA buyer or both.

6. Richter (1997, 12) observed that '(a)nother important indirect source of intra-CEFTA liberalisation and harmonisation of the legal system has been (and will be in the future) the OECD membership of the Czech Republic (December 1995), Hungary (May 1996), and Poland (November 1996) ... it is worth mentioning that, although the liberalisation of capital movements was not addressed in the CEFTA Document, the compliance with the OECD

Codes of Liberalisation of Current Invisible Operations and Capital Movements will leave no room for restrictions in intra-CEFTA capital movements once all the five CEFTA members have become OECD members, and when the transitional restrictions are lifted presumably in about three to four years'.

7. The explanation of Polish Prime Minister, Jozef Oleksy, was that (BBC, 13/9/95, A3) 'the remaining CEFTA states decided that they were not yet ready for it'. For now, movement of labour between CEFTA countries continues to be regulated by bilateral agreements. Czech–Slovak arrangements allow for free movement of labour for the nationals of the two countries.

8. With hindsight the Brno proposals to move to what, in effect, would have been an extension of the EEA to the CEFTA area were optimistic if not naive given the range of practical difficulties (exchange controls, banking sector problems, the interplay of free trade in services and free movement of labour, different stages of privatisation of the service sector and particularly of banks) to be overcome. No doubt the CEFTA countries made a link between their agenda for subregional cooperation in CEFTA and the EC Commission's assessment of their EU applications. No matter what the intentions really were, the tendency of problems of agricultural trade to dominate the CEFTA agenda in recent years along with the time and energy taken up by the three enlargements has left little time for other matters. Very important also is the lack of suitably qualified personnel to devote to this issue (all such resources must be employed in the EU accession effort which in turn already lacks sufficient numbers of suitably qualified personnel).

9. As far as the transparency of state aid measures is concerned, the Joint Committee also agreed that the notifications required by the WTO in this respect would suffice in CEFTA too.

10. Some moves to start implementing this CEFTA Article did in fact get off the ground following a November 1996 meeting of the CEFTA ministers with responsibility for public procurement which resulted in agreement on a process to facilitate liberalisation in public orders by ending discriminatory measures which favour domestic firms and create national databases of public orders.

11. The Czech eagerness to spread its network of free trade arrangements has been interpreted in two, not necessarily mutually exclusive, ways. First, in line with the minimalist approach to subregional cooperation, to promote widening of CEFTA as a way to ensure that the economic cooperation remained limited. Kolankiewicz (1994, 483) wrote that the Czechs were 'accordingly not averse to the expansion of the group to include Slovenia, which however has not yet signed association agreements with the EC. This highlights the "deepening" and "widening" alternatives for Visegrad, with the Czechs preferring the latter to dilute and if possible pre-empt the former'. Second, as a natural feature of its neoliberal open-door economic policies and desire to exploit its strong export position in the CEE region.

12. Some commentators have argued that the Europe Agreement condition was included so as to ensure that CEFTA members do not liberalise trade with countries who are not at the same stage as themselves in EU relations. This view has a logic but it is only really since the opening of accession talks that the CEFTA countries have begun applying this principle. It is the case that the CEFTA countries' trade arrangements with other post-socialist countries are generally not harmonised and have tended to develop at different speeds and in different directions. If the Europe Agreement condition was originally intended primarily to avoid future problems of having to reverse trade arrangements with non-Europe Agreement countries upon EU accession then this would surely have reflected a strictly enforced component of national policies. Yet Slovenia signed free trade agreements with Croatia (December 1997) and FYR Macedonia (July 1996) which are not only without Europe Agreements but also still outside the WTO. Also, a free trade agreement with Ukraine has been on the agenda of all the CEFTA states for some time now. Indeed, following the 1997 (Portoroz) summit it was reported that Ukraine was poised to sign free trade agreements with all the CEFTA states. The then Ukrainian Minister of Foreign Trade and Economic Ties Sergei Osynka said that (RFE/RL Newsline, 15/9/97) 'the Polish and Slovak prime ministers want to complete talks with Ukraine on such agreements later this year. The Slovenian prime minister expressed the wish to sign bilateral accords with Kiev by the end of this year or by early 1998'. See Chapter 6 for further discussion of bilateral trade accords between CEFTA members and non-associated CEE.

13. Since a greater proportion of trade in industrial products and most of agricultural trade were subject to bilateral arrangements it made good sense to have the bilateral agreements in place prior to CEFTA accession. When Romania joined in 1997, by contrast, most industrial goods were tariff-free and the multilateral component of agricultural concessions was greater.

14. Poland's success in achieving some exemptions from the provisions of Additional Protocol 3 in the concessions applying to its food and agricultural imports from Bulgaria meant that the CEFTA countries were not 100 per cent successful in this respect.

15. Existing free trade agreements are cancelled and replaced by the provisions of the protocols which are included (and which are the 'meat' of) in the accession treaties.

16. Moldova expressed interest in CEFTA during bilateral meetings with Hungarian officials in 1999 but it is important to note that it has not yet lodged an official application to join CEFTA.

17. In 1998, for example, of the CEFTA countries only Poland figured in the top fifteen export markets of Latvia (14th position) and Lithuania (9th) respectively. See Wyzan (1998, 55).

18. Comments of Nenad Porges, Croatian Minister of Economy, in an interview given to *Banka International*, July 1997 (on-line version, via http//:alf.tel.hr/banka-mzb/97-07/1lets.html).

19. Looking at the dynamics of CEFTA enlargement from the point of view of integration theory and drawing some comparisons with past EC/EU enlargements, two possible processes can be identified. First the 'EFTAn' model (Baldwin, 1994), according to which business lobbies in 'outsider countries' push their governments to pursue ever closer relations with the core integration area as they feel the effects of intensifying discrimination in the core area markets in which they were once well established. In Western Europe, this situation gave rise first to the 1973 enlargement of the then EC as well as the (rump) EFTA–EC free trade agreement in the 1970s, as responses to the EC's customs union, then the European Economic Area as a response to the Single European Act of 1986 and culminated in EU membership for most 'EFTAn' states by 1995. Alternatively the 'Club-Med' model, under which Portugal, Greece and Spain pursued membership for strong political reasons along with an expectation, though not proved either way prior to joining, that the net economic effect will be positive. The 'EFTAn' model does not really fit due to the small share of exports to CEFTA as a proportion of total exports of the aspirant countries and the likelihood that the pro-protection lobbies fearing competition from outside producers are usually more active. The Club-Med model, however, corresponds neatly with the pronounced club-joining tendencies of post-communist states.

20. Balazs (1997, 362–3) divides the CEE countries into three categories. First, the *avant-garde* (Czech Republic, Hungary, Poland, Slovenia), second, the *follow-up* countries (other CEE countries with Europe Agreements) and third, the *non-associated countries* (CIS and other ex-Yugoslav states). From the outside CEFTA can be seen as an entity which can include countries from each of these categories. From the point of view of the *follow-up* and *non-associated* CEE countries, acceding to CEFTA is a chance to graduate to the *avant-garde*.

21. SECI was a post-Dayton initiative launched by the USA in 1996 with a view to support stability in South Eastern Europe, particularly through emphasising links between the relatively stable countries of central Europe (such as Hungary, Romania) and the more unstable ones in the former Yugoslavia. Apart from the obvious factor of the renewed outbreak of conflict in Kosovo, SECI has in case remained somewhat embryonic, suffering from lack of finance and widespread reluctance to join in the initiative. See Dunay (1998).

22. Described as 'a peculiar fear of loneliness in the time of transformations'.

23. In fact Ukraine's interest in joining CEFTA was reported at the time of CEFTA's founding, though at that time 'none of the Visegrad troika countries have shown an interest in concluding an agreement with a CIS country after experiences with trade links with the former Soviet Union' (*Prague Business Week*, 5 March 1993).

24. It should be pointed out that elements of this were evident at least in the very early phase of CEFTA. According to EBRD economists (EBRD, 1994, 118) the Visegrad countries even went so far as to actively resist multilateral cumulation of local content with Bulgaria and Romania so as to support the Westward orientation of their trade.

25. When asked, during an interview with the author in Sofia in December 1997, about when Bulgaria's application for CEFTA membership was seriously activated, officials at the

Bulgarian Ministry of Trade and Tourism stated that it was during the bilateral trade liberalisation negotiations with Czech and Slovak officials.

26. It should be mentioned that some CEFTA members (Poland, for example) had reservations about the agricultural competition from Bulgarian and Romanian producers.

27. As an indication of how this potential looked at the time of Madej's analysis, a summit between the Polish and Ukrainian leaders which took place in Warsaw in January 1997 (*New Europe*, 2–8 February 1997, 9) noted that Poland's trade with Ukraine grew by 39 per cent in 1996 with 'the balance of trade firmly in Poland's favour' while Poland 'also has investments in some 400 firms there and Kuchma said a planned tax reform would encourage further investment by Poland's fast-growing economy'. In the case of the Czech Republic, exports to the CIS were up 19.1 per cent in the first 9 months of 1996, with particularly high growth in exports of consumer goods (33 per cent) while machinery exports were little changed (*Czech Trade*, January 1997, 75–6). Looking at overall values of Czech–Ukraine trade, Czech exports grew by 37.9 per cent in 1995 and by 3.15 per cent in 1996, while Czech imports grew by 30.15 per cent and declined 15.5 per cent respectively (*Monthly Statistics of the Czech Republic*, 3–96 and *Statistical Information–External Trade* January–December 1996).

28. The Slovak enthusiasm for CEFTA institutions fits in well with the idea of Slovakia's desire to raise the profile of CEFTA, especially as the Slovaks were also very actively promoting enlargement of CEFTA. It is worth remembering however, that the Czech–Slovak customs union already had a set of institutions, including a permanent secretariat located in Bratislava. Thus a different influence on Slovakia could be inferred. The Slovak position also had a practical dimension as Slovak officials had the task of organising the various CEFTA meetings in 1996 (the year of the Slovak presidency of CEFTA) and were convinced that it would be a better use of expert resources if the mundane and the time-consuming duties of that role were carried out by a small team of permanent staff. Also, maybe the Czechs' approach was somewhat selective as they would probably have approved the establishment of an arbitration committee in CEFTA.

29. The first meeting took place in Bratislava on 14 May 1999. 'Visegrad 2' is discussed further in Chapter 6.

6. European Union Enlargement and the Future of CEFTA

INTRODUCTION

For CEFTA, 1997 was a landmark year. 1 January 1997 marked the point at which the core objective of establishing a tariff-free area for trading industrial goods was more or less achieved, at least for the original members, and the year ended with the European Council's formal confirmation that four of the then six CEFTA members would open formal EU accession negotiations during 1998. Though the AGENDA 2000 proposals naturally commanded most of the attention, some scholars were also reflecting on the significance of this juncture for CEFTA. Slovenian specialists Lavrac and Rojec (1997, 47), for example, observed that

> CEFTA as a form of regional integration has come to the point where it will have to redefine its identity and reconsider its future strategy. CEFTA faces challenges of deepening and widening to which appropriate solutions will have to be found ... CEFTA may opt for a process of deepening modelled on EU-type integration or it will remain a free-trade area of a transitional character like EFTA, with member countries clearly defining their accession to EU as their primary goal.

Raising the question of the longer-term trajectory of CEFTA, Grela (1997, 142) asked the following:

> Membership of the European Union will mean the renouncing of all economic agreements, that is withdrawal from CEFTA. Can it be assumed that CEFTA's role will be merely that of an instrument of transition, or will the present cooperation have some continuity and influence on the countries of the region in the following decades?

Since its primary function is to support the member countries' approach to full EU membership, it follows that CEFTA should have a naturally transient existence. Yet precisely because CEFTA is in so many ways a by-product of CEE–EU integration, the uncertainties and many dilemmas surrounding the current EU enlargement strategy mean that the fate of CEFTA is not necessarily so clear-cut. The first question to ask is for how long CEFTA can be expected to remain in existence? The prime influences on this are without doubt the time scale and parameters of the EU enlargement process, the first phase of which will force a reconfiguration of CEFTA. The newly acceded EU states will have to withdraw from CEFTA and their trade relations with the remaining CEFTA will come under the umbrella of the respective Europe Agreements.[1] What is not known, however, is how long it will take to conclude the EU accession process. Before and around the release of AGENDA 2000, the most optimistic scenario forecast that a leading cluster of CEE would enter the EU by 2000/1. It was, however, always pretty clear that the basis of this was more to do with the rash promises of the leaders of certain EU member states rather than a realistic assessment of the complexity and scale of the enlargement project. Though the AGENDA 2000 proposals contained no explicit target date, even for the 'ins', the details of the proposals inferred a five-year process. Yet these days, as Gower (1999, 15–16) wrote, 'the earliest possible date for the first wave enlargement to take place is 2002/3. However, this is recognised as optimistic as it depends on the ratification of the treaties of accession by the applicant states, all 15 EU member states and the European Parliament'. Representing the least optimistic response to AGENDA 2000, some critics have even warned that the EU's 'business as usual' eastward enlargement strategy is 'too narrow and mechanistic ... (n)either the potential new members, nor the present members, are set on a safe course to manage enlargement and the wider European integration that it implies' (Eatwell et al., 1997, 1–2). According to this perspective the internal reforms and compromises required by enlargement are simply not politically feasible for the EU and, moreover, the rapid and uncompromising adoption of the EU's '*acquis communautaire*' will impose social and economic costs which will turn domestic opinion against EU membership in the applicant countries.

Thus the views on the EU membership prospects of the *first batch* of CEE candidates range from a prediction that the whole process is in serious risk of being derailed unless the EU strategy is radically redesigned, to the idea that enlargement is essentially manageable, but entry roundabout 2005 is the most reasonable target date.[2] The uncertainty surrounding the timing of the accession of the rearguard group is clearly much greater. Grabbe and Hughes (1997, 57) argue that the completion of the overall process of expanding the EU is likely to be very slow, with some of the applicants having to wait for 15 or even 20 years. There is not even complete confidence that all of the CEE10 will actually achieve their objective of acceding to the EU. According to Phinnemore (1999a, 79) 'it is arguably the case that the obstacles standing in the way of a second wave are considerably more daunting and potentially even insurmountable. Not only will the EU have to deal (again) with issues already raised in the context of a first wave of enlargement, it will also have to contend with the impact of any new members on the EU'. In this scenario, it may well turn out that Romania and

Bulgaria, and indeed any other CEE country which loses ground, will remain in the limbo of permanent associate status with the EU (and '*de facto* satellisation' as a result). For countries in such a position, the absence of a cast-iron guarantee that full EU membership will automatically follow on from associate membership could draw attention to the costs of that status to the effect of undermining its viability (Phinnemore, 1999b, 129):

> Indeed, in the case of those states which are weakest economically and lagging behind in the transition process (e.g. Romania), there is the possibility that the criteria for EU membership may never be met. In such cases, association could become permanent. Whether such a relationship could be sustained given the shortcomings involved is open to question. Certainly, if the association is seen as having failed to provide the stepping-stone to membership envisaged, then enthusiasm for it will be limited. The commitment to economic and political reforms may falter too.[3]

The prevailing views on the time scale for EU enlargement all indicate that the existing CEFTA members will remain part of it for at least a further four to six years, and the rump CEFTA will be around for some time after. Thus, the impact of EU enlargement on the future development of CEFTA seems to centre on two main questions. First, what are the prospects, if any, for any further intensification of cooperation in CEFTA in the context of the current stage of the EU accession process and the staggered entry of the CEFTA countries? Is the potential for integration in the CEFTA framework in fact already more or less exhausted? Do the existing CEFTA have both the political will and resources to further develop CEFTA and/or to what extent will energy and resources be diverted to other vehicles for subregional cooperation which come to the fore in order to deal with accession-specific issues? Second, what kind of future roles, if any, does the EU enlargement process imply for CEFTA and what influences will determine the most likely outcome? Alternative scenarios which will be discussed include the 'wither away' route, the hypothesis (borne of alleged deficiencies of the current EU enlargement approach) that CEFTA might evolve into a lifeline to connect the more peripheral CEE states (*outs*) to the European integration process and a more extreme (if, say, Phinnemore's suggestion that association with the EU may not be sustainable were to prove accurate) notion that CEFTA could even develop beyond a bridge to the EU and become some kind of alternative integration project.

6.1 PROSPECTS FOR FURTHER DEVELOPMENT OF CEFTA COOPERATION

6.1.1 Policy Statements

Looking first at the development of official attitudes towards subregional cooperation in CEFTA in the post-AGENDA 2000 period, despite the reasonable expectation that the EU fast-track CEFTA members at least would lose some interest in further development of CEFTA the early policy statements of the leading officials of the CEFTA countries did not suggest that this was the case. At the September 1997 (Portoroz) CEFTA summit, which came just two months after the publication of the EC Commission's enlargement proposals, the overall sentiment was that further development of CEFTA was very much on the agenda. In his opening address Slovenian Premier Janez Drnovsek spoke of the 'importance of mutual economic cooperation' and vowed that the CEFTA countries were 'ready to move forward, wishing to further promote the free trade and widen the areas of economic and commercial cooperation'.[4] Vaclav Klaus told a Portoroz news conference that: '(w)e all clearly said that CEFTA is a very positive grouping. We all said clearly that we wanted to deepen CEFTA' (BBC, EE/3024 C/2, 15/9/97), while Gyula Horn (BBC, EE/3025 C/2, 16/9/97) remarked that there had not been 'sufficient progress in freeing the flow of capital and in the further liberalisation of services. Also, despite frequent proposals, there have been few results in making joint efforts to tackle organised crime over the past year'. A little later in the year, the Polish Prime Minister Jerzy Buzek, in his first policy address to the Polish parliament, said that '(a)fter five years in existence, the Central European Free Trade Agreement, CEFTA, has turned out to be a success in the political and economic sphere. We are thinking about deepening and widening it' (BBC, EE/3075 C/13, 13/11/97). In fact, the main way in which the AGENDA 2000 proposals directly impinged on the Portoroz summit was the row that ensued as a result of Hungary's insistence that a clause committing the CEFTA members to support each other's application for EU membership be excluded from the joint declaration.

The 'deepening' rhetoric so characteristic of the 1995–97 period was, however, conspicuous by its absence in the cases of the 1998 and 1999 CEFTA summits. As has already been discussed in Chapter 5, approaches to the development of CEFTA cooperation have gradually moved in a more pragmatic direction connected to fine-tuning the operation of the free trade provisions and exploiting the full potential of the existing CEFTA articles. In the context of the influence of engagement in the EU accession negotiations proper, and the implementation of the Accession Partnerships, the following factors probably played a part in the shifting attitudes towards CEFTA away from an emphasis on 'deepening' in the sense of qualitative leaps forward to the more pragmatic 'integration-enhancing' approach. First, the line-up of politicians attending the CEFTA summit and Joint Committee meeting in 1998 changed considerably, breaking the continuity and sense of community established at previous meetings. While attention to CEFTA cooperation had not been high on the electoral campaign/political agenda of this new set of leaders, getting to grips with the new phase in EU relations would have been occupying them considerably.[5] Second, this group met during the high point of the most serious – in fact the first *really* serious – trade dispute since the start of CEFTA. This context focused attention on some important tasks connected to deficiencies in the functioning of CEFTA highlighted by the agricultural trade difficulties. Third, the problems of accelerating the liberalisation of capital movements and trade in services at the intra-CEFTA level were reported to the Joint Committee by the relevant working parties. This led to a logical postponement of those more ambitious (to be resolved in any case in the WTO, EU and OECD frameworks) objectives in favour of focusing on solutions to existing trade problems as well as the important, more feasible CEFTA articles yet to be activated. Fourth, the 1998 Joint Committee and summit meetings were informed by the CEFTA countries' own jointly prepared analysis of the outcomes and functioning of CEFTA – entitled *Results and Experiences of the First Five Years of CEFTA* – which recommended that priority should be given to improving cooperation within the already existing parameters (see Appendix Three).

6.1.2   The 'Deepening' Agenda

The agenda for intensification of CEFTA cooperation during the next few years is basically as per the resolutions of the 1999 CEFTA summit which endorsed the following recommendations concerning the development of CEFTA cooperation during the next few years (*Declaration of the Prime Ministers of the CEFTA Countries,* 1999, 3):

> the examination of the possibilities and conditions of the elimination or further reduction of the existing barriers to trade; continuing the cooperation in the development and improvement of CEFTA functioning; the intensification of bilateral negotiations concerning mutual recognition of certificates and/or test results [for industrial and agricultural products]; supporting the joint organisation of conferences on capital investment in the CEFTA countries as well as other trade promoting events; supporting the cooperation of the CEFTA countries in the fight against organised crime and the establishment of a Subcommittee for this purpose.

In addition, it will be necessary to persist with attempting to find ways to tackle the problems of agricultural trade, an issue which will no doubt continue to feature in forthcoming CEFTA Joint Committee and summit discussions and for which a CEFTA Subcommittee was (as noted in Chapter 3) convened in summer 1999.[6] The extent to which any serious harmonisation of agricultural policies will be achieved remains to be seen, but some take the view that whatever the results the exercise is extremely valuable in itself. It was reported in the *Prague Post* that the 'members of the Central European Free Trade Agreement (CEFTA) are struggling to formulate common policies on agricultural trade and the effort is a good "training exercise" for looming European Union membership, according to Czech Agriculture Minister Jan Fencl' (Moran, 1998).

Irrespective of whether there is significant progress with the above, integration-deepening should continue on two other fronts. First, further market integration as a consequence of growth of mutual trade.[7] Central Europe is, with one or two exceptions at present, a fast-growing component of the European economy (see Table 6.1). Furthermore, the recent accession of Bulgaria and Romania means that gains from liberalisation of trade with those new members are still materialising.[8] It can also be expected that ongoing reforms and restructuring together with continuing (and maybe accelerating) FDI inflows will continue to fuel mutual market penetration through improvements in the quality and range of goods available for export and their marketing. The benefits of the recently-established pan-European cumulation zone, which will further encourage FDI, should also be coming on stream. Second, deepening integration of the CEFTA countries will continue to proceed as a by-product of the current stage of the EU pre-accession/accession process.

Table 6.1   Real GDP change of CEFTA members

	1997	1998	1999*	2000**
Bulgaria	− 7.0	3.5	1.0	3.0
Czech R.	1.0	− 2.7	− 0.5	1.4
Hungary	4.6	5.1	3.8	3.5
Poland	6.8	4.8	3.5	5.2
Romania	− 6.9	− 7.3	− 4.5	1.0
Slovakia	6.5	4.4	2.0	2.0
Slovenia	4.6	3.9	3.5	3.5

Notes:
* Projection.
** Forecast.

Source: Business Central Europe, The Annual 2000, 56.

The CEFTA states (along with the Baltic states) are all still engaged in the process of adopting the rules and regulations of the EU's single market, a process which began in a limited way with the Europe Agreements and accelerated following the EU's 1995 White Paper and subsequent incorporation into the 'Accession Partnerships' established as part of the AGENDA 2000 programme. Thus the

EU pre-accession strategy automatically forms part of an intra-CEFTA integration-deepening and gives it an imperative by extending regulatory alignment to the subregion. Inotai (1997a, 133) has referred to this process as 'unconscious subregional harmonisation' in which '(e)very country is adjusting in its own way, but in the final outcome we will have, in case of successful adjustment of course, practically the same economic policy framework'. Even the lagging CEE10 candidates are involved in this process, meaning that the division of CEFTA countries into 'ins' and 'pre-ins' was less restrictive for development of CEFTA states' economic integration than might appear. In the light of this, earlier arguments that this differentiation was a reason why CEFTA should not have expanded to Romania and Bulgaria (see, for example, Dunay, 1997, 24) needed to take more account of the distinction between CEFTA enlargement to CEE10 and non-CEE10.

6.1.3   Political Cooperation

The traditional tendency of the CEE countries to resist any direct coordination of their approaches to the EU (see Chapter 4) has been labelled as somewhat short-sighted by certain scholars (for example, Richter 1997; Skjalm 1999) mainly because of the idea that lack of coordination of bargaining positions will enable the EU to fully exploit the fact that 'accession negotiations in the EU are an extraordinary asymmetrical exercise compared with other international negotiations. Typically, the EU has an unusually strong structural power position due to economic and political institutional factors' (Skjalm, 1999, 38). Despite the well-documented long-standing disinclination of the CEE to seriously coordinate their approaches to the EU, it has always been reasonable to assume that as the accession negotiations proceed into hard bargaining on the various dimensions of the *acquis*, the pressure for further political cooperation between the CEE will intensify. In addition, accession-specific matters have already been forcing the subregional cooperation agenda, including for example policy towards the eastern borders of the CEE candidates and the subregional implications of different EU entry timetables (particularly concerning Slovakia). In the light of this, what can be said about the prospect that this new environment for political cooperation among EU candidates will result in CEFTA cooperation 'deepening' in the political sphere so as to become a direct as well as indirect tool for the EU pre-accession process?

Both the 1998 and 1999 CEFTA summit[25] made identical declarations as follows: 'future CEFTA activities should take into account the objective of all CEFTA countries to become members of the European Union. They [the CEFTA Prime Ministers] agreed that it would be useful to exchange information and experience gained on the process of accession to the European Union' (*Declaration of the Prime Ministers of the CEFTA Countries*, 1999, 4). These statements were, however, essentially referring to the need to keep CEFTA developments (for example, concerning relations with third parties, intra-CEFTA agricultural trade policies) tailored to the EU accession requirements and do not alter the conclusion that CEFTA is not going to upgrade its role to a formal device for coordination of the EU accession negotiations. Apart from the decisive lack of political willingness, a key reason CEFTA cannot fulfil this function is the absence of a sufficiently common agenda due to differences within CEFTA in terms of the stage of relations with the EU. This situation will only be further exacerbated by the introduction of the 'regatta approach' expected to be confirmed by the 1999 EU Helsinki summit.

The other main factor which limits the potential for CEFTA to develop a more formal political role in the EU accession is the fact that the emerging EU-related subregional cooperation agenda is being served by more suitable vehicles. While this new subregional cooperation agenda was the background to a Czech proposal, tabled at the 1998 Prague summit, that CEFTA be given 'a political dimension along the lines of the Visegrad accords' (RFE/RL Newsline, 177, 2, 14/9/98) the main result of this was to pave the way for the reconvening of the Visegrad group.[9] The agenda of 'Visegrad 2', as set out during the May 1999 inaugural session, includes 'EU and NATO integration in the region, joint economic policies, cross-border transport and telecommunications projects, efforts to reduce organised crime and illegal migration' (RFE/RL Newsline, 14/5/99). As for the broader issue of CEE cooperation during accession negotiations, such as it is so far, the heads of the negotiating teams of the five (in pre-Helsinki terminology) 'ins' and Cyprus have been meeting regularly since 1997. Up until early 1999, the role of this coordination forum had been restricted to harmonising the timetable for submitting to the EU position papers on various chapters of the *acquis*. Zoltan Becsey, a senior member of the Hungarian team, explained in an interview with Radio Free Europe/Radio Liberty that though the cooperation is 'amicable' (RFE/RL Newsline, 13/1/99) it is to do with 'mainly the procedure, not the content, so we do not discuss the content of our position papers to the EU. After the presentation of our position papers to the EU, of course, we inform the other candidates about our views, but there is no concrete obligation for consultation among us on the content of our positions'.[10]

Finally, the idea that CEFTA might eventually become a more explicit political unit in the form of a Central European circle (the Nordic Council and other such groupings legitimately existing within the larger structures are cited as possible precedents), once its members have joined the EU and CEFTA's economic integration function has been absorbed by the enlarged EU, is not convincing for largely the same reasons which prevent the development of more political cooperation in CEFTA during the approach to EU accession – that is, more appropriate and more cognate subregional groupings (for this obviously the Visegrad group plus perhaps Slovenia) are available. On balance, it seems that

CEFTA's main contribution in the political sense will be as an indirect instrument to support EU accession and the continuing development of interdependence and the less overt 'subtle' security effects already discussed in Chapter 4.

6.2   THE ENLARGEMENT AGENDA

The enlargement agenda for CEFTA is particularly significant because it will determine whether CEFTA can continue as an important element of the European landscape beyond the first stage of the EU's eastward enlargement. For this, CEFTA will have to reconfigure, which means absorbing countries which are currently outside of the CEE10 group. Regarding interest in joining CEFTA from non-CEE10 states, as noted in Chapter 5, the 'accession queue' has featured Ukraine, Croatia, FYR Macedonia and, most recently, Moldova. The obstacles to any further enlargement of CEFTA to this group are, however, such that none of them would be likely to enter CEFTA before the first wave of EU enlargement takes place and the realisation of this has also meant that the interest of the more established non-CEE10 candidates at least can no longer be taken for granted.[11]

Before discussing the specific problems of extending CEFTA to the non-CEE10, it should be mentioned that Lithuania and Latvia have long been earmarked as future CEFTA members. Had their WTO membership been achieved earlier they would most likely have entered CEFTA before Bulgaria and maybe even ahead of Romania. Though that matter is now settled, the two Baltic candidates certainly have had the option of following Bulgaria as the next states to accede to CEFTA.[12] However, by 1999 it appeared that their interest had waned, albeit on the basis that CEFTA membership had become regarded as something which was no longer really necessary rather than unattainable in a meaningful time-scale, which may turn out to be the case for the non-CEE10. Though Latvia has already acceded to the WTO, ahead of Lithuania, so far there has been no attempt to activate CEFTA membership and there was no request from Lithuania for an invitation to the 1999 CEFTA summit.[13] Though the BFTA enabled Lithuania and Latvia, as well as Estonia, to satisfy the EU's subregional cooperation conditionality, and bilateral free trade arrangements have been a means of unifying the CEFTA and BFTA free trade areas, CEFTA membership had been on their policy agenda as a means of emphasising their Central European, rather than post-Soviet, identity and enhance their credentials as EU candidates. As it has become increasingly clear that Latvia and Lithuania's progress towards EU membership is dependent on their own progress and determination, and as they have become increasingly optimistic (during 1999 especially) of being invited to open their full EU accession negotiations sooner rather than later, CEFTA membership has ceased to have any real value added for the Baltic countries.

The easing of the CEFTA accession queue created by the apparent withdrawal of Latvia and Lithuania has had little if any impact on the prospects of the remaining CEFTA candidates because, with the possible exception of Croatia, the main problem is to do with the CEFTA membership criteria. None of the four non-CEE10 CEFTA aspirants are yet WTO members, though they are all engaged in the (invariably lengthy) accession process. No estimates of the times-cale for this process are available, though in its own 1998 assessment of the state of play of individual accession endeavours the WTO (1998) described the negotiations as 'advanced' only in the case of Croatia. Ukraine and Moldova were 'actively engaged' in negotiations while those with FYR Macedonia had yet to begin.

As for the question of when the EU will extend associate status and free trade agreements beyond the CEE10, the only sensible approach is to avoid any predictions. Prior to the Kosovo crisis, the official line was that the EU would be forthcoming with EAs upon evidence of the requisite progress in economic and political transformation. The most commonly used assessments of the reform status of individual countries (the EBRD *Transition Report* and EU verdicts prepared in the framework of bilateral agreements, for example) continue to show that Ukraine, FYR Macedonia and Moldova are clear laggards and can expect a long period of continuing to prepare for association, while the Croatian situation was more fluid with politics explaining the contradiction between its relatively advanced economic condition and retarded place in the European integration process. There was also suspicion that the EU's official approach, pre-Kosovo, was that it would prove more expedient for the EU to deal with the enlargement to the current CEE applicants (or at least the five 'ins') before creating a new group of associated countries. These days it is clear that the Kosovo crisis (and maybe the installation of a new team of EC Commissioners) has imparted a new dynamic and sense of urgency to the EU enlargement process. While this seems to have resulted in a reconfiguration of the formal status of the current batch of CEE candidates, the strategy for the arguably more critical situation of the 'outs' was not clear at the time of writing. The rather vague 'Balkan Stability Pact' details released so far do not suggest that traditional association agreements will be included. Apart from the recognition that a more direct and practical programme of aid and assistance is needed, the view prevails that the structural economic weakness and slower reform progress in countries like FYR Macedonia and Albania would have made reciprocal free trade with the EU premature even before the Kosovo war further deepened the economic difficulties of the region.[14] The main question seems to be what kind of financial resources are going to be forthcoming and whether the EU may grant duty-free access to exports of non-associated Stability Pact countries which would, of course, be relevant for CEFTA accession prospects. As far as Ukraine is concerned, though a 'new strategy' for the Ukraine was also among the EC

Commission's proposals going forward to the December 1999 Helsinki summit, up to that point there had been no indication that the provision in the EU–Ukraine Partnership and Cooperation Agreement to instigate 'at some point in the future' discussions about a possible free trade area between the two parties was going to be activated.

The prospects of the CEFTA aspirants have also become further dimmed by negative signals from within CEFTA itself. As far as the need for unanimous approval for enlargement is concerned, though Bulgaria and Slovakia at least seemed to remain more open and flexible towards CEFTA expansion, in sharp contrast with previous occasions the message from the 1998 (Prague) summit was that 'widening' had become subject to a more pragmatic approach.[15] As noted in Chapter 5, no guest countries were invited to the Prague CEFTA summit and when questioned about whether the candidacy of Ukraine and Macedonia had been discussed, Czech spokesman Frantisek Peer confirmed that 'the entry of these countries was not discussed. At present Macedonia and the Ukraine are not members of the World Trade Organisation and do not have a preferential agreement with the EU' (*Central European Business Weekly*, 18–24/9/98, 3).[16] The Declarations of the Prague and Budapest summits stated simply that 'CEFTA remains open for enlargement subject to fulfilment by the candidate countries of the conditions previously agreed'(*Declaration of the Prime Ministers of the CEFTA Countries*, 1998, 1999).

As with the diminishing ambitions for CEFTA- 'deepening' (or at least more realistic assessment of the prospects for it), the combination of new personalities and qualitative changes in position to the EU relations combined with a number of practical considerations acted to halt the CEFTA enlargement momentum and bring expectations into line with objective conditions. The need for the CEFTA countries to concentrate their energies and limited resources on tackling intra-CEFTA issues has been one important factor, and it must also be mentioned that the lengthy and complicated processes which surrounded the accession of Romania and, in particular, Bulgaria gave rise to what could be called enlargement 'fatigue', at least on the part of those who are working at the operational level of CEFTA. The teams of government officials responsible for CEFTA are often small and carry a substantial workload. It is the case that each CEFTA enlargement becomes increasingly intricate because of the growing number of parties to be satisfied. As CEFTA moved in the direction of countries where the reform process is less advanced, as was the case with Bulgaria and Romania of course, these problems became increasingly relevant. Exhausted by the Bulgarian accession process the CEFTA expert teams certainly had no wish to repeat the process with even more problematic countries and it is therefore no surprise that they supported the view that it is necessary to focus resources on the many internal issues facing CEFTA cooperation.[17] Moreover, the need to cope with the evident shortage of qualified and experienced personnel to deal with the EU accession procedures could place a further strain on human resources available to devote to CEFTA issues.

The problems of formal CEFTA expansion may, however, be offset by further developments in bilateral economic relations as long as these avenues for cooperation remain open. As noted in Chapter 5, up to now, the real significance of full CEFTA membership has perhaps been overstated because some non-CEE10 countries have been able to engage in some opening with the CEFTA market on the basis of bilateral free trade agreements with the individual CEFTA members. Slovenia has been implementing free trade agreements with FYR Macedonia and Croatia since 1 September 1996 and 1 January 1998 respectively. It may even be argued that bilateral arrangements are more appropriate than full CEFTA membership because the latter involves the need for a condensed transition period in order to align with the CEFTA schedule. In this way, relatively economically weaker/less reformed countries (as most of the non-CEFTA CEE tend to be) could avoid the potential shocks which may arise from a rapid rather than gradual liberalisation of trade with CEFTA countries.[18]

Yet the increasingly cautious approach to CEFTA enlargement has come about because the EU accession process is compromising the further development of bilateral relations too, due to the need for the CEE10 to ensure that trade arrangements with third parties stay in line with those of the EU. In April 1998 the Croatian Minister of Economic Affairs Nenad Porges (Kiseljak and Ivankovic, 1998, 1) said that it had become

> clear that there will be plenty of difficulties in negotiations with CEFTA countries which have practically one foot in the European Union already. There is some hesitation on the part of the Czech Republic and the latest CEFTA newcomer, Romania. They put the beginning of free trade negotiations into a package regulating our relations with the European Union.

Also, during the (November) 1998 CEI summit Victor Urban explained that while Hungary wanted to establish free trade with both Croatia and Ukraine, integration with the EU meant that 'if Hungary concludes free trade agreements with countries that do not have even association accords with the EU, it may cause some problems concerning our EU integration. Also, such agreements will have to be revised after our EU accession'(*New Europe*, 29/11–6/12/98, 15).[19]

At the same time it should be mentioned that since the Kosovo crisis some CEE10 have already been showing some discretion in this policy sphere especially where particularly important bilateral relations are concerned. In October 1999 Bulgaria signed a free trade agreement with neighbour and strategic trade partner FYR Macedonia, which was expected to enter into force on January 2000 and which targets duty-free trade in industrial goods from 2005 onwards (*New Europe*, 11–17/10/99, 35). Also, in August 1999 Hungary and Croatia agreed the main provisions of a free trade agreement 'similar to that of the free trade agreement between Hungary and the EU' (*New Europe*, 26/7-1/8/99, 15) which was planned to enter into application on 1 January 2000.[20] In this case the background was the Hungarian concern to develop closer relations with Croatia in connection with the security of ethnic Hungarians in Northern Yugoslavia. Discussing the agreement with Croatia, a spokesman for the Hungarian Ministry of Economic Affairs stated that 'Hungary does not intend to sign further free trade agreements with other countries since it has to cancel all of its bilateral free trade agreements when Hungary joins the EU' (*New Europe*, 26/7–1/8/99, 15).

In sum, not only is formal enlargement of CEFTA subject to delays to the extent that the main reasons for further countries to join have largely evaporated, the EU accession process has also been hampering the arguably more important '*de facto*' participation in CEFTA. The possibility that the EU may grant duty-free access to industrial products to certain non-associated Balkan countries as part of the Stability Pact will be a positive move as far as those countries' prospects for bilateral trade agreements with the CEFTA countries are concerned, but problems will remain with respect to the countries to the east of CEFTA (Ukraine, Moldova). In these cases it should be remembered that as well as free trade arrangements with CEFTA members having to await the EU's discretion in this same respect, these countries also face serious disruption to existing areas of economic and cross-border cooperation which entail important costs for those countries in the CEFTA area too.[21]

6.3   LONGER-TERM SCENARIOS FOR CEFTA

As noted above the existing CEFTA members' integration can continue during the next few years, both directly within the specific confines of the CEFTA arrangements and indirectly through the preparations to join the EU. As far as the period after the first stage of the EU's eastward expansion is concerned, three potential scenarios can be considered. The first hypothesis is that CEFTA will simply wither away. The second hypothesis is that CEFTA may continue its role as a support for full EU membership but with an expanded line-up. The third hypothesis is for CEFTA to develop a more independent role as an alternative integration framework for CEE who face or opt for long-term exclusion from the EU.

The 'wither away' scenario assumes no further enlargement in the foreseeable future. Apart from the factors presently blocking further CEFTA enlargement, it may well be that some alternative subregional integration frameworks, perhaps based on the CEFTA model, will emerge. The need to develop subregional cooperation is a core element of the Stability Pact concept and in this connection,

George Soros, for example, has called for the Balkan states to come up with a 'plan of their own to win accession to the EU. The plan, Soros said, should include a common Balkans customs union – which he had been advocating since June – and a common market interacting with the EU' (*New Europe*, 20–26/9/99, 5). Also, in October 1999 Radio Free Europe/Radio Liberty reported that the Prime Ministers of the CIS countries (Belarus was not represented) met in Yalta in order to 'discuss the introduction of a CIS free-trade zone. The participants signed an agreement on reducing customs regulations and other deals oriented toward making the CIS a free-trade zone' (*RFE/RL Newsline*, 11/10/99).[22] Whatever patterns of subregional cooperation develop in the coming years, in the absence of any further enlargement once the first group of CEFTA have withdrawn to take up full EU membership, CEFTA will reduce to a smaller free trade complex linked, as far as trade arrangements are concerned, to the expanded EU through their Europe Agreements and to other CEE by various bilateral free trade agreements. The diminished CEFTA would then either 'wither away' or remain in a kind of limbo due to serious delays in the second wave of EU enlargement.

In 1998 former Czech Trade and Industry Minister Karel Kuhnl stated that 'after some of the CEFTA countries, including the Czech Republic, have joined the EU, CEFTA will remain a good starting point for its remaining countries in their efforts to enter the EU ... these countries can practise rules for trade liberalisation, for example' (CEBW, 26/6-2/7/98, 60). This role could be extended if further enlargement enables the reconfigured CEFTA to more or less continue as a bridge/stepping stone to the EU but with a more pan-European identity, a scenario which more or less corresponds with one of the hypotheses Grela (1997, 142) has advanced for the future of CEFTA in which it will 'remain, though in a changed line-up, an important regional free-trade zone and will have stronger links with both the (enlarged) European Union and the eastern part of the Continent'. This would probably be the most productive role CEFTA could play but as noted above the main doubts concern the assumptions that underpin this scenario: that the CEFTA candidates achieve the accession criteria in due course, that they lock into an extending and inclusive EU enlargement process and continue to view CEFTA as the most appropriate subregional integration rather than something which has rather lost its essence once the founder countries have departed it.

As with the above, scenario three assumes enlargement to the south and east but takes into account that the members of the reconfigured CEFTA, or a significant group of them, could either fail to become engaged in the EU accession process or, in line with the potential consequences of '*de facto* satellisation' as elaborated by Phinnemore (1999b), downgrade their relations with the EU. In these circumstances could CEFTA, having shifted its centre of gravity further towards Europe's eastern and southern periphery, develop into something beyond a component of the broader pan-European free trade complex, perhaps even as an alternative integration? Without even considering the complication of other subregional organisations, such as the Black Sea Economic Cooperation (BSEC), becoming more active, or the potential emergence of a Balkan subregional integration initiative, it is clear that chances of any subregional cooperation in CEE developing into a genuine alternative to integration in the EU are even less realistic than the countries concerned abandoning their EU ambitions. If we simply consider what the process of developing beyond a free trade area would mean, the extra layers of integration would involve emulating the EC/EU since the mid-1980s which represented, as Tsoukalis (1997, 2) has written, 'a major qualitative change: European integration is now largely about economic regulation, redistribution, and increasingly through the locking of exchange rates, macroeconomic policies'. Such developments would clearly be a long way down the line even for the existing CEFTA members, let alone the slower reforming, economically weaker states that could make up the reconfigured CEFTA.

It is also the case that the available evidence suggests that it is only viable to attempt to substitute subregional cooperation for engagement with a wider regional integration framework if certain conditions prevail which are as follows (Inotai, 1997b, 5–6). First the necessary 'material conditions' have to be present, that is the 'development anchor (modernisation anchor) should be located within the sub-region'. Second, the existence of 'an overwhelming external threat may force countries to cooperate' though in this case the cooperation will be second-best and will disentangle when the external pressure disappears. Third, the subregional cooperation may represent some kind of independent 'preparation for membership of the larger scheme' and will be viable as long as the cooperation entails adjustment to the rules of the larger integration. None of these would be relevant for a rump CEFTA looking to develop an alternative integration to the EU. Inotai also makes the important and connected argument that it is only in the context of full membership that subregional cooperation and integration can reach its full potential – that is the main gains at the subregional level will come after accession to the EU as important barriers to cooperation are removed and key financial resources to support infrastructure developments become available. On the prospects for what is presently intra-CEFTA and intra-BFTA trade, for example

(t)he case of Portugal and Spain (and indirectly, the earlier case of the Benelux countries) shows that EU membership gives a substantial boost to subregional trade flows ... Intra-regional trade can be expected to grow faster than trade with the present EU members, to a proportion of 12-15 percent of the total...Among the factors behind this will be higher growth rates, booming investment (domestic and foreign), deeper intra-industry specialisation, economic-policy coordination, enhanced security (also in psychological terms), financial transfers, and the establishment of a more efficient subregional infrastructure.

Inotai's assumptions concerning the range of benefits of EU membership may well be up for debate and the accessibility of the EU for the more peripheral east, south and south-east European states may not be a question of choice, but it seems difficult to argue that the countries concerned could independently achieve an effective and advanced form of integration.

NOTES

1. As things stand, of course, the main discrepancy between CEFTA and the trade chapters of the Europe Agreements concerns agricultural trade. It is a possibility, therefore, that the first wave of entrants may have to reverse market access for agricultural exports of the remaining CEFTA.

2. At the time of writing it was looking increasingly unlikely that the original first wave of CEE candidates were going to enter the EU together. Part of the problem is that the categories established in July 1997 are already becoming unravelled less than two years later. The run-in to the EU Helsinki summit even featured speculation that the Czechs could drop out of the fast-track group due to a second successive damning progress report while Slovakia, because of significant improvements in the political dimension of transition, could be promoted to it, which would have been a truly farcical scenario. The most likely outcome was that the two-tier system would be formally scrapped and the former 'pre-ins' would begin proper negotiations, opening up the prospect of the strongest and best prepared nations not being held back by lack of progress in other countries. In September 1999 the EU Commissioner for Enlargement Günther Verheugen said that it 'was uncertain whether admission will be implemented in groups. He added that there was also the possibility of individual admission when asked whether the Czech Republic would be in the first group of admitted countries' (*Central European Business Weekly*, 17–23/9/99, 6).

3. While the new sense of urgency attached to enlargement caused by the Kosovo crisis was behind the EC Commission's recommendation (released 13 October 1999) that the approaching Helsinki summit should formally end the two-tier system and invite all current candidates to come to the negotiating table this will not in itself accelerate particular EU entry dates. Günther Verheugen has already made it clear that he does not favour allowing the renewed political momentum for enlargement to force any relaxation of the EU accession conditions. Otherwise 'the union could pay a heavy price' (*New Europe*, 20–26/9/99, 6).

4. The source of this quote is the transcript of the opening address, supplied in my case by the Ministry of Economy and Development of Slovenia.

5. It should, however, be mentioned that in comparison with the Klaus team the new Czech government had a much more positive view as far as subregional cooperation in general was concerned.

6. The main task of the newly formed CEFTA Subcommittee on Agricultural Trade is to carry out a 'detailed analysis of the existing concessions, of all agricultural policy measures and mechanisms, related to trade among the CEFTA countries' (*Declaration of the Prime Ministers of the CEFTA Countries*, 1999, 3) in order to inform all decisions connected to attempts to develop and improve the agricultural trade system of CEFTA.

7. According to certain Hungarian economists there is 'no doubt about a huge growth potential in regional trade...subregional trade, which now accounts for 8 per cent in the total trade of Hungary, may be raised to 12 to 14 per cent without any difficulty' (Inotai, 1997a, 137).

8. Bulgarian Trade and Tourism Minister forecasts a 30 per cent increase in Bulgaria's trade with the CEFTA area in 1999 (BBC, EE/3284 B/1, 21/7/98). There is, however, as the experience of Romania in 1998 showed, that as CEFTA expands to economically weaker, less reformed and FDI-rich states, a danger that export growth will tend to be one-sided in favour of the original CEFTA members.

9. Not least by signalling the intentions of the Czech government in this respect. The removal from office of Vladimir Meciar (Meciar's reason for rejecting the 1998 Czech proposal on a formal political role for CEFTA was because it would be discussed during Hungary's presidency of CEFTA) and his government not long after the Prague summit enabled Slovakia to fill its 'empty chair' and the first meeting of 'Visegrad 2' took place in Bratislava in May 1999.

10. Signs of the emergence of a more coordinated approach to the substance of the negotiations became evident during October 1999 during a meeting of the Foreign Ministers of the 'five plus one'. The *Financial Times* (12/10/99, 9) reported that the meeting produced a collective letter to Romano Prodi requesting the acceleration of negotiations and that the meeting, held in Tallin, 'represents the fast-track applicants' efforts to pool resources to strengthen their bargaining position. In particular the six are hoping to seek concessions over farming subsidies, and raise concerns over traditional trade ties with other eastern countries'.

11. Official statements have continued to affirm that CEFTA membership is still an important goal for Ukraine. For example in May 1999 Olexander Danyleiko, Head of the Division of Bilateral and Regional Economic Cooperation Division of the Ukrainian Ministry of Foreign Affairs, stated that 'Ukraine, watching the formation of a new trade regime near its borders, realising the great potential of CEFTA, expedience of bilateral and multilateral cooperation between our countries does not want to be outside the orbit of European processes and declared its willingness to be a member of CEFTA' (Danyleiko, 1999, 95). Despite such statements, it appears that full CEFTA membership is no longer being stressed in Ukrainian debates and policy statements to the extent that it was a couple of years ago (I am grateful to Dr Oleksander Pavliuk of the Kiev Centre of the EastWest Institute for advising me on this matter) suggesting that the further development of bilateral relations with the individual CEFTA (and BFTA) states are recognised as being the main practical way forward. One can expect that Croatia and FYR Macedonia may be drawing the same conclusions about full CEFTA membership. In fact the signs were there much earlier anyway in Croatia's case. In 1997, some Croatian spokesmen were arguing that as far as CEFTA was concerned the boat had already been missed. Croatian Ambassador to the USA Miomir Zuzul took the view that since the 'CEFTA countries, and Zuzul specifically mentioned Hungary, the Czech Republic and Poland, are the first candidates for entry into the European Union, and when this has been achieved, something that is sure to happen very soon, CEFTA will in fact lose its meaning' (*Banka International*, 1997b).

12. Following the signing of Bulgaria's Accession Treaty in July 1998 Deputy Czech Minister for Industry and Trade Pavel Dvorjak, speaking for the CEFTA chair, said that 'the next applicant to be considered for CEFTA membership will be Lithuania' (*Warsaw Voice*, 26/7/98).

13. I was advised by the Hungarian Ministry of Economic Affairs that Lithuania would have been granted an invitation.

14. In April 1999 senior EU official Dirk Buda said that while he expected 'rapid forward movement on some form of association for Macedonia ... he cautioned that this agreement might fall short of the association agreement, known as Europe Agreement, currently enjoyed by countries like Bulgaria and Romania ... current thinking in the EU Executive Commission is that it would be better to create a type of technical association for newcomers, without the perspective of accession as new members' (*RFE/RL Newsline*, 23/4/99).

15. As would have been expected, when questioned about the future of CEFTA at the Prague summit Vladimir Meciar stressed the importance of further enlargement of the organisation and reaffirmed Slovakia's readiness to offer concrete support to candidate states such as Ukraine and Croatia (BBC, EE/3331 C/3, 14/9/98). Similar sentiments were indicated by a statement made on the occasion of the Bulgarian parliament's ratification of its CEFTA accession treaty by Trade and Tourism Minister Valentin Vasilev who said that the 'aim of the government now is to sign identical agreements with other European countries next year' (BBC, EE/3329 B/2, 11/9/98).

16. The more encouraging attitude to the non-associated CEFTA aspirants was still very much in evidence at the Portoroz summit. Five guest countries attended and the Slovenian premier welcomed them as 'other states in the area which want to take a share in the results of our

mutual cooperation'. Vaclav Klaus stated that '(o)f course CEFTA has a future regardless of whether some countries get or do not get into the European Union' (BBC, EE/3024 C/2, 15/9/97) and confirmed that all the CEFTA members had said they wanted to 'widen it to include other countries'. For new CEFTA entrant Romania, Victor Ciorbea said that his government 'favoured CEFTA's enlargement by admitting new members such as Bulgaria, Lithuania, Latvia, Macedonia, Ukraine' (BBC, EE/3024 B/3, 15/9/97). Concrete action towards the widening of CEFTA was also in evidence, mainly in the form of the resolution, duly implemented, to commence the accession negotiations with Bulgaria. There was also a reported attempt by the Czech side to get approval for a proposal which 'would have eased the system of conditions linked to membership in CEFTA' (BBC, EE/3024 C/9, 15/9/97). If this proposal had concerned either the WTO or Europe Agreement conditions (no details were given, but it is possible that the proposal was to waive the need to have signed bilateral free trade agreements with all the incumbent CEFTA members in advance of accession, given that they would be cancelled in favour of the relevant protocols contained in the accession treaties – the context for this was the delay facing Bulgaria) this would help explain some subsequent confusion. Shortly after the Portoroz summit it was reported that during the meeting: 'Ukrainian Prime Minister Valery Pustovoitenko has agreed with CEFTA on a plan for Ukraine's entry into the organisation ... the scheme envisages concluding bilateral free-trade agreements with CEFTA members' (*RFE/RL*, 15/9/97). Later in the year it was also heralded that 'the (Croatian) government formalised a deal with Central European Free trade Agreement (CEFTA) members to gain full membership' (*New Europe*, 28/12/97–3/1/98, 10). There may have been a connection with the idea of Associate Membership of CEFTA which had been circulating in certain quarters, notably in the Czech Foreign Ministry (for instance see Winkler, 1997, 82), evidently with certain of the less advanced CEFTA candidates in mind.

17. This observation is based on conversations between the author and a former member of the Slovak CEFTA expert group.

18. The example of Romania is relevant here. The huge deficit in CEFTA trade which developed in 1998, particularly in agricultural trade with Hungary, caused a political backlash and even prompted some calls for Romania's withdrawal from CEFTA.

19. The pressure on the EU candidate countries in this respect is clearly real rather than inferred. The UNECE reported that Hungary's decision (in February 1999) to begin free trade negotiations with Croatia 'prompted a rather negative reaction on the part of the EU' (*Economic Survey of Europe*, No. 1, 1999, 151). Of course in this case, the EU's reaction may have been more to do with the contradictions with its own political approach to Croatia rather than worries about incompatible trade regimes *per se*.

20. In the end the agreement was not signed, mainly due to Croatia's reservations over agricultural trade liberalisation.

21. According to the *Economist* (2/10/99, 49) '(m)ore than 100,000 people from Transcarpathia probably work illegally outside Ukraine. Trade between Transcarpathia and the neighbouring region of Hungary may be worth $200m a year. The tight visa regime, which the EU wants the Central European countries to impose on visitors from farther east before joining the European club would kill all of this. The Central Europeans, however, have their own reasons for keeping their borders open. Hungary likes its links with some 3m-odd ethnic Hungarians living south and east of Hungary, some in Ukraine. And Poland sees Ukraine as a strategic partner, to be pulled westwards and away from Russia. Besides, like Hungary, Poland has a vast black-market trade with Ukraine, and hires many cheap Ukrainian workers. It would be wretched for the Uzhgorodtsi if a new iron curtain came down between them and their neighbours to the West'. Also, for policy statements by Polish politicians arguing in favour of maintaining visa-free traffic with Ukraine when Poland is in the EU see also 'EU membership must not alter relations with eastern states' (*New Europe*, 13–19 September 1999, 9) and 'Poland wants Ukrainian border open even when in EU' (*New Europe*, 5–11/7/99, 8).

22. It should be mentioned that this is not seen by many as a practical possibility because the CIS countries are simply not yet ready to implement an effective free trade area. It does, however, throw light on the difficult situation of Ukraine in terms of its further development of its

external economic relations. Association with the EU remains elusive, the CEFTA door has closed (or at least the illusion that it was open has gone) and bilateral economic relations with the CEE10 – except with Estonia and Lithuania for now – look unlikely to materialise, and Ukraine appears to have no viable avenues for subregional economic cooperation.

7. Conclusion

The short period since the end of the cold war has been marked by significant developments in the scope and spread of subregional and regional economic cooperation. In the European arena the associations which formed in the first major phase of post-war regionalism have undergone major reconfiguration. The CMEA no longer exists, EFTA has virtually disappeared, and the EU has not only further widened and deepened but also has had its role transformed by the need to accommodate former socialist countries in the European integration process. Many new cooperation initiatives have also emerged, both in Europe and other parts of the globe. In the case of the various subregional groups (CEI, BSEC) which have emerged in post-cold war Europe, most of them have a mixture of economic and more broadly defined agendas for cooperation. The non-European initiatives which have proliferated in the last decade or so tend to be more strictly economic associations usually based on preferential trade arrangements.

One of the most important factors which distinguished CEFTA from the other 'second wave' economic associations was that its member states had previously been together in a failed integration project for over 40 years. Moreover, CEFTA was preceded by not only the disintegration of the CMEA but also of the broader edifice of communism and Soviet power in Eastern Europe and rather than find reasons to cooperate the Central and East European states wanted to deconstruct the region and align themselves with 'mainstream' Europe. Thus in the aftermath of the fall of communist regimes the new elites' strategic priorities were based on assumptions and policy preferences that were hardly conducive to an early renewal of economic cooperation among former CMEA states, despite the considerable economic shock associated with the rapid extrication from the regional, and particularly Soviet, market. While the CEE states' determination to anchor themselves to Euro–Atlantic economic and security organisations is usually explained in terms of political imperatives, potent economic arguments were also deployed to the effect of a strong intellectual case for the policy of trade reorientation rather than reintegration. Economists from the CEE region, particularly in Hungary where the argument for open-door foreign economic policies preceded the debates of the transformation context, reasoned that overintensive, preferential trade with the ex-USSR had been a principle cause of economic backwardness and measures to artificially sustain exchanges would threaten transformation not vice-versa as claimed by certain eminent Western specialists.

The dominant position of the former USSR in intra-CMEA trade meant that the economic grounds for a reintegration of the CEE5 (which itself faced covert political opposition) were generally much weaker and the situation was further complicated by the reform gap that opened up between the Visegrad countries on the one hand and Bulgaria and Romania on the other. In order to send the correct message to the Western institutions, however, the governments of the Visegrad3 proved willing to bring their mutual trading conditions into line with those negotiated with the EC and EFTA during 1991. Czechoslovakia, Hungary and Poland had already been coordinating their Eastern and Western foreign policies to some extent in the framework of the Visegrad triangle. The roots of CEFTA were therefore the Visegrad cooperation and the EU's preference for aspirant members to engage in mutual cooperation as a forerunner. Yet though officials from the CEFTA countries were anxious to stress that their subregional cooperation did not represent the formation of a new 'bloc' in Europe and that CEFTA was restricted to a mutual exercise in free trade, the link between CEFTA cooperation and relations with the EU was nevertheless interpreted differently in some quarters. While views expressed in some parts of the Polish administration that CEFTA could evolve along EU lines had little serious support, the seemingly more practical idea that CEFTA cooperation could be extended to more active collaboration to further EU integration, particularly in coordinating overall economic reform strategies, was a topic of more serious debate in Polish circles, at least for a while. The Czech government's more outspoken opposition to further development of political cooperation and increasingly neo-liberal economic policy approach has tended to credit them with the blame for the suspension of Visegrad cooperation at about the same time as CEFTA was signed and for the free market form of economic cooperation which prevailed. Yet different national circumstances and varying approaches to the unprecedented and the hugely experimental process of systemic transformation were the most important impediments to coordination of transformation strategies and economic integration policies. CEFTA was the only multilateral economic cooperation initiative to emerge, hesitantly, out of the debris of the former CMEA and the only appropriate model in the circumstances of the time. It was also clearly in line with the basic approach of the EU in its economic relations with CEE. The main questions were therefore whether what was essentially a strategic response to the imperatives of the 'return to Europe' could facilitate a recovery and further expansion of trade in Central Europe and whether there would be scope for CEFTA cooperation to both widen and deepen in due course.

The CEFTA countries were able to rely on a number of existing international trade agreements, including ones drawn up for their own external trade liberalisation programme, as a basis for the form and content of the CEFTA treaty. Though the CEFTA countries as a result (maybe even unwittingly) incorporated some integration provisions which may be seen as contradictory to the relatively modest intentions and ambitions of the time as far as mutual economic cooperation was concerned, the acceleration of the trade liberalisation timetable was as a clear sign of a move to a more positive assessment of mutual economic cooperation. According to the available data on the extent of tariff removal/reduction after the first five years of CEFTA it is clear that the overall implementation of the CEFTA trade liberalisation programme has proceeded successfully, at least for the industrial goods trade. The various reversals of market access for agricultural goods, especially from 1998 onwards, and the decision to postpone the move to complete free agricultural trade in CEFTA have certainly been setbacks but should not necessarily be interpreted as a failure of CEFTA cooperation. An alternative conclusion is that the CEFTA countries were simply overambitious. Despite the fact that the duty-free area for industrial goods was in place, at least for the original CEFTA and Slovenia, by the beginning of 1997, the implementation of CEFTA is still ongoing. Duties still apply to the industrial goods included in the various 'lists of exceptions' which have been subject to a more delayed liberalisation and the major question of how to proceed with the liberalisation of agricultural goods still remains. There are also the less publicised provisions of the CEFTA treaty which are more concerned with non-tariff barriers. These have been subject to more gradual implementation as the tendency has been to deal with the tariff and quantitative barriers first before shifting to the more indirect aspects of market integration.

Turning to the results of CEFTA cooperation, intra-CEFTA trade growth has kept pace with (and for the most part expanded faster than) overall external trade growth of the CEFTA members. CEFTA has clearly contributed to an effective rebuilding of trade ties within the CEFTA area which itself has expanded following three successful enlargements. Since the main intention of the intra-CEFTA trade liberalisation has been to align the preferences given to CEFTA producers with those available to producers in the CEFTA states' main trading partners in EFTA and the EU, no major negative consequences of CEFTA (connected to trade diversion) should be inferred. Even where some discrimination against EU producers could be claimed, due to the asymmetrical nature of the Europe Agreement trade arrangements, preferential conditions for subregional as well as domestic producers in CEFTA is not inconsistent with the general principles upon which industrial trade relations between CEE and the EU have been based. As far as agriculture is concerned CEE–EU agricultural trade arrangements are clearly no example and the subregional liberalisation which has resulted in considerable increase in agricultural trade must simply be seen as a progressive step.

The intra-CEFTA trade patterns have undergone some realignment over the years since CEFTA began operation. Some developments are due to the rearrangements generated by CEFTA enlargement but some important changes have also been observable within the V4 – the original CEFTA and still its core – which can be linked to broader trends in the transformation process and which also indicate that CEFTA has really been functioning as a market. The different experiences of the V4 in terms of FDI inflows seems to have been particularly telling, especially as far as the weakening position of Slovakia and strengthening position of Hungary are concerned. The role of FDI in the reintegration of the CEFTA market is clearly a key one and FDI will no doubt underwrite any sustained expansion of intra-CEFTA trade, further demonstrating that regional and subregional integration is a function of a successful all-round engagement with the global economy. In this sense, CEFTA shares the same characteristics of other 'second wave' regional economic associations which '(u)nlike the episode of the 1930s, the current initiatives represent efforts to facilitate their members participation in the world economy rather than withdrawal from it. Unlike those in the 1950s and 1960s, the initiatives involving developing countries are part of a strategy to liberalise and open their economies to implement export- and foreign-investment-led policies rather than to promote import substitution' (Mansfield and Milner, 1999, 601, quoting Lawrence, 1996).

The economic effects of CEFTA have been useful, though it is necessary to avoid exaggerating them since CEFTA constitutes a small component of the external trade of its members and will continue so. Nevertheless, as Vaclav Klaus said in 1996 'we all feel the positive impacts on our economies that CEFTA has created' (*Radio Free Europe/Radio Liberty Newsline,* 17/9/96). Coupled with the (again modest but useful) direct and indirect support that CEFTA cooperation has offered to the EU accession endeavours and the subconscious inputs to stable subregional political relations, the many official endorsements of the success of CEFTA which have come from inside and outside of CEE seem justified. While the CEFTA experience fits well with the general idea about how the subregional initiatives which have emerged in the 'new' Europe generate valuable soft security effects, the question of how significant these contributions are remains open. An advantage that CEFTA, and its 'smaller cousin' the BFTA, may have stems from its more restricted but nevertheless focused and concrete agenda which has meant that the generic soft security effects are supplemented by a range of more tangible economic outcomes which in turn further enhance the political dimension of cooperation through the interdependence factor. The lesson could be that while participation in subregional initiatives with more vague, or less committal cooperation agendas encounters less resistance, especially when existing NATO and /or EU countries are involved too, these looser arrangements may generate less benefits and be more prone to identity crisis problems than those initiatives which have a more ambitious agenda but are more difficult to convene, perhaps to the extent that they need an outside pressure to do so.

Once successful implementation of a given regional economic cooperation agenda has been achieved, the pressure to strive for new areas of cooperation always seems to assert itself and the attention of outsider countries is attracted. Despite its self-acclaimed lack of ambition, the developmental momentum generated by success has been relevant for CEFTA too. According to some official statements from within CEFTA it is 'not an integration organisation but merely [a] free trade agreement. This means that it has no permanent institution and that its Parties have full sovereignty in making decisions (CEFTA is not an entity of international law)' (Joint Committee, 1998, 5). Apart from the fact that few, if any, scholars would argue that trade is not a cornerstone of the integration of national economies, modelling CEFTA on the Europe Agreements meant that the provision to go beyond a classic free trade area was in place right from the start. CEFTA has already begun the process of transformation to a single market, an inevitable consequence of the interplay between subregional economic cooperation in CEFTA and the process of furthering regional and global integration, with the influence moving primarily from the latter to the former. This brings to mind some parallels with the EFTA experience. Apart from the fact that the three objectives listed under Article 1 of CEFTA are virtually identical, even in wording, to those of the (1960) EFTA treaty, the approach to integration in CEFTA seemed to closely resemble the EFTA experience where an aversion to a more serious and committed integration project was also at the time characteristic of the countries which signed the (1960) Stockholm Convention. States favouring these types of regional arrangements are usually following the 'pluralist' approach to integration which entails 'a minimum degree of integration to attain certain limited economic and political objectives, principally trade liberalisation in an international environment of peace and security' (Hitiris, 1998, 39). The key difference was that whereas the strategic thinking underlying the formation of EFTA had largely been defensive vis-à-vis the EU, it was mainly the fact that CEFTA fitted an offensive strategy towards the EU that led to its creation. In the case of the CEFTA countries the pluralist approach applied to the subregional integration project only and existed alongside a clear commitment to a much deeper model of integration in the broader European context. A second analogy with the EFTA experience concerns the interactions between parallel regional associations through which the dominant partner imparts an integration-deepening effect on the subordinate one. This was relevant for the last batch of EFTA countries to transfer to the EU, which initially prepared to engage in a mutual deepening exercise through the European Economic Area (EEA) which still exists for certain members of the rump EFTA.

CEFTA's further development – while having featured debates which illustrated that the various actors within the region had different perceptions of and preferences for its role, functioning and evolutionary path – has been stimulated largely by external impulses coming from the higher layers of the trade liberalisation, economic cooperation and integration framework CEFTA is located within. Of those, which include also the WTO and OECD, by far the most the important influence has been and will be the EU. As Inotai (1997a, 69) put it, the general principle is that 'the sequence runs not from subregional to regional (or global) cooperation, but in the opposite direction. Widespread international experience of successfully modernising countries indicates that efficient policies have always proceeded from the global (regional) to the subregional level'. Inotai also distinguishes between subregional cooperation which has had 'pioneer' status in the European integration process (that is, has had an important influence in creating and developing it) and subregional cooperation which has had 'follower' status (that is, has copied elements of what has gone before in other subregions or larger groupings). His decision to place CEFTA clearly in the category of 'follower' status seems perfectly justified in terms of the broader European integration process but it might be suggested that CEFTA has been a pioneer subregional cooperation of sorts in the specific CEE context.

CEFTA also quickly moved on from being an exclusive economic club based on the Visegrad group to become a broader subregional economic association of post-communist states. This has not only expanded the free trade network and opened new export opportunities within the subregion but has also meant that CEFTA has become a subregional component of the EU pre-accession process which brings together EU candidate states at different stages of the EU enlargement process (that is, 'ins' and 'pre-ins'). Though the key influences on the further development of CEFTA have been external ones, it is also the case that the economic and political interests of the member states have also played their parts. From the economic point of view, the overall need to expand exports and reverse trade diversion caused by biased opening to EC and EFTA economies has been a factor in the push to accelerate and enhance the liberalisation of the CEFTA market and to expand it through enlargement.

In fact, it is clear that the economic case for CEFTA was developed retrospectively. In the political sphere, attempts to strengthen and/or widen integration in CEFTA have been seen variously as the tactic of utilising all bilateral and multilateral tools available to deal with a more substantial Eastern agenda (a perspective on Poland's approach), to attempt to increase the scope and substance of CEFTA as a counterweight to losing ground in the integration with the main Euro–Atlantic economic and security structures (a perspective on Slovakia's approach during the Meciar years), and as a strategy to pre-empt extra layers of cooperation (a perspective on the Czech approach during the Klaus years). This leads to some further observations about the different national approaches to not only CEFTA but subregional cooperation in general. The national approaches have not been constant, which is not uncommon in general experience as far as policies towards regional and subregional integration have been concerned. In this respect, the influence of governmental changes have been particularly important in the case of Slovakia. The post-Meciar regime is now building a completely different relationship with the international community, including the EU and the other Visegrad partners. The enthusiasm for subregional cooperation is if anything stronger but refocused on utilising subregional relations to help resuscitate its EU and NATO accession chances rather than compensate for lack of them by an emphasis on further development of CEFTA. While the political changes in Slovakia tend to have, understandably, been presented as more significant than the change of government in the Czech Republic during the same year, the Czech approach to subregional political cooperation which prevailed after the 1998 elections was also in clear contrast to the previous leadership. At the same time, it would be incorrect to present this as a reversal of the Czechs' minimalist approach because the evidence presented in Chapter 5 shows that the Czech role in developing CEFTA as a vehicle for market integration in CEE was always anything but minimal. Many of the proposals and actual developments connected with the improvement, deepening and widening (to other countries) of CEFTA integration were driven by the Czechs. Though the open-door trade policies of the Klaus regime corresponded well with the general neo-liberal orthodoxy they also reflected a logical approach for a country with an above average stake in trade within CEE.

The years 1995–97 seemed to mark the point when ambitions for CEFTA cooperation were at their highest, since when an increasingly pragmatic and realistic approach has gradually set in. Attempts by certain of the CEFTA parties to push for qualitative leaps forward (intra-CEFTA liberalisation of capital, services and labour) have subsided and energies have been increasingly devoted to dealing with problems of trade liberalisation, especially to do with agricultural trade, and activating/interpreting the various articles of CEFTA. On the latter, some of them deal with certain non-tariff barriers (state aids, public procurement) usually associated with single market programmes. To the extent that the failure to invite guest countries to the 1998 and 1999 CEFTA summits indicates that enlargement has gone on hold, then this is a sign that CEFTA has also become more introspective. The internal agenda of CEFTA seems to have been one factor; but these developments have also coincided with the AGENDA 2000 programme and the opening of full EU accession negotiations for a subset of CEE, which leaves the question of where CEFTA goes from here.

On the future of CEFTA, the internal agenda will remain active for a while yet, though it should be noted that intra-CEFTA cooperation will remain in the parameters of the CEFTA treaty and there appears to be no chance that CEFTA might develop a more direct role in the coordination of its member states' negotiations with the EU. The main reasons for this are that the CEFTA countries are clearly at the different stages of the EU accession process and more suitable subregional coordinating fora are already carrying out this role to the limited extent currently possible. The longer term future of CEFTA and the question of whether it will have one beyond the first phase of EU enlargement is inevitably speculative. What does seem clear is that as well as the widely accepted view that genuine European unity is not achievable on the basis of a restricted enlargement of the EU it is also the case that CEFTA, or any other subregional cooperation which may become established, will not be able to develop in a way that can compensate for a failure of the EU to properly integrate all CEE states that so desire. As far as scaled down (that is, other than an alternative to EU integration) ambitions for CEFTA are concerned, there is limited room for manoeuvre in terms of enlarging CEFTA before the first batch of CEE candidates enter the EU around 2003/2004, though the significant political change in Croatia could conceivably open the door to CEFTA rather rapidly in that particular case.

Though it may appear that the opening of the EU accession talks on the part of some of CEFTA's members led to a loss of momentum for CEFTA, particularly as far as enlargement is concerned, the fact is these developments were not in themselves responsible. Rather, objective conditions asserted themselves, particularly the discrepancies between the existing CEFTA countries (here the emphasis is on CEFTA members at the front of the EU accession queue) and the CEFTA accession candidates. As long as CEFTA remains an exercise in EU pre-accession tied to the EU's own strategy, then the further CEFTA states progress along their pathways to the EU while the CEFTA candidates are stuck at the starting gate for even pre-accession, the less appropriate it has become to think about them sharing the same pre-accession vehicle. By the time the EU enlarges, CEFTA may simply have had its day. At the same time, some useful integration between CEFTA countries and non-CEE10 can be achieved on the basis of bilateral free trade agreements which can also have useful spin-offs in the support they give to the parties' political relations and any other parts of the subregional political agenda. Moreover, this 'de facto' partial integration may be more use than full CEFTA membership because it makes possible a gradual integration of markets rather than a fast liberalisation exercise necessitated by CEFTA entry. The intention of those CEFTA states in EU negotiations to push for retention of bilateral free trade arrangements they already have in place (*Financial Times*, 12/10/99, 9) and the likelihood that the EU may offer certain Balkan countries at least non-reciprocal duty-free access for industrial goods should make this particular issue less complicated to the overall benefit of subregional economic and political relations. If the decisions of the Helsinki summit indicate a genuinely more embracing and flexible EU strategy for eastward enlargement and relations with CEE in general, then the need for CEFTA to develop a pan-European role could become irrelevant anyway and the most important issue will be whether other subregions can emulate the CEFTA experience and make use of subregional cooperation to support their European integration in a way the CEFTA countries have done.

APPENDICES

Appendix 1: Extracts from the CEFTA Treaty

A1.1   PREAMBLE TO THE CEFTA AGREEMENT AND ARTICLE 1 (OBJECTIVES)

PREAMBLE

The Czech Republic, the Republic of Hungary, the Republic of Poland and the Slovak republic (hereinafter called the Parties),

Reaffirming their commitment to pluralistic democracy based on the rule of law, human rights and fundamental freedoms,

Having regard to the Visegrad Declaration of 15 February 1991 and the Cracow Declaration of 6 October 1991 adopted as the results of the meetings of the highest representatives of the Parties,

Recalling their intention to participate actively in the process of economic integration in Europe and expressing their preparedness to co-operate in seeking ways and means to strengthen this process,

Reaffirming their firm commitment to the principles of a market economy, which constitutes the basis for their relations,

Recalling their firm commitment to the Final Act of the Conference on Security and Co-operation in Europe, the Paris Charter, and in particular the principles contained in the final document of the Bonn Conference on Economic Co-operation in Europe,

Resolved to this end to eliminate progressively the obstacles to substantially all their mutual trade, in accordance with the provisions of the General Agreement on Tariffs and Trade,

Firmly convinced that this agreement will foster the intensification of mutually beneficial trade relations among them and contribute to the process of integration in Europe,

Considering that no provision of this agreement may be interpreted as exempting the Parties from their obligations under other international agreements, especially the General Agreement on Tariffs and Trade,

Have decided as follows:

Article 1

Objectives

1. The Parties shall gradually establish a free trade area in accordance with the provisions of the present Agreement and in conformity with Article XXIV of the General Agreement on Tariffs and Trade in a transitional period ending on 1 January 2001, at the latest.

2. The objectives of the present Agreement are:

(a) to promote through the expansion of trade the harmonious development of the economic relations between the Parties and thus to foster in the Parties the advance of economic activity, the improvement of living and employment conditions, and increased productivity and financial stability,

(b) to provide fair conditions of competition for trade between the Parties,

(c) to contribute in this way, by the removal of barriers to trade, to the harmonious development and expansion of world trade.

A1.2   SEPARATE JOINT DECLARATION SIGNED TOGETHER WITH THE AGREEMENT ON 21/12/92

JOINT DECLARATION

The governmental Delegations headed by Mr Vladimir Dlouhy, Minister of Industry and Trade of the Czech Republic, Mr Bela Kadar, Minister for International Economic Relations of the Republic of Hungary, Mr Andrzej Arendarski, Minister for Foreign Economic Relations of the Republic of Poland and Mr Ludovit Cernak, Minister of Economy of the Slovak Republic, signing the Central European Free Trade Agreement in Krakow on 21st December, 1992 have agreed as follows:

1. Reaffirming their strong commitment to the principles of market economy and free trade between the nations and, mindful of the importance of the economic integration within the wider European marketplace the Governments of the Czech Republic, the Republic of Hungary, the Republic of Poland and the Slovak Republic declare that:
They have full trust in the beneficial influence of the free trade on the economic growth of their countries and the welfare of their inhabitants, thus the speed of implementation of the trade liberalisation programme must be increased.

2. With this in mind the four Visegrad countries have decided to initiate immediately negotiations under the auspices of the Joint Committee following the signature of the original Agreement. Consequently they will immediately start to discuss the reduction of the transitional period to five years and to abolish all tariff and non-tariff barriers and to include both industrial and agricultural products into the Agreement.

Source: The Central European Free Trade Agreement, Krakow, 21 December 1992. Author's copy supplied by Ministry of Economy, Republic of Slovakia.

Appendix 2: Activities of CEFTA Joint Committee and CEFTA Summit in 1997

A2.1   AGENDA FOR CEFTA JOINT COMMITTEE MEETING, BLED, SLOVENIA, 3–4 JULY

Session of the Joint Committee of the CEFTA Countries

Each year the presiding country is organising a meeting of the CEFTA Joint Committee, its members being ministers responsible for the foreign economic relations of the Parties to the Central European Free Trade Agreement. In the year 1997 the Republic of Slovenia got the presidency. In April (on the 12 April 1997) Slovenia had organised an extraordinary meeting of the CEFTA Joint Committee in Bucharest and the regular meeting which was held from 3 to 4 July 1997 in Bled. That had been the first participation of Romania as the Party to the CEFTA.

The Joint Committee evaluates the accomplished activities in the framework of the CEFTA agreement and the agreement's application. Furthermore, the Joint Committee also designates activities that have to be accomplished in the current year and in the year 1998.

At the session of the Joint Committee, ministers will be discussing topics from all fields of work being carried out by the countries of the CEFTA agreement and also the activities that are not necessarily directly subject to the Agreement.

At the session of the Joint Committee each minister is going to represent precisely the theme of the field of work his country is responsible for. Marjan Senjur, PhD., Minister of Economic Relations and Development of the Republic of Slovenia will give an up-to-date report on the realisation of the CEFTA Activities for 1997. He will be evaluating the results of the negotiations on Additional Protocol No. 6 to the CEFTA and offer a representation of the preparatory work for the Summit in September in Portoroz. At the same time each minister will have to offer his point of view regarding other topics that will be discussed at the session.

The minister for economy of the Slovak republic, Mr Karol Cesnek whose country namely has been presiding the CEFTA in the year 1996 will give the report on evaluation of the CEFTA functioning in 1996.

The minister for economic relations and development of the Republic Slovenia, Marjan Senjur, PhD, has the task to report on up-to-date realisation of the CEFTA Activities for 1997 in the framework of the Central European Free Trade Agreement.

The minister for industry and trade of the Czech Republic, Mr Karel Kühnl is going to report on the results of the negotiations in respect of dispute settlement and interpretation of the CEFTA agreement. The Czech Republic has been namely co-ordinating the work (and also represents the initiator) of this question.

Both ministers from the Czech Republic and the Slovak Republic are going to inform the Joint Committee on introduced temporary import deposit scheme because of the Balance-of-Payments difficulties.

The minister for economy of the Republic of Poland, Mr Wieslaw Kaczmarek, will be talking about the introduction of specific safeguards measures applicable in Poland from 1 June 1997.

At the session the ministers will be evaluating the results of the negotiations on Additional Protocol No. 6 to the CEFTA. The Republic of Slovenia would with the Additional Protocol No. 6 to the CEFTA adjust its agricultural concessions to the rules adapted by the original Parties to the CEFTA. Ministers will decide on further steps to be taken by the experts groups.

The Joint Committee will determine the date of the beginning of the negotiations with the Republic of Bulgaria on the Agreement on Accession of the Republic of Bulgaria to the CEFTA.

Each Minister will also give the information about the free trade agreements concluded with the third countries.

A2.2   AGENDA FOR CEFTA SUMMIT, PORTOROZ, SLOVENIA, 11–12 SEPTEMBER

Summit of the Prime Ministers of CEFTA Countries, Portoroz, September 1997

At the last year's CEFTA summit in Jasna, Slovak Republic, Slovenia presented its candidacy for hosting this year's gathering. The candidacy was accepted by all Prime Ministers of CEFTA countries. Slovenia is thus organising this year three high-level meetings within the framework of CEFTA: in early July, Bled hosted a meeting of the CEFTA Joint Committee (the highest CEFTA body for decision-making and recommendations), at the end of August the Ministers of Agriculture of CEFTA Countries met in Maribor and on 12 and 13 September, the six Prime Ministers of CEFTA countries will meet in Portoroz.

As agreed by all CEFTA countries, the Prime Minister of the Republic of Slovenia, Dr Janez Drnovsek also invited the Prime Ministers of Bulgaria, Croatia, Macedonia, Lithuania, Latvia and Ukraine to the Portoroz gathering as guests. They expressed their interest in attending the meeting and confirmed their participation in Portoroz, as their countries are interested in closer co-operation.

The great interest of the Central and Eastern European countries to attend the CEFTA summit is a clear sign that CEFTA is becoming an increasingly powerful economic factor in the Central European region. From the original four founding members, CEFTA was enlarged to six member countries. Slovenia joined CEFTA on 1 January, 1996 and Romania on 12 July, 1997. At the Portoroz gathering, the Prime Ministers will give their support to Bulgaria's application for CEFTA membership and it is expected that in 1998 this country will join CEFTA as well, thus enlarging the common free trade area to include a population of over 100 million.

The plenary session of the Prime Ministers will be divided into three parts. In the morning, only the delegations of CEFTA member countries, headed by their respective Prime Ministers, will convene.

The gathering will be addressed by the host, Slovenia's Prime Minister, Dr Janez Drnovsek who will, as the keynote speaker, give an overview of the economic co-operation and trade relations among the CEFTA countries in the period since the last summit. Then the Prime Ministers of the Czech Republic, Hungary, Poland, Romania and Slovak Republic will have a chance to address the gathering. The following topics will be discussed:

1. Activities in the framework of the CEFTA Agreement (implementation of Additional Protocols No. 4 and 5, signing of Romania's Accession Agreement, extraordinary and ordinary sessions of the CEFTA Joint Committee, meeting of the Ministers of Agriculture, activities of expert groups in the area of dispute settlement);

2. Activities beyond the scope of CEFTA Agreement (investment conference in the USA);

3. Introduction of protection measures introduced by some CEFTA member countries in 1997 (Poland – temporary measures applied to importation of steel products; Czech Republic and Slovak Republic – import deposits; Poland – specific protection measures);

4. Progress report on negotiations on Additional Protocol No. 6 (agricultural concessions of Slovenia to founding CEFTA members).

In the second part of the gathering the Prime Ministers will outline the forms of co-operation and activities until the next summit. The following discussion topics will be presented by the Prime Minister of Slovenia:

• Preparation of interpretation of specific articles of the CEFTA Agreement;
• Signing of Additional Protocol No. 6;
• Beginning of negotiations on Bulgaria's accession;
• Restart of negotiations on the liberalisation of trade in services, free flow of capital, recognition of certificates and testing results;
• Agreement on the next meeting of Prime Ministers (venue and date);
• Criteria for inviting guests to the Prime Ministerial meetings;
• Investment conference in Japan (October 1997);
• Future development of CEFTA and its role in relation to those CEFTA members countries which are acceding to the EU.

After the morning part of the meeting, the Prime Ministers will formulate the conclusions and jointly prepare the text of the Joint Declaration of the Prime Minister of CEFTA

Countries of the Portoroz Summit. The Prime Ministers will sign the Declaration at the signing ceremony in the afternoon part of the summit. The conclusions of the Declaration will provide the guidelines for CEFTA's operation until the following Prime Ministerial summit and will also provide the basis for the 1998 activities plan.

In the afternoon part of the gathering, the Prime Ministers of CEFTA Countries will be joined by the Prime Ministers of guest countries (Bulgaria, Croatia, Latvia, Lithuania, Macedonia and Ukraine) who will also have the opportunity to speak and thus contribute to the overall content of the gathering.

In addition to the planned session, several bilateral meetings will also take place and will be organised according to the wishes of the Prime Ministers. These meetings will also take place at the ministerial level, since all the Ministers responsible for international economic relations, who are also members of the Joint Committee of CEFTA, will attend the Portoroz Summit as well.

A2.3 RESOLUTIONS OF CEFTA SUMMIT, PORTOROZ, SLOVENIA, 12–13 SEPTEMBER 1997

Conclusions of the 1997 CEFTA Summit

At the Summit of the prime ministers of the CEFTA countries the prime ministers of the Czech Republic, the Republic of Hungary, the Republic of Poland, Romania, the Slovak Republic and the Republic of Slovenia co-ordinated and signed a declaration.

The prime ministers began by expressing their satisfaction that for the first time the prime minister of Romania participated at the meeting as a regular member.

All the prime ministers agreed that the Central European Free Trade Agreement is generating positive shifts and positive results, and that trade among the signatory countries is growing. They also agreed with the findings that the functioning of CEFTA is less dynamic after the first successful years. Not enough has been done in the last year in the field of free movement of capital, common interpretation of certain articles of the Agreement, liberalisation of trade in services or in the field of mutual recognition of certificates and test results for agricultural and industrial products. Therefore all the prime ministers agreed to continue with these activities in the future.

The prime ministers expressed their opinion that the negotiations on the Additional Protocol No. 6 are approaching a conclusion. The prime minister of the Republic of Slovenia noted with satisfaction that all the CEFTA signatories agreed to the Republic of Slovenia abolishing all exemptions on 1 January 2000. It is expected that the Additional Protocol No. 6 will be applied from 1998.

Support for organising conferences on investment opportunities in the CEFTA countries and all other activities contributing to the promotion of the CEFTA group was also expressed.

The Polish prime minister proposed a comprehensive analysis of the functioning of the Central European Free Trade Agreement in the five years since its creation. In his words such an analysis could define the problems and thus enable further development, the multilateral nature and flexibility of relations between the signatory countries. His proposal was met with approval by all the prime ministers. It is anticipated that Poland will organise a meeting on the ministerial level for the fifth anniversary of the signing of the Central European Free Trade Agreement (21 December 1992) in Krakow, at the end of December 1997.

The openness of the Central European Free Trade Agreement for the accession of other Central European countries that satisfy the accession conditions was emphasised at this Summit. The prime ministers agreed to launch accession negotiations with the Republic of Bulgaria.

At the Summit the prime ministers exchanged views on accession to the European Union. However, on the request of the Hungarian prime minister they did not bind themselves in the declaration to provide mutual support in the process of joining the European Union.

The Czech Republic will take over the presidency and organisation of the next summit of the prime ministers of CEFTA countries in 1998.

Source: Ministry of Economic Relations and Development, Republic of Slovenia (via http://www.uvi.si/CEFTA).

Appendix 3: Summary Assessment, Conclusions and Recommendations for the Improvement of Cooperation

After 5 years of functioning of the Central European Free Trade Agreement the Parties have come to the following conclusions:

The functioning of CEFTA demonstrates that the Agreement has met the expectations and has been a decisive element in the increase of the volume of mutual trade among the CEFTA Parties.

The CEFTA provisions have been implemented thus the gradual abolition of trade barriers and the establishment of fair conditions of competition are proceeding in accordance with the objectives defined by the Parties.

The general trend of liberalisation has shown the growth during this time what was clearly demonstrated in several amendments aiming at deepening and widening trade liberalisation. This fact can be acknowledged even taking into account that in some areas there are still some existing barriers and full liberalisation is not foreseen so far (e.g. in agriculture).

The safeguard measures applied by some Parties have weakened, to some extent, the effect of liberalisation. The general rule is that they should be of exceptional character and limited in time. The basic principle of trade liberalisation among the CEFTA Parties is not disturbed by the introduction of safeguard measures.

A modification of the rules of origin aiming at the pan-European cumulation of origin has contributed to the development of a wider cooperation among the CEFTA Parties.

and make the following recommendations for the improvement of cooperation:

The CEFTA Parties should focus on an active participation in the process of economic integration in Europe and on the co-operation in seeking ways and means to strengthen this process.

Regarding certain areas of co-operation the following may be stated:

- in the process of CEFTA enlargement the criteria and conditions agreed for the accession should be strictly kept,
- in the field of industrial products the liberalisation of nearly the whole of trade should be finished in accordance with the provisions of CEFTA by 1 January 2001,

- the possibilities of further liberalisation in the agricultural sector should be examined on the basis of practical implementation of the existing concessions and taking into account the accession of the EU,
- it appears necessary for the CEFTA Parties to move to a qualitatively higher level of co-operation in more fields and areas (e.g. certification, mutual recognition of test results),
- some provisions of the CEFTA require closer and more intensive co-operation between the Parties. They should aim at intensifying discussions, inter alia, in the field of state aid, opening of government procurement markets, intellectual property rights, sanitary and phitosanitary measures, taking into account the existing WTO regulations and the stage of bilateral negotiations with the European Union.

In harmony with the idea of liberalisation and the procedure provided in the agreement safeguard measures should be adopted only in cases of necessity and only for what is strictly needed to remedy the situation. The CEFTA parties underline the importance of the principle of information and consultations in order to find amicable solutions.

The discussion on improvement of the functioning of CEFTA should continue, particularly on interpretation of some CEFTA provisions and on preparation of new Rules of Procedure of the Joint Committee.

Source: Extract from CEFTA Joint Committee (1998).

Appendix 4: The Customs Union between the Czech Republic and Slovakia

Article 36 of CEFTA ('Trade relations governed by this and other Agreements') clarifies the status of trade relations between the Czech Republic and Slovakia in CEFTA along with the position as far as Customs Unions within CEFTA are concerned. Paragraph 1 of Article 36 states that (CEFTA, 18) '(t)his Agreement shall apply to trade relations among the Czech Republic, the Republic of Poland, the Republic of Hungary and the Slovak Republic but not to the trade relations between the Czech Republic and the Slovak Republic'. The Czech and Slovak Republics' mutual trade is covered by the Customs Union signed in Prague on 29 October 1992 which entered into force upon 1 January 1993. Consequently the Czech and Slovak Republics effectively form one party in the CEFTA as illustrated in, for example, Protocol 1 of Article 3 (Customs duties on imports of industrial products) which sets out the provisions for the abolition of customs duties between (CEFTA, 3) 'the Czech Republic and the Slovak Republic on the one side and the Republic of Hungary on the other side'. Paragraph 2 of Article 36 of CEFTA confirms it (CEFTA, 18) 'shall not prevent the maintenance or establishment of Customs Unions, free trade areas or arrangements for frontier trade to the extent that these do not negatively affect the trade regime and in particular the provisions concerning rules of origin provided for by this Agreement'.

Chapter I of the Czech–Slovak Customs Union agreement sets out the objectives and principles as follows (*Agreement Establishing the Customs Union Between the Czech Republic and Slovakia*):

CHAPTER I: OBJECTIVES AND PRINCIPLES

Article 1

1. A Customs Union of the Czech Republic and the Slovak Republic is hereby established (hereinafter referred to as 'the Customs Union'). The Customs Union is in conformity with the provisions of the General Agreement on Tariffs and Trade.

2. The customs territory of the Customs Unions is a customs territory of the Czech Republic and of the Slovak Republic.

146

3. The Customs Union has the following objectives and principles:

the aim of the Customs Union is to ensure the free movement of goods and services, integration of economies and of economic policy of the Contracting Parties and to provide favourable conditions for the development of trade between the Customs Union and third countries,

the Contracting Parties shall on the customs territory of the Customs Union pursue conforming commercial and customs policy towards third countries,

commercial and customs policy shall be co-ordinated to an agreed extent by the Council of the Customs Union,

the Customs Unions shall apply common customs tariff towards third countries, including the method determining the customs value,

the free movement of goods and services between the two Contracting Parties shall be ensured through the elimination of customs duties and quantitative restrictions,

the Contracting Parties shall apply the same rules of origin of goods as applied in trade with third countries,

the Contracting Parties shall implement the customs legislation, covering conforming regulations for the assessment, payment, refund of and exemption from customs duties, leasing, transmitting of goods, the same prohibitions and restrictions on imports and exports, including non-tariff measures and suspension of customs duties in cases of justified economic interest,

the financial needs of the Customs Union shall be covered by contributions of both Contracting Parties with regard to the fact that the customs duties collected by individual Contracting Parties shall go to their respective budgets,

the Customs Union shall ensure a coordinated application of customs statistics and registration of goods,

both Contracting Parties shall use the same customs documents,

customs clearance shall be effected on a common state and customs frontier between the Czech Republic and the Slovak Republic,

eventual disputes between the Contracting Parties arising from the implementation of this Agreement shall be settled by an arbitration body.

In line with the original hope that the political division of Czechoslovakia could be achieved without significant disruption to the prevailing state of 'complete economic integration' (remembering that it was assumed that the two states would be maintaining a common currency), the provisions of the Czech–Slovak Customs Union were significantly more ambitious than CEFTA. For example, unlike CEFTA, the complete elimination of barriers applied to agricultural as well as industrial products. Also, as paragraph 3 of Article 1 states the original intentions included 'economic policy integration' as well as the free movement of services. In line with the latter, the Czech and Slovak Republics have also maintained free movement of persons, and according to Article 28 (*Agreement Establishing the Customs Union Between the Czech Republic and Slovakia*) 'with respect to trade in services the Contracting Parties shall grant to nationals of the other Contracting Party the treatment equal to that granted to its own nationals'. The Customs Union also provided for the formation of institutions, again unlike CEFTA. Chapter VII, reproduced below, deals with the bodies of the Customs Union which include a 'Council of the Customs Union', 'Permanent Secretariat' and 'Arbitration Commission of the Customs Union':

CHAPTER VII: BODIES OF THE CUSTOMS UNION

Council of the Customs Union

Article 29

1. The Council shall ensure the coordination of foreign commercial and customs policies of the Contracting Parties.

2. The Council shall act on behalf of the Customs Union in foreign relations in all matters provided for this Agreement. For this purpose, it may establish its permanent missions to international governmental organisations upon an agreement with the Contracting Parties.

3. The Council promulgates the common customs tariff and other trade policy measures.

4. The Council shall submit to the Contracting Parties an annual report on the implementation of the Agreement establishing the Customs Union.

5. The Contracting Parties shall agree on the statute of the Council and its rules of procedure.

Article 30

1. The Council shall consist of an equal number of members of the Governments of both Contracting Parties.

2. The Council shall take its decisions by an agreement.

3. The activities of the Council shall be determined by its President whose office will be held alternately, for a six-month period, by a representative of the Czech republic or the Slovak Republic.

4. The Council shall hold at least one session every three months. The President shall convene a session of the Council upon the request of either Contracting Party.

Permanent Secretariat

Article 31

1. The Secretariat shall have its seat in Bratislava.

2. The Secretariat shall be an executive body of the Council which

– exercises the powers conferred on it by the Agreement,

– prepares draft recommendations for the Council,

– fulfils other tasks assigned to it by the Council.

Article 32

The Secretariat shall execute the following tasks, in particular it:

a) keeps under review the implementation of the commercial and customs policies of the Customs Union,

b) keeps under review the harmonisation of the systems whereby the Contracting Parties grant export aids in order to prevent distortion of economic competition between the nationals of the two Contracting Parties,

c) submits to the Council draft annual reports on the implementation of the Agreement establishing the Customs Union,

d) makes recommendations to both Contracting Parties measures affecting foreign trade,

e) co-ordinates the application of customs statistics based on the system of collecting data from the Contracting Parties and ensures their mutual exchange,

f) ensures technical and organisational aspects of activities of the Council and of the Arbitration Commission,

g) keeps under review the developments of customs legislation, particularly in the European Communities,

h) keeps under review the customs legislations of the Contracting Parties.

Article 33

The decisions of the Permanent Secretariat shall be subject to approval by the next session of the Council.

Article 34

The Permanent Secretariat shall be headed by the Director General who will be appointed and recalled by the Council.

Article 35

The Council shall make recommendations which shall become binding upon their approval by the Contracting Parties.

The Arbitration Commission of the Customs Union

Article 36

1. Disputes arising from this Agreement shall be settled by the Arbitration Commission of the Customs Union.

2. The Arbitration Commission shall open its proceedings on a proposal from the Council or from one of the Contracting Parties.

3. The Arbitration Commission shall be established on an ad hoc basis for each particular dispute. It shall consist of an arbitrator appointed from the Government of the Czech Republic, an arbitrator appointed by the Government of the Slovak Republic and a third arbitrator agreed upon by the two appointed arbitrators. The third arbitrator who shall be the Chairman of the Arbitration Commission can be a national of a third country. The Contracting Party which has proposed to open the proceedings shall appoint its arbitrator in its proposal. In other cases this appointment shall be made within 30 days from the date of receipt of the proposal for opening proceedings.

4. The rules governing the Arbitration Commission shall be agreed upon by the Contracting Parties.

5. The decisions of the Arbitration Commission shall be binding upon the Contracting Parties and both Contracting Parties shall undertake to comply with the decisions within the terms specified therein.

Some provisions of the Customs Union which took market integration beyond the basic removal of tariffs and quantitative restrictions on trade in goods were in line with CEFTA provisions although the idea was for immediate effect (or, rather continuity with the single country context) rather than future implementation. These provisions included the openness of public procurement contracts and forbidding the use of state aids which distorted competition by discriminating against producers in either country. The Customs Union Agreement does, however, state in Article 16 that the provisions on state aids (Article 19) and consolidation of systems for granting aid for exports to third countries (Article 26) shall not apply to agricultural products. Depending on the extent of progress in CEFTA as far as harmonisation of agricultural support policies is concerned, this could be one area in which the provisions of CEFTA rather than the Customs Union eventually determine the trade relations of the Czech Republic and CEFTA.

Finally, Article 33 of the Agreement which concerns the procedures for its termination. Either of the 'Contracting Parties may denounce it by a written notification. As a result of such denunciation, the Agreement shall cease to be in force 12 months following the receipt of such a notification by the other Contracting Party' (*Agreement Establishing the Customs Union Between the Czech Republic and Slovakia*). Although the two sides have often accused each other of undermining the Customs Union and threatening to cause its cancellation (usually in the context of the introduction of specific or general discriminatory trade barriers and retaliatory responses – see for example BBC, EE/2939 C/3, 7/6/97 and BBC EE/2942 C/1–C/3, 11/6/97) the Customs Union has survived and these days the two parties stress their desire to maintain it in the event that their accessions to the EU should occur separately.

Sources: The Central European Free Trade Agreement, Krakow, 21 December 1992; *Agreement Establishing the Customs Union Between the Czech Republic and Slovakia*, Prague, 29 October 1992. Author's copies supplied by Ministry of Economy, Republic of Slovakia.

Appendix 5: Statistical Tables

Statistics

A5.1 THE CZECH REPUBLIC IN CEFTA

Table A5.1.1 Trade with CEFTA countries, 1993–98 ($US million)

	1993	1994	1995	1996	1997	1998	Index 1998/93 1993 = 100
Hungary:							
Export	296.1	377.0	377.7	390.6	423.8	503.6	170.1
Import	174.8	170.4	218.1	275.6	351.8	426.6	244.1
Poland:							
Export	359.3	548.3	965.5	1205.1	1296.8	1489.9	414.7
Import	322.6	423.9	681.9	806.8	868.6	971.1	301.0
Slovakia:							
Export	2833.5	2333.1	3005.1	3120.1	2888.5	2806.6	99.1
Import	2248.3	2123.8	2983.3	2650.4	2253.2	2076.0	92.3
Slovenia:							
Export				227.8	206.7	230.8	–
Import				153.5	148.4	158.6	–
Romania:							
Export						167.9	–
Import						24.4	–
Total CEFTA:							
Export	3488.9	3258.4	4348.3	4943.6	4815.8	5198.8	149.0
Import	2745.7	2718.1	3883.3	3886.3	3622.0	3656.7	133.2
Excluding Slovakia:							
Export	655.40	925.33	1343.22	1823.54	1927.3	2392.2	365.0
Import	497.30	594.29	900.00	1235.92	1368.8	1580.5	317.8

Table A5.1.2   Ranking of trade partners in CEFTA, 1998

	Export $US millions	% of total	Imports $US millions	% of total	Balance $US millions
Slovakia	2806.6	54.0	2076.0	56.8	730.6
Poland	1489.9	28.7	971.1	26.6	518.8
Hungary	503.6	9.7	426.6	11.7	77.0
Slovenia	230.8	4.4	158.6	4.3	72.2
Romania	167.9	3.2	24.4	0.6	143.5
Total	5198.8	100.0	3656.7	100.0	1542.1

Table A5.1.3   Export/import coverage: CEFTA and total trade 1994–98

	1994	1995	1996	1997	1998
Hungary	221.3	173.2	141.8	120.5	118.0
Poland	129.3	141.6	149.4	149.3	153.4
Slovakia	109.9	100.7	117.7	128.2	135.2
Slovenia			148.4	139.4	145.5
Romania					688.1
Total CEFTA	119.9	112.0	127.2	132.9	142.2
Total trade	95.2	85.7	79.0	83.8	91.5

Table A5.1.4   CEFTA trade and total trade by commodity groups, 1997 (% of total)

		Imports from CEFTA	Total imports	Ratio of CEFTA imports to total imports	Exports to CEFTA	Total exports	Ratio of CEFTA exports to total exports
SITC0	Food and live animals	6.7	4.8	1.4	5.6	3.5	1.6
SITC1	Beverages and tobacco	1.2	1.1	1.1	2.0	1.1	1.8
SITC2	Crude materials, except fuels	3.1	3.9	0.8	2.8	3.9	0.7
SITC3	Mineral fuels, lubricants, related materials	9.9	8.5	1.2	6.8	4.0	1.7
SITC4	Animal and vegetable oils, fats, waxes	0.2	0.3	0.7	0.4	0.1	4.0
SITC5	Chemicals and related products	15.1	12.0	1.3	14.4	8.5	1.7
SITC6	Manufactured goods, classified chiefly by materials	32.8	19.5	1.7	28.6	26.4	1.1
SITC7	Machinery and transport equipment	22.1	38.3	0.6	30.5	39.4	0.8
SITC8	Miscellaneous manufactured items	8.7	11.6	0.7	8.0	13.0	0.6
SITC9	Others	0.0	0.0	0.0	0.1	0.1	1.0

Table A5.1.5   Balance of CEFTA trade by commodity groups, 1997

		Exports $US millions	Imports $US millions	Balance $US millions
SITC0	Food and live animals	274.2	256.6	17.6
SITC1	Beverages and tobacco	95.6	47.7	47.9
SITC2	Crude materials, except fuels	135.2	117.6	17.6
SITC3	Mineral fuels, lubricants, related materials	330.4	379.2	– 48.8
SITC4	Animal and vegetable oils, fats, waxes	19.5	9.3	10.2
SITC5	Chemicals and related products	700.2	579.4	120.8
SITC6	Manufactured goods, classified chiefly by materials	1390.3	1256.8	133.5
SITC7	Machinery and transport equipment	1482.6	847.7	634.9
SITC8	Miscellaneous manufactured items	432.6	331.6	101.0
SITC9	Others	4.5	1.3	3.2
Total		4865.1	3827.2	1037.9

Note: Table A5.1.5 exports and import totals are slightly higher than figures given in Table A5.1.1 because goods classed as Czech trade with the Czech Republic are included.

Table A5.1.6   Developments in commodity structure of CEFTA trade, 1994–97, exports ($US millions)

	SITC0	SITC1	SITC2	SITC3	SITC4	SITC5	SITC6	SITC7	SITC8	SITC9
1994:value	185.37	59.96	105.89	372.24	21.12	531.98	873.89	828.94	288.73	0.52
% of total	5.8	1.8	3.2	11.4	0.6	16.3	26.7	25.4	8.8	0.0
1995: value	296.19	67.45	140.50	371.51	7.95	649.92	1172.12	1007.65	332.48	0.49
% of total	7.2	1.7	3.5	9.2	0.2	16.1	29.0	24.9	8.2	0.0
1996: Value	289.96	87.16	150.08	393.41	24.50	768.32	1489.48	1353.18	447.96	5.93
% of total	5.8	1.7	3.0	7.9	0.5	15.3	29.7	27.0	8.9	0.1
1997: value	274.24	95.64	135.23	330.44	19.48	700.23	1390.27	1482.60	432.61	4.51
% of total	5.6	2.0	2.8	6.8	0.4	14.4	28.6	30.5	8.0	0.1
Index 1997/94	147.94	159.50	127.71	88.77	92.23	131.63	159.09	178.86	149.83	865.01
Weighted index 1997/94	8.3	3.1	3.6	6.0	0.4	18.9	45.5	54.5	13.3	–

Note: Formula for weighed index is as follows: index 1994/97 × (% of total exports in 1997/ 100).

Table A5.1.7 **Developments in commodity structure of CEFTA trade, 1994–97, imports ($US millions)**

	SITC0	SITC1	SITC2	SITC3	SITC4	SITC5	SITC6	SITC7	SITC8	SITC9
1994:value	174.12	58.88	138.02	237.24	5.63	443.01	939.45	508.32	268.26	0.45
% of total	6.2	2.1	5.0	8.6	0.2	16.0	33.9	18.3	9.7	0.0
1995: value	219.18	47.32	175.40	317.07	9.87	605.20	1274.49	665.18	332.78	0.49
% of total	6.1	1.3	4.8	8.7	0.3	16.6	34.9	18.2	9.1	0.0
1996: Value	246.93	40.60	159.22	366.84	11.05	627.78	1341.68	897.81	382.13	1.18
% of total	6.1	1.0	3.9	9.0	0.3	15.4	32.9	22.0	9.4	0.0
1997: value	256.59	47.69	117.55	379.21	9.30	579.40	1256.75	847.69	331.64	1.29
% of total	6.7	1.2	3.1	9.9	0.2	15.1	32.8	22.1	8.7	0.0
Index 1997/94	147.36	80.99	85.16	159.84	165.23	130.79	133.77	166.76	123.62	286.17
Weighted index 1997/94	9.87	0.89	2.64	15.82	0.33	19.75	43.88	36.85	10.75	–

Note: Formula for weighed index is as follows: index 1994/97 × (% of total exports in 1997/100).

Sources A5.1.1–A5.1.7: own calculations; *CESTAT Statistical Bulletin* (various issues). *The Czech Republic in the International Economy*; Richter (1997).

A5.2   HUNGARY IN CEFTA

Table A5.2.1   Trade with CEFTA countries, 1993–98 ($US millions)

	1993	1994	1995	1996	1997	1998	Index 1998/93 1993 = 100
Czech Republic:							
Export	170.1	197.8	207.4	294.9	321.4	373.1	219.3
Import	266.0	348.7	364.0	491.6	509.6	554.5	208.5
Poland:							
Export	163.4	222.9	337.1	392.3	510	530.1	324.4
Import	149.4	194.4	248.6	289.9	358	459.2	307.4
Slovakia:							
Export	128.1	144.5	212.9	252.9	265.1	332.4	259.5
Import	239.9	357.2	369.7	384.2	400.5	427.4	178.2
Slovenia:							
Export				222.8	290.7	240.6	–
Import				88.1	109.6	139.5	–
Romania:							
Export						562.8	–
Import						185.4	–
Total CEFTA:							
Export	461.6	565.2	757.4	1162.9	1387.2	2039.0	441.7
Import	655.3	900.3	982.3	1253.8	1377.7	1766.0	269.5

A5.2.2.   Ranking of trade partners in CEFTA, 1998

	Exports $US millions	% of total	Imports $US millions	% of total	Balance $US millions
Romania	562.8	27.6	185.4	10.5	377.4
Poland	530.1	26.0	459.2	26.0	70.9
Czech R.	373.1	18.3	554.5	31.4	– 181.4
Slovakia	332.4	16.3	427.4	24.2	– 95.0
Slovenia	240.6	11.8	139.5	7.9	101.1
Total	2039.0	100.0	1766.0	100.0	273.0

Table A5.2.3   Export/import coverage: CEFTA and total trade, 1994–98

	1994	1995	1996	1997	1998
Czech R.	56.7	56.9	60.0	63.1	67.3
Poland	114.7	135.6	135.3	142.5	115.4
Slovakia	40.4	57.6	65.8	66.2	77.7
Slovenia			252.9	265.2	172.5
Romania					303.6
Total CEFTA	62.8	77.1	92.7	100.7	115.5
Total trade	74.2	83.2	86.6	89.9	89.5

Table A5.2.4   CEFTA trade and total trade by commodity groups, 1997 (% of total)

		Imports from CEFTA	Total imports	Ratio of CEFTA imports to total imports	Exports to CEFTA	Total exports	Ratio of CEFTA exports to total exports
SITC0	Food and live animals	4.6	3.8	1.2	23.3	11.6	2.0
SITC1	Beverages and tobacco	0.1	0.5	0.2	1.3	1.4	0.9
SITC2	Crude materials, except fuels	6.3	2.8	2.3	4.8	2.9	1.7
SITC3	Mineral fuels, lubricants, related materials	21.1	9.9	3.1	6.3	2.6	2.4
SITC4	Animal and vegetable oils, fats, waxes	0.3	0.5	0.6	3.0	0.9	3.3
SITC5	Chemicals and related products	13.3	11.4	1.2	20.1	8.6	2.3
SITC6	Manufactured goods, classified chiefly by materials	34.8	19.8	1.8	18.3	13.4	1.4
SITC7	Machinery and transport equipment	14.8	41.4	0.4	16.0	45.2	0.4
SITC8	Miscellaneous manufactured items	4.7	9.9	0.5	6.9	13.4	0.5
SITC9	Others	–	–	–	–	–	–

Table A5.2.5 **Balance of CEFTA trade by commodity groups, 1997**

		Exports $US millions	Imports $US millions	Balance $US millions
SITC0	Food and live animals	323.6	63.1	260.5
SITC1	Beverages and tobacco	17.9	1.3	16.6
SITC2	Crude materials, except fuels	66.3	86.5	− 20.2
SITC3	Mineral fuels, lubricants, related materials	86.8	290.5	− 203.7
SITC4	Animal and vegetable oils, fats, waxes	41.7	3.7	38.0
SITC5	Chemicals and related products	279.4	183.9	95.5
SITC6	Manufactured goods, classified chiefly by materials	253.9	479.1	− 225.2
SITC7	Machinery and transport equipment	221.7	204.4	17.3
SITC8	Miscellaneous manufactured items	95.9	65.2	30.7
SITC9	Others	–	–	–
Total		1387.2	1377.7	9.5

Table A5.2.6   Developments in commodity structure of CEFTA trade, 1994–97, exports ($US millions)

	SITC0	SITC1	SITC2	SITC3	SITC4	SITC5	SITC6	SITC7	SITC8
1994: value	90.56	26.37	36.11	48.65	21.05	138.72	94.49	65.76	43.50
% of total	16.02	4.67	6.39	8.61	3.72	24.54	16.72	11.63	7.70
1995: value	151.90	14.48	42.41	20.87	18.08	199.75	157.92	92.32	59.67
% of total	20.06	1.91	5.60	2.76	2.39	26.37	20.85	12.19	7.88
1996: value	286.03	19.80	65.07	63.83	34.91	246.64	219.61	145.69	81.32
% of total	24.60	1.70	5.60	5.49	3.00	21.21	18.88	12.53	6.99
1997: value	323.60	17.87	66.33	86.78	41.65	279.35	253.96	221.71	95.94
% of total	23.33	1.29	4.78	6.26	3.00	20.14	18.31	15.98	6.92
Index 1997/94	357.34	67.77	183.71	178.38	197.88	201.38	68.78	337.16	220.56
Weighted index 1997/94	83.36	0.87	8.78	11.16	5.94	40.55	49.21	53.89	15.25

Note: Formula for weighed index is as follows: index 1994/97 × (% of total exports in 1997/100).

159

Table A5.2.7   Developments in commodity structure of CEFTA trade, 1994–97, imports ($US millions)

	SITC0	SITC1	SITC2	SITC3	SITC4	SITC5	SITC6	SITC7	SITC8
1994: value	32.91	0.68	102.68	250.33	5.32	111.29	250.84	117.04	29.24
% of total	3.65	0.08	11.41	27.80	0.59	12.36	27.86	13.00	3.25
1995: value	30.43	0.15	105.22	217.96	0.87	136.57	337.46	116.61	37.04
% of total	3.10	0.02	10.71	22.19	0.09	13.90	34.35	11.87	3.77
1996: value	29.29	0.69	87.28	366.88	0.47	168.30	399.43	148.84	52.60
% of total	2.34	0.06	6.96	29.26	0.04	13.42	31.86	11.87	4.20
1997: value	63.05	1.32	86.53	290.46	3.70	183.85	479.14	204.42	65.23
% of total	4.58	0.10	6.28	21.08	0.27	13.34	34.78	14.84	4.73
Index 1997/94	191.60	195.54	84.27	116.03	69.58	165.20	191.02	174.66	223.06
Weighted index 1997/94	8.77	0.19	5.29	24.46	0.19	22.04	66.43	25.92	10.56

Note: Formula for weighed index is as follows: index 1994/97 × (% of total imports in 1997/100).

Sources A5.2.1–A5.2.7: own calculations; CESTAT Statistical Bulletin (various issues); Statistical Yearbook of Hungary, 1994, 1995, 1996, 1997; Richter (1997).

A5.3   POLAND IN CEFTA

Table A5.3.1   Trade with CEFTA countries, 1993–98 ($US millions)

	1993	1994	1995	1996	1997	1998	Index 1998/93 1993 = 100
Czech Republic:							
Export	341.4	456.1	698.2	847.4	912.2	1023.1	299.7
Import	350.4	501.7	891.7	1150.5	1318.8	1463.2	417.6
Hungary:							
Export	174.5	183.6	267.3	310.2	383.0	470.0	269.3
Import	168.7	220.6	352.3	426.0	572.6	591.8	350.8
Slovakia:							
Export	164.5	183.3	279.4	280.0	314.0	336.3	204.4
Import	163.1	196.2	380	432.5	519.3	588.8	361.0
Slovenia:							
Export				43.2	49.5	73.0	–
Import				151.5	174.3	199.3	–
Romania:							
Export						123.6	–
Import						130.9	–
Total CEFTA:							
Export	680.4	823.0	1244.9	1480.8	1658.7	2026.0	297.8
Import	682.2	918.5	1624.0	2160.5	2585.0	2974.0	435.9

Table A5.3.2   Ranking of trade partners in CEFTA, 1998

	Exports $US millions	% of Total	Imports $US millions	% of Total	Balance $US millions
Czech R.	1023.1	50.5	1463.2	49.2	– 440.1
Hungary	470.0	23.2	591.8	19.9	– 121.8
Slovakia	336.3	16.6	588.8	19.8	– 252.5
Romania	123.6	6.1	130.9	4.4	– 7.3
Slovenia	73.0	3.6	199.3	6.7	– 126.3
Total	2026.0	100.0	2974.0	100.0	– 948.0

Table A5.3.3   Export/import coverage: CEFTA and total trade, 1994–98

	1994	1995	1996	1997	1998
Czech Republic	90.9	78.3	73.7	69.2	69.9
Hungary	83.2	75.9	72.8	66.9	79.4
Slovakia	93.4	73.5	64.7	60.5	57.1
Slovenia			28.5	28.4	36.6
Romania					94.4
Total CEFTA	89.6	76.7	68.5	64.2	68.1
Total Trade	79.9	78.8	65.8	60.9	60.0

Table A5.3.4   CEFTA trade and total trade by commodity groups, 1997 (% of total)

		Imports from CEFTA	Total imports	Ratio of CEFTA imports to total imports	Exports to CEFTA	Total exports	Ratio of CEFTA exports to total exports
SITC0+1	Food and live animals, beverages, tobacco	8.2	7.6	1.1	8.8	12.2	0.7
SITC2	Crude materials, except fuels	3.3	4.2	0.8	3.6	3.2	1.1
SITC3	Mineral fuels, lubricants, related materials	4.5	8.8	0.5	15.6	6.7	2.3
SITC4	Animal and vegetable oils, fats, waxes	1.3	0.6	2.2	0.1	0.2	0.4
SITC5	Chemicals and related products	22.5	13.8	1.6	13.8	7.8	1.8
SITC6	Manufactured goods, classified chiefly by materials	29.9	19.6	1.5	30.4	26.5	1.2
SITC7	Machinery and transport equipment	23.9	36.0	0.7	17.7	21.6	0.8
SITC8+9	Miscellaneous manufactured items, others	6.4	9.6	0.7	10.1	21.8	0.5

Table A5.3.5   Balance of CEFTA trade by commodity groups, 1997 ($US millions)

		Exports $US millions	Imports $US millions	Balance $US millions
SITC0	Food and live animals	145.5	200.0	− 54.5
SITC1	Beverages and tobacco	0.8	13.0	− 12.2
SITC2	Crude materials, except fuels	58.6	85.0	− 26.4
SITC3	Mineral fuels, lubricants, related materials	258.3	115.5	142.8
SITC4	Animal and vegetable oils, fats, waxes	1.2	32.6	− 31.4
SITC5	Chemicals and related products	229.5	581.9	− 352.4
SITC6	Manufactured goods, classified chiefly by materials	504.2	773.0	− 268.8
SITC7	Machinery and transport equipment	293.9	619.1	− 325.2
SITC8	Miscellaneous manufactured items	166.8	165.0	1.8
Total		1658.7	2585.0	− 926.3

Table A5.3.6 Developments in commodity structure of CEFTA trade, 1994–97, exports ($US millions)

	SITC0	SITC1	SITC2	SITC3	SITC4	SITC5	SITC6	SITC7	SITC8	SITC9
1994: value	47.81	1.4	60.72	190.6	0.05	113.86	215.5	126.18	66.88	0.16
% of total	5.81	0.17	7.38	23.16	0.00	13.83	26.18	15.33	8.13	0.02
1995: value	67.68	0.47	72.37	254.66	0.98	166.43	378.24	198.05	106.02	–
% of total	5.44	0.04	5.81	20.46	0.08	13.37	30.38	15.91	8.52	–
1996: value	74.33	2.37	78.02	278.72	1.31	281.18	423.71	268.24	149.79	0.36
% of total	4.77	0.15	5.01	17.89	0.08	18.05	27.20	17.22	9.61	0.02
1997: value	145.53	0.81	58.61	258.25	1.12	229.48	504.19	293.89	166.84	–
% of total	8.77	0.05	3.53	15.57	0.07	13.83	30.39	17.71	10.06	–
Index 1997/94	304.39	57.86	96.53	135.49	2240.00	201.55	233.96	232.91	249.46	–
Weighted index 1997/94	26.70	0.00	3.40	21.10	1.50	27.90	71.10	41.30	25.10	–

Note: Formula for weighed index is as follows: index 1994/97 × (% of total exports in 1997/100).

164

Table A5.3.7 *Developments in commodity structure of CEFTA trade, 1994–9, imports ($US millions)*

	SITC0	SITC1	SITC2	SITC3	SITC4	SITC5	SITC6	SITC7	SITC8	SITC9
1994: value	57.53	5.92	46.54	45.50	16.75	268.63	258.81	151.18	67.65	0.05
% of total	6.26	0.64	5.07	4.95	1.82	29.24	28.18	16.46	7.36	–
1995: value	200.01	8.57	64.85	112.87	20.18	405.62	460.55	260.06	92.04	–
% of total	12.31	0.53	3.99	6.95	1.24	24.97	28.35	16.01	5.66	–
1996: value	166.04	12.38	80.96	110.74	32.84	481.82	637.02	419.07	142.13	–
% of total	7.97	0.59	3.89	5.32	1.58	23.13	30.58	20.12	6.82	–
1997: value	199.98	12.95	84.96	115.45	32.62	581.87	772.99	619.13	165.02	–
% of total	7.74	0.50	3.29	4.47	1.26	22.51	29.90	23.95	6.38	–
Index 1997/94	347.61	218.75	182.55	253.74	194.75	216.61	298.67	409.53	243.93	–
Weighted index 1997/94	26.9	1.09	6.0	11.34	2.45	48.76	89.3	98.1	15.6	–

Note: Formula for weighed index is as follows: index 1994/97 × (% of total imports in 1997/100).

Sources A5.3.1–A5.3.7: own calculations; *CESTAT Statistical Bulletin* (various issues); *Yearbook of Foreign Trade Statistics*, Warsaw, Central Statistical Office, 1995, 1996, 1997, 1998; Richter (1997).

A5.4   ROMANIA IN CEFTA

A5.4.1 Trade with CEFTA countries, 1993–98 ($US millions)

	1994	1995	1996	1997	1998	Index 1998/93 1993 = 100	Index 1996/96 1996 = 100
Czech Republic:							
Export	75.7	21.0	17.6	17.3	12.6	131.3	74.6
Import	50.2	61.8	82.3	104.7	194.5	540.3	236.3
Hungary:							
Export	161.4	174.4	171.5	182.6	219.2	187.4	127.8
Import	167.2	315.0	288.8	346.4	547.0	326.2	189.4
Poland:							
Export	14.0	39.1	52.9	101.0	82.3	407.4	155.6
Import	29.8	57.1	85.6	90.4	145.6	439.9	170.1
Slovakia:							
Export	7.5	16.1	30.0	24.6	21.4	369.0	71.3
Import	31.8	48.6	59.1	72.2	107.1	459.7	181.2
Slovenia:							
Export	17.3	22.0	21.6	16.3	33.5	281.5	155.1
Import	12.6	11.8	25.1	27.9	45.8	462.6	182.5
Total CEFTA:							
Export	258.6	250.6	293.6	341.8	369.0	241.8	125.7
Import	279.0	482.5	540.9	641.6	1040.0	399.8	192.3

Notes:
Free trade area between Romania and Slovakia signed on 11 November 1994 and between Romania and the Czech Republic on 24 October 1994.
Total CEFTA for 1993, 1994, 1995 = Czech Republic, Hungary and Poland.
Total CEFTA since 1996 = Czech Republic, Hungary, Poland and Slovenia.

A5.4.2   Ranking of trade partners in CEFTA, 1998

	Exports $US millions	% of total	Imports $US millions	% of total	Balance $US millions
Hungary	219.2	59.4	547.0	52.6	−327.8
Poland	82.3	22.3	145.6	14.0	−63.3
Slovenia	33.5	9.1	45.8	4.4	−12.3
Slovakia	21.4	5.8	107.1	10.3	−85.7
Czech R.	12.6	3.4	194.5	18.7	−181.9
Total	369.0	100.0	1040.0	100.0	−671.0

Table A5.4.3   **Export/import coverage: CEFTA and total trade 1994–98**

	1994	1995	1996	1997	1998
Czech Republic	150.8	34.0	21.4	16.5	6.5
Hungary	96.5	55.4	59.4	52.7	40.1
Poland	47.0	68.5	61.8	111.7	56.5
Slovakia	23.6	33.1	50.8	34.0	20.0
Slovenia	137.3	186.4	86.1	58.4	73.1
Total CEFTA	92.7	51.9	54.3	53.3	35.5
Total trade			70.7	74.7	70.2

Sources Tables A5.4.1–A5.4.3: own calculations; *CESTAT Statistical Bulletin*, 98/4; data supplied by Ministry of Industry and Trade of Romania.

A5.5   SLOVAKIA IN CEFTA

Table A5.5.1   **Trade with CEFTA countries, 1993–98 ($US millions)**

	1993	1994	1995	1996	1997	1998	Index 1998/93 1993 = 100
Czech Republic:							
Export	2310	2502	3011	2738	2358	2164	93.7
Import	2275	1958	2333	2682	2352	2390	105.1
Hungary:							
Export	247	366	390	403	414	469	189.9
Import	85	111	189	217	225	317	372.9
Poland:							
Export	159	189	377	427	487	584	367.3
Import	123	157	235	270	285	324	263.4
Slovenia:							
Export			95	88	98	88	
Import			48	56	53	78	
Romania:							
Export					62	92	
Import					16	13	
Total CEFTA:							
Export	2716	3057	3778	3656	3357	3397	125.1
Import	2483	2226	2757	3225	2915	3122	125.7
Excluding Czech Republic:							
Export	406	555	767	918	999	1233	303.7
Import	208	268	424	543	563	732	351.9

Table A5.5.2   **Ranking of trade partners in CEFTA, 1998**

	Exports $US millions	% of total	Imports $US millions	% of total	Balance $US millions
Czech R.	2164	63.7	2390	76.6	−226
Poland	584	17.2	324	10.4	260
Hungary	469	13.8	317	10.1	152
Romania	92	2.7	13	0.4	79
Slovenia	88	2.6	78	2.5	10
Total	3397	100.0	3122	100.0	275

Table A5.5.3 **Export/import coverage: CEFTA and total trade 1994–98**

	1994	1995	1996	1997	1998
Czech Republic	127.8	129.1	102.1	100.3	90.5
Hungary	329.7	206.4	185.7	184.0	147.9
Poland	120.4	160.4	158.2	170.9	180.2
Slovenia			157.1	184.9	112.8
Romania					707.7
Total CEFTA	137.3	137.0	113.4	115.2	108.8
Total trade	101.2	98.4	79.4	80.4	82.3

A5.5.4 **CEFTA trade and total trade by commodity groups, 1997 (% of total)**

		Imports from CEFTA	Total imports	Ratio of CEFTA imports to total imports	Exports to CEFTA	Total exports	Ratio of CEFTA exports to total exports
SITC0	Food and live animals	7.6	6.3	1.2	4.3	3.7	1.2
SITC1	Beverages and tobacco	3.0	1.2	2.5	1.3	0.7	1.9
SITC2	Crude materials, except fuels	2.4	4.6	0.5	5.0	4.5	1.1
SITC3	Mineral fuels, lubricants, related materials	9.3	17.8	0.5	10.1	5.0	2.0
SITC4	Animal and vegetable oils, fats, waxes	0.3	0.2	1.5	0.3	0.2	1.5
SITC5	Chemicals and related products	14.0	12.3	1.1	15.8	11.4	1.4
SITC6	Manufactured goods, classified chiefly by materials	25.8	15.1	1.7	36.3	34.7	1.0
SITC7	Machinery and transport equipment	27.8	33.6	0.8	19.8	27.5	0.7
SITC8	Miscellaneous manufactured items	9.8	8.9	1.1	7.1	12.1	0.6
SITC9	Others	0.0	0.0	0.0	0.0	0.1	–

Table A5.5.5   Balance of CEFTA trade by commodity groups, 1997

		Exports $US millions	Imports $US millions	Balance $US millions
SITC0	Food and live animals	144.9	224.4	− 79.5
SITC1	Beverages and tobacco	45.0	89.7	− 44.7
SITC2	Crude materials, except fuels	167.0	69.3	97.7
SITC3	Mineral fuels, lubricants, related materials	339.5	272.2	67.3
SITC4	Animal and vegetable oils, fats, waxes	8.5	9.6	− 1.1
SITC5	Chemicals and related products	532.3	412.1	120.2
SITC6	Manufactured goods, classified chiefly by materials	1218.3	758.4	459.9
SITC7	Machinery and transport equipment	666.6	816.5	− 149.9
SITC8	Miscellaneous manufactured items	237.8	287.3	− 49.5
SITC9	Others	0.9	2.2	− 1.3
Total		3360.8	2941.7	419.1

Note: Table A5.5.5 export and import totals are slightly higher than figures given in Table A5.1 because goods classed as Slovak trade with Slovakia are included.

Table A5.5.6 Developments in commodity structure of CEFTA trade, 1994–97, exports ($US millions)

	SITC0	SITC1	SITC2	SITC3	SITC4	SITC5	SITC6	SITC7	SITC8	SITC9
1994: value	171.58	43.73	188.77	235.34	4.44	487.47	632.53	583.17	266.35	2.15
% of total	6.56	1.67	7.22	9.00	0.17	18.63	24.18	22.29	10.18	0.08
1995: value	231.91	46.01	220.65	280.85	6.71	632.06	1424.18	676.06	298.95	0.61
% of total	6.07	1.20	5.78	7.36	0.18	16.55	37.30	17.71	7.83	0.02
1996: value	176.47	36.63	203.13	328.31	9.14	592.89	1380.82	687.98	313.97	1.45
% of total	4.73	0.98	5.44	8.80	0.24	15.89	37.01	18.44	8.42	0.04
1997: value	144.88	45.02	166.97	339.46	8.45	532.28	1218.31	666.61	237.82	0.93
% of total	4.23	1.32	4.88	9.92	0.25	15.55	35.59	19.47	6.95	0.03
Index 1997/94	84.44	102.95	88.45	144.24	190.28	109.19	192.61	114.31	89.29	43.17
Weighted index 1997/94	3.60	1.40	4.40	14.60	0.50	17.30	69.80	22.70	6.30	–

Note: Formula for weighed index is as follows: Index 1994/97 × (% of total exports in 1997/100).

Table A5.5.7 *Developments in commodity structure of CEFTA trade, 1994–97, imports ($US millions)*

	SITC0	SITC1	SITC2	SITC3	SITC4	SITC5	SITC6	SITC7	SITC8	SITC9
1994: value	156.16	58.98	78.52	252.09	12.41	333.54	645.59	488.02	196.32	5.19
% of total	7.01	2.65	3.53	11.32	0.56	14.98	28.99	21.91	8.82	0.23
1995: value	220.16	67.24	102.93	311.04	8.23	418.03	856.55	644.57	229.77	0.63
% of total	7.70	2.35	3.60	10.88	0.29	14.62	29.96	22.55	8.04	0.02
1996: value	239.68	87.19	91.63	309.09	8.88	467.49	908.32	843.52	288.85	2.90
% of total	7.38	2.68	2.82	9.52	0.27	14.39	27.97	25.97	8.89	0.09
1997: value	224.44	89.72	69.29	271.23	9.57	412.05	758.38	816.47	287.28	2.16
% of total	7.59	3.04	2.34	9.18	0.32	13.94	25.66	27.62	9.72	0.07
Index 1997/94	143.73	152.14	88.24	107.59	77.16	123.54	117.47	167.30	146.33	41.72
Weighted index 1997/94	10.9	4.60	2.10	9.90	0.20	17.20	30.10	46.20	14.20	–

Note: Formula for weighed index is as follows: index 1994/97 × (% of total imports in 1997/100).

Sources A5.5.1–A5.5.7: own calculations; data supplied by Slovak Ministry of Economy; data supplied by Slovak Statistical Office; *CESTAT Statistical Bulletin* (various issues).

172

A5.6 SLOVENIA IN CEFTA

Table A5.6.1 Trade with CEFTA countries, 1993–98 ($US millions)

	1993	1994	1995	1996	1997	1998	Index 1998/93 1993 = 100	Index 1998/95 1995 = 100
Czech Republic:								
Export	48.4	82.5	132.0	146.6	147.4	149.9	309.7	113.6
Import	104.6	177.8	246.9	236.6	233.9	263.9	252.3	106.9
Hungary:								
Export	77.0	98.7	114.6	105.4	120.5	141.1	183.2	123.1
Import	151.3	192.6	266.8	238.6	292.9	243.6	161.0	91.3
Poland:								
Export	84.5	96.3	104.9	141.5	155.5	181.2	214.4	172.7
Import	13.4	22.5	37.7	48.4	58.3	78.3	584.3	207.7
Slovakia:								
Export	26.1	30.3	51.7	57.2	56.4	72.9	279.3	141.0
Import	26.5	58.1	82.3	92.2	103.3	89.9	339.2	109.2
Romania:								
Export						42.9		
Import						48.6		
Total CEFTA:								
Export	236.0	307.8	403.2	450.7	479.8	588.0	249.2	145.8
Import	295.8	451.0	633.7	615.8	688.4	724.3	245.1	114.4

Note: Prior to joining CEFTA in 1996 free trade agreements between Slovenia and individual CEFTA members had already been signed as follows: Hungary (6/4/94), the Czech Republic (4/12/93), Slovakia (22/12/93), Poland (17/7/95).

Table A5.6.2 Ranking of trade partners in CEFTA, 1998

	Exports $US millions	% of total	Imports $US millions	% of total	Balance $US millions
Poland	181.2	30.8	78.3	10.8	102.9
Czech R.	149.9	25.5	263.9	36.5	− 114.0
Hungary	141.1	24.0	243.6	33.6	− 102.5
Slovakia	72.9	12.4	89.9	12.4	− 17.0
Romania	42.9	7.3	48.6	6.7	− 5.7
Total	588.0	100.0	724.3	100.0	− 136.3

Table A5.6.3   Export/import coverage: CEFTA and total trade, 1994–98

	1994	1995	1996	1997	1998
Czech Republic	46.40	53.46	61.96	63.02	56.80
Hungary	51.25	42.95	44.17	41.14	57.90
Poland	428.00	278.25	292.36	266.72	231.40
Slovakia	52.20	62.80	62.04	54.60	81.10
Romania					88.3
Total CEFTA	68.30	63.60	73.20	69.70	81.20
Total trade	93.50	87.60	88.20	89.40	89.60

Table A5.6.4   CEFTA trade and total trade by commodity groups, 1997 (% of total)

		Imports from CEFTA	Total imports	Ratio of CEFTA imports to total imports	Exports to CEFTA	Total exports	Ratio of CEFTA exports to total exports
SITC0+1	Food and live animals, beverages, tobacco	15.8	7.0	2.3	1.6	3.7	0.4
SITC2	Crude materials, except fuels	7.9	5.2	1.5	0.8	2.0	0.4
SITC3	Mineral fuels, lubricants, related materials	12.4	8.3	1.5	2.0	1.2	1.7
SITC4	Animal and vegetable oils, fats, waxes	2.2	0.4	5.4	0.4	0.2	1.9
SITC5	Chemicals and related products	10.8	12.1	0.9	39.2	11.3	3.5
SITC6	Manufactured goods, classified chiefly by materials	33.7	20.5	1.6	30.9	27.1	1.1
SITC7	Machinery and transport equipment	11.7	33.1	0.4	16.9	33.6	0.5
SITC8+9	Miscellaneous manufactured items, others	6.3	13.3	0.5	8.2	20.9	0.4

A5.6.5   Balance of CEFTA trade by commodity groups, 1997

		Exports $US millions	Imports $US millions	Balance $US millions
SITC0	Food and live animals	5.9	103.4	97.5
SITC1	Beverages and tobacco	1.9	0.5	1.4
SITC2	Crude materials, except fuels	3.9	54.5	– 50.6
SITC3	Mineral fuels, lubricants, related materials	9.7	85.6	– 75.9
SITC4	Animal and vegetable oils, fats, waxes	1.8	14.8	– 13.0
SITC5	Chemicals and related products	188.0	74.6	113.4
SITC6	Manufactured goods, classified chiefly by materials	148.0	231.7	– 83.7
SITC7	Machinery and transport equipment	81.2	80.5	0.7
SITC8	Miscellaneous manufactured items	39.4	42.2	– 2.8
SITC9	Others	0.0	0.8	– 0.8
Total		479.7	688.5	– 208.8

Table A5.6.6 Developments in commodity structure of CEFTA trade, 1994–97, exports ($US millions)

	SITC0	SITC1	SITC2	SITC3	SITC4	SITC5	SITC6	SITC7	SITC8	SITC9
1994: value	6.24	2.21	4.31	4.92	0.00	128.39	71.13	63.97	21.95	4.81
% of total	2.03	0.72	1.40	1.60	0.00	41.71	23.11	20.78	7.13	1.56
1995: value	10.03	1.88	6.67	1.96	0.01	152.10	110.07	81.20	32.23	7.05
% of total	2.49	0.47	1.65	0.49	0.00	37.73	27.30	20.14	7.99	1.75
1996: value	7.85	1.71	2.79	7.01	0.00	177.66	133.81	83.60	36.27	0.00
% of total	1.74	0.38	0.62	1.560	39.42	29.69	18.55	8.05	0.00	0.00
1997: value	5.91	1.88	3.90	9.67	1.83	188.00	148.00	81.15	39.38	0.00
% of total	1.23	0.39	0.81	2.02	0.38	39.19	30.85	16.92	8.21	0.00
Index 1997/94	94.74	84.84	90.55	196.63	–	146.43	208.06	126.85	179.39	
Weighted index 1997/94	1.17	0.33	0.73	3.97	–	57.39	64.19	21.46	14.73	

Note: Formula for weighed index is as follows: index 1994/97 × (% of total exports in 1997/100).

Table A5.6.7 Developments in commodity structure of CEFTA trade, 1994–97, imports ($US millions)

	SITC0	SITC1	SITC2	SITC3	SITC4	SITC5	SITC6	SITC7	SITC8	SITC9
1994: value	65.44	0.50	63.00	39.49	15.08	49.75	147.70	59.23	10.56	0.90
% of total	14.51	0.11	13.97	8.76	3.34	11.03	32.76	13.14	2.34	0.20
1995: value	100.14	0.66	84.16	48.74	15.64	74.71	219.60	66.58	22.90	0.57
% of total	15.80	0.10	13.28	7.69	2.47	11.79	34.65	10.51	3.61	0.09
1996: value	91.65	0.47	46.16	53.11	18.12	70.37	222.50	79.10	33.57	0.82
% of total	14.88	0.08	7.49	8.62	2.94	11.43	36.13	12.84	5.45	0.13
1997: value	103.36	0.51	54.45	85.56	14.81	74.61	231.66	80.49	42.23	0.83
% of total	15.01	0.07	7.91	12.43	2.15	10.84	33.65	11.69	6.13	0.12
Index 1997/94	157.95	103.64	86.43	216.66	98.25	149.95	156.85	135.90	400.07	92.32
Weighted index 1997/94	23.71	0.07	6.84	26.93	2.11	16.25	52.78	15.89	24.52	0.11

Note: Formula for weighed index is as follows: index 1994/97 × (% of total imports in 1997/100).

Sources A5.6.1–A5.6.7: own calculations; data supplied by Slovenian Statistical Office; CESTAT Statistical Bulletin (various issues).

Bibliography

Additional Protocol to the Central European Free Trade Agreement Concerning the Amendments to the Protocols 1 to 6, Budapest, 29 April 1994.

Additional Protocol No. 2 to the Central European Free Trade Agreement, Warsaw, 18 August 1995.

Additional Protocol No. 3 to the Central European Free Trade Agreement, Warsaw, 21 December 1995.

Additional Protocol No. 4 to the Central European Free Trade Agreement, Jasna, 13 September 1996.

Additional Protocol No. 5 to the Central European Free Trade Agreement, Jasna, 13 September 1996.

Additional Protocol No. 6 to the Central European Free Trade Agreement, Warsaw, 19 December 1997.

Agreement Amending the Central European Free Trade Agreement, Brno, 11 September 1995.

Agreement Establishing the Customs Union between the Czech Republic and the Slovak Republic, Prague, 29 October 1992.

Agreement on Accession of the Republic of Bulgaria to the Central European Free Trade Agreement, Sofia, 17 July 1998.

Agreement on Accession of Romania to the Central European Free Trade Agreement, Bucharest, 12 April 1997.

Agreement on Accession of the Republic of Slovenia to the Central European Free Trade Agreement, Ljubljana, 25 November 1995.

Agreement Establishing the Customs Union between the Czech Republic and the Slovak Republic, Prague, 29 October 1992.

Avery, G. and Cameron, F. (1998), *The Enlargement of the European Union*, Sheffield: UACES/Sheffield Academic Press.

Bailes, A. (1997), 'Sub-regional organisations: the Cinderellas of European security', *NATO Review*, **45** (2) (March), 27–31 (via: http://www.mfa.ee/nato/docu/review/articles/9702-8.htm).

Bakos, G. (1993), 'After COMECON: a free trade area in Central Europe?, *Europe–Asia Studies*, **45** (6), 1025-1044.

Balazs, P. (1997), 'Globalisation: Symptoms and Consequences,' in M. Mareaceau (ed.), *Enlarging the European Union: Relations Between the EU and Central and Eastern Europe*, New York: Addison Wesley Longman.

Baldwin, R. (1994), *Towards An Integrated Europe*, London: Centre for Economic Policy Research.

Banka International, (1997b), *Trade Burden*, (via: http://www.banka-mzb.tel.hr/banka-mzb/97-07/1lets.html)

Banka International, (1997b), *Optimism Without Caution*, (via: http://www.banka-mzb.tel.hr/banka-mzb/97-07/2optim.html)

BBC, *Summary of World Broadcasts*, London: BBC Monitoring.

Bobek, V., Potocnik, J., Ravbar, V., Rocek, M., Stanovnik, P., Stiblar, F., (1996), *The Strategy of International Economic Relations of Slovenia*, Ljubljana: Ministry of Economic Relations and Economic Development of the Republic of Slovenia.

Brabant, J. van (1980), *Socialist Economic Integration – Aspects of Contemporary Economic Problems in Eastern Europe*, New York: Cambridge University Press.

Brabant, J. van (1989), *Economic Integration in Eastern Europe: A Handbook*, Hemel Hempstead: Harvester Wheatsheaf.

Brabant, J. van (1991), 'Renewal of cooperation and economic transition in Eastern Europe', *Studies in Comparative Communism* **XXIV**, (2), 151–172.

Brabant, J. van (1998), 'Eastern Europe and the World Trade Organisation: The Present Position and Prospects of Accession', in I. Zloch-Christy (ed.), *Eastern Europe in the Global Economy*, Cheltenham: Edward Elgar.

Bremner, I. and Bailes, A. (1998), 'Sub-regionalism in the newly independent states', *International Affairs*, **74** (1), 131–148.

Brinar, I. (1999), 'Slovenia: From Yugoslavia to EU', in K. Henderson (ed.), *Back to Europe*, London: UCL Press.

Bulletins of the Ministry of Economic Relations and Development, Republic of Slovenia.

Business Central Europe, various issues.

CEFTA Joint Committee (1998), *Results and Experiences of the First Five Years of CEFTA* (copy of text supplied by Ministry of Trade and Industry of Romania).

Central European Business Weekly (formerly Prague Business Week), various issues.

Central European Express, various issues.

Central European Free Trade Agreement, Krakow, 21 December 1992 (abbreviated to CEFTA in the text for referencing purposes).

CESTAT Statistical Bulletin.

Cottey, A. (1996), *Multi-layered Integration: The Sub-regional Dimension*, Summary of an Inter-Governmental Conference, Bucharest 7–8 October 1996, Warsaw: Institute for EastWest Studies.

Cottey, A. (ed.) (1999), *Subregional Cooperation in the New Europe. Building Security, Prosperity and Solidarity from the Barents to the Black Sea*, Basingstoke: Macmillan.

Croatian Investment Promotion Agency (1998), 'Croatian Diplomacy – the Economic Aspects of its Work: Interview with Mate Granic, Minister of Foreign Affairs', CIPA Communication, 12, June (via: http://www.tel.hr/hapu/newsletters/no_12/interview.htm).

Csaba, L. (1992), 'How to Survive Reorientation and Liberalisation: The Example of Hungary', in J. Flemming and J. Rollo (eds.), *Trade, Payments and Adjustments in Central and Eastern Europe*, London: RIIA/EBRD.

CzechTrade (formerly Centre For Foreign Economic Relations), *The Czech Republic in the International Economy*, Prague: CzechTrade, (various issues).

Dabrowski, P. (1991a), 'East European Trade (Part I): The loss of the Soviet Market', *Report on Eastern Europe*, Radio Free Europe/Radio Liberty, 4 October, 28–37.

Dabrowski, P. (1991b), 'East European Trade (Part II): Creative Solutions by the Former Eastern Bloc', *Report on Eastern Europe*, Radio Free Europe/Radio Liberty, 11 October, 28-36.

Dabrowski, P. (1991c), 'East European Trade (Part III): Getting the West Involved', *Report on Eastern Europe*, Radio Free Europe/Radio Liberty, 18 October, 30-37.

Dangerfield, M. (1997), 'The Central European Free Trade Agreement (CEFTA): A Free Trade Area That Is Not?', Seminar Programme of Russian and East European Research Centre, University of Wolverhampton, 7 May, mimeo, University of Wolverhampton, School of Humanities, Languages and Social Sciences.

Dangerfield, M. (1998a), 'Bulgaria's Accession to the Central European Free Trade Agreement (CEFTA): Alternative or Complement to European Union Membership?', in M. Dangerfield, G. Hambrook and L. Kostova (eds), *Europe: Real and Imagined,* Proceedings of Second International Contemporary European Studies Conference held in Varna, 3–5 June 1997, Veliko Turnovo: PIC.

Dangerfield, M. (1998b), 'The Central European Free Trade Agreement (CEFTA): Towards and Beyond the Eastward Enlargement of the European Union', paper presented at the 3rd EPRC/ISA Conference, Vienna, 16–19 September 1998, mimeo, University of Wolverhampton, School of Humanities, Languages and Social Sciences.

Dangerfield, M. (1999a), 'Croatia and the Central European Free Trade Agreement (CEFTA): Road to the European Union or Dead End?', in S. Goic (ed.), *Enterprise in Transition* (proceedings of the 3rd International Conference on Enterprise in Transition, Split, 22–27 May 1999), Split, Faculty of Economics of University of Split.

Dangerfield, M. (1999b), 'Sub-regional Cooperation in CEFTA: Past Performance and Future Prospects', in M. Stepanek (ed.), *The Role of CEFTA in the Process of EU Enlargement,* (proceedings of the International Conference, 28–29 May 1999, Prague), Prague, Institute of International Relations/Association for the Study of International Relations.

Dangerfield, M. (1999c), 'Integrating the New Europe: What Role (If Any) Does The Central European Free Trade Agreement (CEFTA) Have?', paper presented at the conference *Beyond Boundaries II: New Europe ... Pan Europe? Trajectories and Destinations,* University of Salford, 19–21 February 1999, mimeo, University of Wolverhampton, School of Humanities, Languages and Social Sciences.

Danyleiko, O. (1999), 'Ukraine and European Integration Processes' in M. Stepanek (ed.), *The Role of CEFTA in the Process of EU Enlargement,* (proceedings of the International Conference, 28–29 May 1999, Prague), Prague, Institute of International Relations/Association for the Study of International Relations.

Declaration of Cracow, 6 October 1991 (copy of text supplied by Czech Ministry of Foreign Affairs).

Declaration of Prague, 6 May 1992 (copy of text supplied by Czech Ministry of Foreign Affairs).

Declaration of the Prime Ministers of the CEFTA Countries, Prague, 11–12 September 1998 (copy of text supplied by Slovak Ministry of Economy).

Declaration of the Prime Ministers of the CEFTA Countries, Budapest, 19–20 October 1999 (copy of text supplied by Slovak Ministry of Economy).

Deutsches Institut für Wirtschaftsforschung (1998), *Wirtschaftslage und Reformprozesse in Mittel-und Osteuropa,* Sammelband 1998.

Drabek, Z. (1992), 'Convertibility or a Payments Union? – Convertibility', in J. Flemming and J. Rollo (eds), *Trade, Payments and Adjustments in Central and Eastern Europe,* London: RIIA/EBRD.

Dunay, P. (1997), 'Hungarian–Romanian Relations: A New Paradigm?', in M. Wohfeld (ed.), *The Effects on Enlargement on Bilateral Relations in Central and Eastern Europe,* Chaillot Papers, 26, June.

Dunay, P. (1998), 'Regional Cooperation: Much Ado About Nothing?', paper presented to the 3rd EPRC/ISA Conference, Vienna, 16–19 September 1998, mimeo, Geneva Centre for Security Policy.

Eatwell, J., Ellman, M., Karlsson, M., Nuti, M. and Shapiro, J. (1997), *Not Just Another Accession,* London: Institute for Public Policy Research.

El-Agraa, Ali M. (1998), *The European Union,* Hemel Hempstead: Prentice Hall.

Elteto, A. and Sass, M. (1998), 'Motivations and Behaviour by Hungary's Foreign Investors in Relation to Exports', Working Paper of the Institute for World Economics, Budapest, Hungarian Academy of Sciences, No. 88, January.

European Bank for Reconstruction and Development, *Transition Report*, London, EBRD, 1994, 1995, 1996, 1997, 1998.

Faini, R. and Portes, R. (1995), 'Opportunities Outweigh Adjustment', in R. Faini and R. Portes (eds), *European Union Trade with Eastern Europe. Adjustment and Opportunities*, London: Centre for Economic Policy Research.

Financial Times, various issues.

Flemming, J. and Rollo, J. (eds) (1992), *Trade, Payments and Adjustments in Central and Eastern Europe*, London: RIIA/EBRD.

Gower, J. (1999), 'EU Policy to Central and Eastern Europe', in K. Henderson (ed.), *Back to Europe*, London: UCL Press.

Grabbe, H. and Hughes, K. (1997), *Eastward Enlargement of the European Union*, London: RIIA.

Grela, M. (1997), 'CEFTA and Pan-European Political and Economic Cooperation', in H. Machowski (ed.), *The Further Development of CEFTA: Institutionalisation, Deepening, Widening?*, Warsaw: Friedrich Ebert Foundation.

Handl, V. (1999), 'CEFTA – More Than Merely Free Trade?', draft paper for the conference *Beyond Westpolitik – East European Foreign Policies in Transition*, Essen, 1–2 March 1999, mimeo, University of Birmingham, Institute for German Studies.

Henys, O. (1974), 'The Council for Mutual Economic Assistance established twenty five years ago', *Soviet and East European Foreign Trade*, Summer, 3–16.

Hitiris, T. (1998), *European Union Economics*, London: Prentice Hall Europe.

Hurrell, A. (1995), 'Explaining the resurgence of regionalism in world politics', *Review of International Studies*, 21, 331–358.

Inotai, A. (1997a), 'Impacts of the European Union on Regional Cooperation in CEFTA', in H. Machowski (ed.), *The Further Development of CEFTA: Institutionalisation, Deepening, Widening?*, Warsaw: Friedrich Ebert Foundation.

Inotai, A. (1997b), 'Correlations Between European Integration and Sub-regional Cooperation. Theoretical Background, Experience and Policy Impacts', Working Paper No. 87 of the Institute for World Economics, Budapest, Hungarian Academy of Sciences, September.

Kaczurba, J. (1997), 'The Impact of CEFTA', in H. Machowski (ed.), *The Further Development of CEFTA: Institutionalisation, Deepening, Widening?*, Warsaw: Friedrich Ebert Foundation.

Kaser, M. (1965), *Comecon*, Oxford: Oxford University Press.

Kiseljak, F. and Ivankovic, Z. (1998), 'Joining the Queue' (interview with Nenad Porges), *Banka International*, 30 April (via: http://www.banka-mzb.tel.hr/.banka-mzb/98-01/4queue.html).

Kiss, J. (1997), 'Agricultural Trade Within CEFTA (A Substitute or Supplement to EU Accession?)', Working Paper of the Institute for World Economics, Budapest, Hungarian Academy of Sciences, December.

Kiss, J. (1999), 'Hungary's Experience with Agricultural Trade in CEFTA: Developments, Problems and Possibilities', in M. Stepanek (ed.), *The Role of CEFTA in the Process of EU Enlargement* (proceedings of the International Conference, 28–29 May 1999, Prague), Prague: Institute of International Relations/Association for the Study of International Relations.

Kolankiewicz, G. (1994), 'Consensus and competition in the eastern enlargement of the European Union', *International Affairs*, 70 (3), 477–495.

Kopec, U. (1997), 'Progress of Poland's Integration with the CEFTA Countries', in U. Plowiec (ed), *Foreign Economic Policy of Poland 1996–1997*, Warsaw: Foreign Trade Research Institute.

Kornai, J. (1992), *The Socialist System: The Political Economy of Communism*, Oxford: Oxford University Press.

Köves, A. (1992), *Central and Eastern Europe in Transition: The External Dimension*, Oxford: Westview.

Köves, A. and Oblath, G. (1994), 'The Regional Role of the Former Soviet Union and the CMEA: A Net Assessment', Kopint-Datorg Discussion Paper No. 24, Budapest, September.

Lavigne, M. (1991), *International Political Economy and Socialism*, Cambridge: Cambridge University Press.

Lavigne, M. (1995), *The Economics of Transition*, London: Macmillan.

Lavrac, V. and Rojec, M. (1997), 'A Common CEFTA Capital Market: An Attraction for Foreign Investors?', in H. Machowski (ed.), *The Further Development of CEFTA: Institutionalisation, Deepening, Widening?*, Warsaw: Friedrich Ebert Foundation.

Lawrence, R. (1996), *Regionalism, Multilateralism and Deeper Integration*, Washington, DC: Brookings Institution.

Linden, R. (1992), 'The new international political economy of East Europe', *Studies in Comparative Communism*, **XXV** (1), 3–21.

Machowski, H. (1997), 'Introduction: Basic Question, Main Answers', in H. Machowski (ed.), *The Further Development of CEFTA: Institutionalisation, Deepening, Widening?*, Warsaw: Friedrich Ebert Foundation.

Madej, Z. (1997), 'Is it Possible for CEFTA to be Enlarged Eastward?', in H. Machowski (ed.), *The Further Development of CEFTA: Institutionalisation, Deepening, Widening?*, Warsaw: Friedrich Ebert Foundation.

Mansfield, E. and Milner, H. (1999), 'The new wave of regionalism', *International Organisation*, **3**, 589–627.

Marer, P. (1976), 'Prospects for integration in the CMEA', *International Organisation*, **4**, 631–643.

Maresceau, M. (1997), 'On Association, Partnership, Pre-accession and Accession', in M. Maresceau (ed.), *Enlarging the European Union: Relations Between the EU and Central and Eastern Europe*, New York: Addison Wesley Longman.

Marrese, M. (1986), 'CMEA: effective but cumbersome political economy', *International Organisation*, **40**, 287–327.

Marrese, M. and Vanous, J. (1983), *Soviet Subsidisation of Trade with Eastern Europe: A Soviet Perspective*, Berkeley: University of California, Institute of International Studies.

Metcalf, L. (1997), *The Council for Mutual Economic Assistance: The Failure of Reform*, New York: Columbia University Press.

Ministry of Economic Relations and Development, Slovenia (1997), 'Opening Address by Prime Minister of the Republic of Slovenia, Dr Janez Drnovsek' (via: http://www.uvi.si/CEFTA).

Monthly Statistics of the Czech Republic, Prague; Czech Statistical Office.

Moran, D. (1998), 'Prepping for European Union', *The Prague Post Online* (via http://www.praguepost.cz/archive/busi90998e.html).

New Europe, various issues.

Obrman, J. (1992), 'Czechoslovakia overcomes its initial reluctance', *RFE/RL Research Report*, **1** (23), 5 June, 19–24.

Okolicsanyi, K. (1993), 'The Visegrad triangle's free trade zone', *RFE/RL Research Report*, **2** (3), 15 January, 19–22.

OMRI Daily Digest

Outrata, R. (1999), 'Foreign Trade and the Competitiveness of CEFTA Member States in the European Integration Process', in M. Stepanek (ed.), *The Role of CEFTA in the Process of EU Enlargement* (proceedings of the International Conference, 28–29 May 1999, Prague), Prague: Institute of International Relations/Association for the Study of International Relations.

Paleckis, J. (1997), 'The Lithuanian Road through CEFTA into the EU?', in H. Machowski (ed.), *The Further Development of CEFTA: Institutionalisation, Deepening, Widening?*, Warsaw: Friedrich Ebert Foundation, 121–129.

Perczynski, M. (1993), 'Subregional Cooperation among the Visegrad Group Countries', WERI Working Papers, No. 83, Warsaw, World Economy Research Institute, November.

Phinnemore, D. (1999a), 'The Challenge of EU Enlargement: EU and CEE Perspectives', in K. Henderson (ed.), *Back to Europe*, London: UCL Press.

Phinnemore, D. (1999b), *Association: Stepping-stone or Alternative to EU Membership?*, Sheffield: UACES/Sheffield Academic Press.

Pinder, J. (1976), 'Economic Diplomacy', in J. Rosenau, K. Thompson and G. Boyd (eds), *World Politics. An Introduction*, New York: The Free Press (Macmillan).

Preston, C. (1997), *Enlargement and Integration in the European Union*, London: Routledge.

Radio Free Europe/Radio Liberty, *Radio Free Europe/Radio Liberty Daily Report, Slovak Selection* (via: http://www.eunet.sk/media).

Reisch, A. (1992), 'Hungary sees common goals and bilateral issues', *RFE/RL Research Report*, **1** (23), 5 June, 25–32

Reisch, A. (1993), 'The Central European Initiative: to be or not to be?, *RFE/RL Research Report*, **2** (34), 27 August, 30–37.

Richter, S. (1992), 'Is There a Future for Regional Economic Cooperation in Eastern Europe?', in M. Keren and G. Ofer (eds), *Trials of Transition. Economic Reform in the Former Communist Bloc*, Oxford: Westview.

Richter, S. (1997), *European Integration: The CEFTA and the Europe Agreements*, Research Report No. 237, Vienna Institute for Comparative Economic Studies, Vienna, May.

Robson, P. (1980), *The Economics of International Integration*, London: Allen and Unwin.

Romanian News Agency, *Mediafax*, April 1997 (via http://www.mediafax.ro).

Rosati, D. (1992), 'The CMEA demise, trade restructuring, and trade destruction in Central and Eastern Europe', *Oxford Review of Economic Policy*, **8** (1), 58–81.

Rudka, A. and Mizsei, K. (1995), 'East Central Europe between disintegration and reintegration. Is CEFTA the solution?', *The Rose Occasional Paper Series*, **1** (1), USA and Poland: Institute for EastWest Studies.

Skjalm, K. (1999), 'CEFTA and the EU Enlargement Process: An Asymmetrical Bargaining Exercise', in M. Stepanek (ed.), *The Role of CEFTA in the Process of EU Enlargement* (proceedings of the International Conference, 28–29 May 1999, Prague), Prague, Institute of International Relations/Association for the Study of International Relations.

Slovak Information Agency, *Slovakia Today* (via: http://www.sia.gov.sk).

Smith, A. (1979), 'Plan coordination and joint planning in CMEA', *Journal of Common Market Studies*, **XVIII** (1), 3–21.

Smith, A. (1992), 'Integration Under Communism and Economic Relations after Communism in Eastern Europe', in D. Dyker (ed.), *The European Economy*, London: Pitman.

Statistical Information–External Trade, Prague Czech Statistical Office.

Stepanovsky, J. (1995), 'Cooperation within the Central European Visegrad Group. A Czech Perspective', *Perspectives*, Winter 1994–95, 91–98.

Toth, L. (1994), 'Trade Among the CEFTA Countries in the mid 1990s: How to Promote the Expansion of Intra-regional Trade Flows in Central Europe', Kopint-Datorg Discussion Paper No. 27, Budapest, November.

Tsoukalis, L. (1997), *The New European Economy Revisited*, Oxford: Oxford University Press.

UNECE (1997), *Economic Survey of Europe in 1996–97*, Economic Commission for Europe, New York and Geneva: United Nations.

UNECE (1998), *Economic Survey of Europe, 1998, No. 3*, Economic Commission for Europe, New York and Geneva: United Nations.

UNECE, (1999), *Economic Survey of Europe, 1999, No.1*, Economic Commission for Europe, New York and Geneva: United Nations

United Nations (1998), *World Investment Report*, New York: United Nations.

Vachudova, M. (1993), 'The Visegrad Four: no alternative to cooperation?', *RFE/RL Research Report*, **2** (34), 27 August, 38–47.

Vukadinovic, R. (1995), 'From Visegrad to CEFTA – Part 1', *Peace and the Sciences*, **XXVI**, December, 11–19.

Vukadinovic, R. (1996), 'From Visegrad to CEFTA – Part 2', *Peace and the Sciences*, **XXVII**, March, 13–29.

Warsaw Voice (via: http://www.warsaw.voice.com.pl).

Weydenthal, J. de (1992), 'Poland supports the triangle as a means to reach other goals', *RFE/RL Research Report*, **1** (23), 5 June, 15–18.

Winkler, J. (1997), 'CEFTA Enlargement: Small Steps or a Big Leap?', in H. Machowski (ed.), *The Further Development of CEFTA: Institutionalisation, Deepening, Widening?*, Warsaw: Friedrich Ebert Foundation.

World Economy Research Institute, *Poland. International Economic Report*, Warsaw: Warsaw School of Economics, various issues.

World Trade Organisation (1998), *Accession to the WTO–State of Play*, Geneva: WTO (via: http://www.wto.org).

Wyzan, M. (1998), 'Economic liaisons. The Baltics look toward the European Union', *Transitions*, December, 54–55.

Zagorski, A. (1997), 'Russia and European Institutions', in V. Baranovsky (ed.), *Russia and Europe: The Emerging Security Agenda*, Oxford: Oxford University Press.

Zakrowska, K. (1997), 'Polish Trade with CEFTA Countries: in Search of the Promising Sectors', *Economic Developments and Reforms in Cooperation Partner Countries: External Economic Relations with Particular Focus on Regional Cooperation*, Colloquium 1997, Brussels: NATO.

Index